The Evaluation
of Personal
Constructs

The Evaluation
of Personal
Constructs

D. BANNISTER

M.R.C. External Scientific Staff,
Bexley Hospital, Kent

J. M. M. MAIR

Senior Lecturer in Psychology,
Academic Department of Psychiatry,
Middlesex Hospital Medical School,
London

ACADEMIC PRESS
London and New York
1968

ACADEMIC PRESS INC. (LONDON) LTD
Berkeley Square House
Berkeley Square
London, W.1

U.S. Edition published by
ACADEMIC PRESS INC.
111 Fifth Avenue
New York, New York 10003

Library of Congress Catalog Card Number: 68–17673

PRINTED IN GREAT BRITAIN BY
WESTERN PRINTING SERVICES LTD
BRISTOL

to the late George Alexander Kelly
to whose work it is a footnote

Preface

Prefaces often authorise a book by claiming that it fills some startling gap in the literature, integrates hitherto unrelated areas or provides a timely summary of promising lines of study. These seem reasons why books are read rather than reasons why books are written.

This present work was born of an inability to accept that the impossible is unattainable. Three years ago, we began work on a journal paper defining grid methods as techniques of psychological investigation. We blandly agreed that we would write a paper which did not end with customary phrases about how many questions had been left unanswered and how much more work was needed. Experiments to answer key questions multiplied, more and more relevant studies were examined and the paper underwent cell division into parts I, II, and III. Eventually it was realised that there was little point in talking of grid methods without examining their relationship to personal construct theory and the assumptions about what people are in business for, which underlie both. The three-part paper coalesced into a monograph. We saw that all we had written about construct theory as a way of understanding people meant little unless we showed, of course, its revolutionary implications for psychology in all its forms. So the monograph fattened into its final form leaving numberless questions unanswered and much more work to be done.

This being said we set about providing the book with a truly unbiased preface by asking the first author's nine-year old daughter to forecast what the book would be like. Her presaging is given *verbatim*.

'I think its something to do with psychology, and I won't understand a word of it. I think thiers something about Prof. Kelly in it, and it dosen't mean a thing to me (expect the MONEY dad'll get for it.'

This seems to us a cogent summary of the key points of the venture.

January, 1968
D. Bannister
J. M. M. Mair

Acknowledgements

The first author gratefully acknowledges the support of the Medical Research Council, whose grants financed much of the work he has contributed to the study.

The second author wishes to express thanks for encouragement and opportunities afforded by Dr Victor Meyer, Professor Sir Denis Hill and Professor John Hinton.

Both authors are in debt to Dr Phillida Salmon for transmuting tangled arguments into English prose and grateful for the discussions of construct theory which she, Dr Fay Fransella and Neil Warren have inspired.

We also thank Messrs Methuen & Co. for permission to reproduce pp. 284–6 from "Personality Assessment" by P. E. Vernon, and Dr D. N. Hinkle of Colorado University for permission to quote from his Thesis. We are very grateful to Mrs Gladys Kelly for permission to quote so extensively from the work of the late George Kelly.

Contents

CHAPTER 1

Personal Construct Theory

PSYCHOLOGY is often described, especially in introductory textbooks, as the *science of behaviour*. This phrase claims for psychologists the status and dignity of scientists, engaged in predicting and controlling the behaviours of subjects who are submitted to tasks designed by the experimenter. It simultaneously claims that the important thing to study in their subjects – other human beings – is agreed units of observable behaviour, agreed between experimenters, not between subject and experimenter. There seems to be relatively little concern with the possibility that the subject, in his own way, may be experimenting, even in the experimenter's experiment, and seeking to do some predicting, controlling and even understanding, on his own account.

That such a possibility can be seriously entertained, about at least the human section of the subject matter of psychology, places psychology in a unique position in relation to the older natural sciences. No one suggests that the subject matter which the physicist, the chemist, the botanist, or geologist seeks to order and make sensible, at the same time may seek to order and make sense of him. This, however, is perhaps the single most outstanding feature of the field of events which the psychologist has chosen to study – people.

It is at least arguable that psychology, basing so many of its methods, assumptions and standards on the mechanistic view of nature popular in the nineteenth century in the then established sciences, is basically ill equipped to deal with this unprecedented state of affairs. Only in that erstwhile Queen of the Sciences – theology – has such a problem been faced before. There the main subject matter – God – was all along assumed, by the committed at least, to have a better than average grasp of the business of prediction, control and understanding. Psychologists in general have been rather slow to admit that their human subjects may be in the same league as themselves in this business of prediction, control and understanding, and some still refuse to regard them as being interested in the game at all.

George Kelly was concerned with just this problem and in his writings elaborated a theory of psychological functioning, entitled *The Psychology of Personal Constructs* (1955),[1] which gave primary emphasis to the active,

---

[1] All quotations with only a page number reference are from this work.

exploratory propensities of the individual. His theory and methodology may come to hold a special place in any science of behaviour since he is concerned explicitly to conceptualize the theories, methodologies and behaviours of scientists. The scientists he is concerned with are not just those who wear white coats, work in laboratories or have gained a Ph.D., but rather he invites his readers to consider the theoretical and practical possibilities ensuing from viewing men – all men – in their scientist-like aspects. He is not here saying that the professional scientist does just the same things as the man-in-the-street scientist or that all men are good scientists. Rather he suggests that some benefits may accrue from contemplating the scientist-like qualities and endeavours of all men.

Many may object to parallels being drawn between the strategies of science and ordinary human behaviour, and certainly psychologists have worked hard to distinguish the processes they consider important for explaining their behaviour from that of other people.

Kelly (1966) points out

"Psychologists are likely to be very much in earnest about making their discipline into a science. (Unfortunately, not many are as concerned as they might be about making science into something.) And they are never more deadly serious about staking a claim to scientific respectability than they are when they are writing elementary textbooks. It struck me rather suddenly one day that all the elementary texts I had read contained at least two theories of personality – one covert, lucid, and facile, and the others labeled, abstruse and labored.

'Psychology is a science,' each author would say as soon as he had finished his initial exhortation to his young readers to stop relying upon common sense, 'and a scientist is one who observes, construes relationships, articulates theories, generates hypotheses, ventures predictions, experiments under controlled conditions, and takes candid account of outcomes.' This is to say that if the student is to understand a psychologist's commitment to life, here is the way to make sense out of it. Not bad! It gives us a pretty clear picture of what it is like to be a psychologist. Altogether it is a most penetrating and perceptive theory of personality, albeit one reserved for the scientifically elite.

Later on in the book, after the writer has explained that the eye really sees things upside down, that dogs' mouths water when they hear the dinner bell, and that the child's confrontation with the school system at age sixteen turns out about the same way it did when he was six (proving that it is *the child's* intelligence that does not change) he takes up the matter of personality theories, making it clear that he is really talking about organisms and being careful not to anthropomorphize his explanations – even his explanations of man. And how do organisms, such as human organisms (still being careful to avoid the use of such a compromising term as *persons*), behave? Why, they are *conditioned* (meaning that learning is something they must have had done to them – probably when they weren't looking), they are propelled by drives (anyone can see that otherwise they would just sit and do nothing at all), deluded by their motives (why else would they disagree with us?), and stalked by the ghosts of their childhood fantasies (note how they read the comic strips in the newspaper).

But what would happen if one were to envision all human endeavour in those same terms the psychologists have found so illuminating in explaining themselves to their students? And, indeed, might it not be that in doing so one would see the course of individual life, as well as human progress over the centuries, in clearer perspective? Scientists are men, and, while it does not follow that men are scientists, it is quite appropriate to ask if it is not their human character that makes scientists what they are. This leads us to the question of how that human character can better be construed so as to account for scientists, and whether our construction can still explain as well the accomplishments that fall far short of what we, at this transient moment in our history, think good science is.

This is not a question of whether or not men do, in fact, live by the canons of science. That, except to an accumulative fragmentalist, is not even an appropriate question. We are not in search of such a neat conclusion, but of a strategic advantage in a long term quest for understanding. No theory can offer us more than that. The issue, then, is what this constructive alternative of seeing man as an incipient scientist will contribute at the present state in the search for a psychological understanding of him. Who knows – a by-product of this venture may be new light on scientific endeavour itself."

A further observation which directed Kelly's attention to the possible fruitfulness of regarding human and scientific endeavours as sharing some important similarities is noted in the following passage (Kelly, 1963c).

"One of my tasks in the 1930s was to direct graduate studies leading to the Masters Degree. A typical afternoon might find me talking to a graduate student at one o'clock, doing all those familiar things that thesis directors have to do – encouraging the student to pinpoint the issues, to observe, to become intimate with the problem, to form hypotheses either inductively or deductively, to make some preliminary test runs, to relate his data to his predictions, to control his experiments so that he will know what led to what, to generalize cautiously and to revise his thinking in the light of experience.

At two o'clock I might have an appointment with a client (i.e. patient). During this interview I would not be taking the role of the scientist but rather helping the distressed person work out some solutions to his life's problems. So what would I do? Why, I would try to get him to pin-point the issues, to observe, to become intimate with the problem, to form hypotheses, to make test runs, to relate outcomes to anticipations, to control his ventures so that he will know what led to what, to generalize cautiously and to revise his dogma in the light of experience.

At three o'clock I would see a student again. Likely as not he was either dragging his feet, hoping to design some world shaking experiment before looking at his first subject to see first hand what he was dealing with, or plunging into some massive ill-considered data-chasing expedition. So I would again try to get him to pin-point the issues, to observe open-mindedly, to become intimate with the problem, to form hypotheses – all the things that I had to do at one o'clock.

At four o'clock another client! Guess what! He would be dragging his feet, hoping to design a completely new personality before venturing his first change in behavior, or plunging into some ill-considered acting-out escapade, etc., etc. But this, of course, was not my hour for science; it was my hour for psychotherapy. And what I had done with that student back in the hour before, that was obviously not psychotherapy; it was science!"

Is it legitimate or useful, however, to talk about man-the-scientist and more particularly, man-the-psychologist? Certainly from the position Kelly has adopted, it is legitimate to consider man in terms of this model, just as one can contemplate *man-the-closed-circuit-habit-system* or *man-the-biochemical-miracle* or *man-the-walking-computer*. Within appropriate contexts these and many other interpretations of man's condition may have relevance but their usefulness has to be tested over time in accordance with the criteria set up by their originators or by others employing them. Kelly was clearly fascinated by the unifying possibilities of attempting to explain and chart the strategies of human endeavour, both in the life span of the individual man and in the progress of mankind through the centuries, within the same language and with the assumptions at present reserved for encompassing only the scientist's operations. For psychology, the introduction of a single language for describing the processes of man and the psychological nature of scientific enquiry would be a unique and exciting event, offering the possibility of new insights into the potentialities of man and the nature of science. Kelly himself makes no such sweeping claim but offers an attempt at reaching such a goal. He invites exploration of the concept of *man-the-scientist*.

BASIC ASSUMPTIONS

Kelly introduces his psychology of personal constructs by revealing the preconceptions which helped to shape the theory he produced. Of course, all psychological theories are erected on the basis of prior assumptions about man and his relation to the world but they are seldom made explicit. Kelly starts by stating his assumptions about the nature of the universe and the nature of man.

He makes three assumptions about the universe – that it is real and not a figment of the imagination; that it can be understood only on a time line; and that it is integral, so that in the light of complete knowledge and a broad enough perspective, all events can be seen as inter-related. Each of these points has important implications for the kind of psychological theory he originated.

In accepting that the universe contains real events and objects, Kelly also assumed that events internal to a person were equally real, so that thoughts or ideas about external things have a reality which is as convincing as the things themselves. Man comes to know something about the universe only in so far as he can make interpretations of it, and approaches an accurate awareness of events by successive approximations. The theory, then, is one which avoids the groundlessness and subjectivity of the purely phenomenono-logical or existential approaches, by seeing man as testing out his interpreta-tions or constructions for their adequacy in predicting the world which he is gradually coming to know. Furthermore, in accepting that a man's thoughts are as real as any other events in the universe, he emphasizes his conviction that a viable psychology of man can be built without recourse to the underpinning insurance which many psychologists seek in the supposedly more substantial events handled by the physiologist, neurologist or biochemist.

The assumption that the world really *exists*, directly implies a state of permanence or persistence which necessitates the idea of time, but Kelly argues that some aspects of the world more than others, can only be adequately understood or be open to the possibility of being understood, if the perspective offered by the concept of time is used. A man's life is one aspect of the world which cannot be comprehended without recourse to the notion of time. For a psychological theory, this idea is important in emphasizing that behaviour cannot be understood if only the present is considered, or if the present is considered simply in relation to the immediate or distant past. The events of a man's life may make sense only if he is seen as acting in relation to the future as well as the present and past.

The relevance to a psychological theory of assuming that the universe is integral, with everything affecting everything else, is somewhat more difficult to define, since an integrated system of thought for knowing such a universe is likely to be long, if not infinitely, delayed in coming. Even in the situation which exists, where the universe has to be studied piecemeal, the notion of underlying integration may encourage attempts to achieve some degree of consistency and unity in the concepts used to organize different partial views of the world. Kelly's contribution is in relation to a psychological view of man, and he attempts to elaborate a psychology where one set of principles and concepts can subsume and organize events otherwise conceptualized within disparate and less coherent systems. A further aspect of Kelly's psychology of personal constructs is consistent with the notion of an integral universe. Since any degree of integration in the universe can only be appreciated by means of a system of ideas operated by an individual, attention needs to be directed to exploring and analyzing the *system* of interrelated interpretations of the world used by individuals to bring coherence to their view of it. Kelly sought to conceptualize and describe how such systems might operate.

In essence the assumption of an integral universe is both a philosophical statement underpinning personal construct theory, and a psychological statement which refers to the continual effort of men to construe relationships where none were "seen" before. Construing is the perpetual attempt to relate what was hitherto seen as diverse and thereby envisage a more integral universe.

What is man like in this universe assumed to be real, making sense in time and integral? Kelly accepts that living things – men in particular – are distinguished by their capacity not merely to react to external events but to *represent* their environment. Because of this, man is in a position to make different kinds of representations of his environment and so is not bound by that environment but only by his interpretations or representations of it. Thus, while the universe is real, to the living creature it need not be inexorable unless it is represented as being so. Man can only come to know the world by means of the constructions he places upon it and he will be bound by events to the extent that his ingenuity limits his possibilities for reconstruing these events. Each man erects for himself a representational model of the world which allows him to make some sense out of it and which enables him to chart a course of behaviour in relation to it. Such a representational model or construct system, which may be explicitly formulated or implicitly acted out, may constitute a crude facsimile of many features of the world. However, a crude set of constructs is better than none at all, and as the world rolls along, constructions of reality may be tested out and modified to allow better predictions in the future.

From the beginning, therefore, Kelly refuses to accept that any once-and-for-all or absolute construction of the universe, or any part of it, is possible. He suggests instead that all our present interpretations of the universe are subject to revision or replacement.

"Like other theories, the psychology of personal constructs is the implementation of a philosophical assumption. In this case the assumption is that whatever nature may be, or howsoever the quest for truth will turn out in the end, the events we face today are subject to as great a variety of constructions as our wits will enable us to contrive. This is not to say that one construction is as good as any other, nor is it to deny that at some infinite point in time human vision will behold reality out to the utmost reaches of existence. But it does remind us that all our present perceptions are open to question and reconsideration, and it does broadly suggest that even the most obvious occurrences of everday life might appear utterly transformed if we were inventive enough to construe them differently.

This philosophical position we have called *constructive alternativism*, and its implications keep cropping up in the psychology of personal constructs. It can be contrasted with the prevalent epistemological assumption of *accumulative fragmentalism*, which is that truth is collected piece by piece. While constructive alternativism does not argue against the collection of information, neither does it measure truth by the size of the collection. Indeed it leads one to regard a large accumulaton of facts as an open invitation to some far-reaching reconstruction which will reduce them to a mass of trivialities." (Kelly, 1966)

Kelly was well aware of the questioning and unsettling implications of taking this standpoint seriously, for he went on to write

"A person who spends a great deal of his time hoarding facts is not likely to be happy at the prospect of seeing them converted into rubbish. He is more likely to want them bound and preserved, a memorial to his personal achievement. A scientist, for example, who thinks this way, and especially a psychologist who does so, depends upon his facts to furnish the ultimate proof of his propositions. With these shining nuggets of truth in his grasp it seems unnecessary for him to take responsibility for the conclusions he claims they thrust upon him. To suggest to him at this point that further human reconstruction can completely alter the appearance of the precious fragments he has accumulated, as well as the direction of their arguments, is to threaten his scientific conclusions, his philosophical position, and even his moral security. No wonder, then, that, in the eyes of such a conservatively minded person, our assumption that all facts are subject – are wholly subject – to alternative constructions looms up as culpably subjective and dangerously subversive to the scientific establishment.

None of this is a denial that men customarily share each other's insights and prejudices. Our ingenuity in devising alternative constructions is limited by our feeble wits and our timid reliance upon what is familiar. So we usually do things the way we have done them before or the way others appear to do them. Moreover, novel ideas, when openly expressed, can be disruptive to ourselves and disturbing to others. We therefore often avoid them, disguise them, keep them bottled up in our minds where they cannot develop in the social context, or disavow them in what we believe to be loyalty to the common interest. And often, against our better judgment, we accept the dictates of authority instead, thinking thus to escape any personal responsibility for what happens.

But though our devices for interpreting circumstances are still meagre, and the human adventure continues to be fraught with dire uncertainties, it does not follow that facts ever dictate our conclusions, except by the rules we impose upon our acts. Events do not tell us what to do, nor do they carry their meanings engraved on their backs for us to discover. For better or worse we ourselves create the only meanings they will ever convey during our lifetime. The facts of life may even be brutal, but they are nonetheless innocent of any evil intent, and we can scarcely accuse them of taking sides in our epistemological disputes. Our ever present task is to devise ways of anticipating their occurrences, and thus to prepare ourselves for assuming a more and more responsible role in the management of the universe." (Kelly, 1966)

THE NATURE OF A GOOD PSYCHOLOGICAL THEORY

When any new psychological theory is being considered, it may be understood better if the theoretician's assumptions about the "goodness" of good theories are made clear. What Kelly says directly about the features he values and requires in a good psychological theory, reflects also some aspects of his evaluation of the theoretical endeavours of ordinary men.

While a theory may be considered as a way of binding together a large collection of facts so that they may be comprehended more quickly and easily, it also provides a basis for charting an active approach to life and the problems on hand. In psychology, more perhaps than in other disciplines, a theory is a means by which its user can become involved in events and perhaps even change them; it is not simply a window through which events can be viewed and anticipated in a dispassionate manner. Certainly a theory aids prediction and, if the resulting predictions are precise, the theory may be considered more scientific than when the predictions generated are elastic and vague. However, in science, as in daily life, a theory need not generate consistently precise predictions in order to be useful. Some theory is better than no theory at all.

In daily life, explanations are not often sought to problems which do not exist and in erecting a psychological theory Kelly suggests that the theorist should start by having something to theorize about. A theory should have a *focus of convenience*, some set of events which it is specifically designed to subsume and in relation to which it may initially be seen as particularly effective. "The focus of convenience which we have chosen for our own theory-building efforts is the psychological reconstruction of life. We are concerned with finding better ways to help a person reconstrue his life so that he need not be the victim of his past. If the theory we construct works well within this limited range of convenience, we shall consider our efforts success-ful, and we shall not be too much disturbed if it proves to be less useful elsewhere." (p. 23)

Perhaps, above all other qualities, Kelly values a theory for its *fertility* in producing new ideas, and in opening up new realms in which hypotheses can be formulated and experiments effected. In psychology, he suggests, a good theory should allow predictions concerning people's behaviour in a wide range of circumstances and it should encourage and inspire the invention of new approaches to the solution of problems facing man and society. His enthusiasm for fertility in a theory is still qualified, however, by a recognition of the need for *testable hypotheses*. Yet while a good scientific theory should yield precise predictions which can receive incontrovertible confirmation or negation, the theory itself need not be so fragile. In fact it is rare that any theory in science stands or falls on the outcome of a single crucial experiment and this is perhaps especially true in psychology.

This point of view has, of course, been expressed by others and succinctly by Thouless (1951) as follows

"If we agree that a scientific hypothesis must be stated in a form that is falsifiable by some observation of fact, it plainly does not follow that it must be stated in a form that enables it to be falsified by a simple observation of fact. That seems to be what is assumed in some current discussions of the problem. It may be, however, that a valid and useful hypothesis is only to be tested by a complicated and difficult act of judgment involving observation of a wide range of facts. Of course, there are advantages in working with simple hypotheses; it is better to be able to make an easy test than be forced to make a difficult one. But there is no reason for supposing that the hypotheses most fruitful for psychological understanding will necessarily be those most easy to verify."

Although the fate of a psychological theory need not turn on the outcome of a particular experiment or the validity of a particular prediction, its *validity* cannot be maintained if a succession of hypotheses, when put to adequate experimental test, do not turn out to be palpably true. Since Kelly views a theory as an implement in a man's quest for a better understanding of the future, it cannot be considered as serving its purpose if predictions based upon it are consistently misleading. The theory can only become valid when someone is able to make use of it to produce verifiable and largely verified hypotheses.

While arguing that a psychological theory should be structured initially for its convenience in dealing with problems within a narrow focus, Kelly also suggests that it should have considerable *generality*, being expressed in terms of abstractions which are of a sufficiently high order to be traced through nearly all of the phenomena with which psychology must deal. Furthermore, in its original formulation the theory should deal with properties rather than categories, and while properties may eventually be used as grounds for erecting categories, the original formulation should avoid the concretism inherent in the pigeon-hole idea.

Kelly considers two further points, relevant to theory use rather than theory construction – namely the achievement of operational definitions of theoretical concepts and the modifiability of these concepts. On the question of *operationalism*, Kelly takes the stand that it is primarily the concern of the experimenter, not the theorist. "The terms in which a theory is stated do not need to carry their own operational definitions on their backs, though if the theory is to be productive it should, in the hands of experimentally minded psychologists, lead to research with operationally defined variables." (pp. 29–30) Just as with categorization, too early a concern with operational definitions may lead to undue concreteness in thought and so stunt the fertility, the generality and eventually the usefulness of the theory.

Modifiability should be seen as a property of those who use a theory, rather than of the theory itself. In line with the philosophical position of constructive alternativism outlined earlier, which holds that all present constructions of the universe are subject to modification and eventual abandonment, Kelly argues that any psychological theory should be considered similarly alterable and ultimately expendable. How long different theory users will hang on to their assumptions about the validity of the theory in the face of mounting evidence to the contrary will be very much a matter of taste, and a reflection of their commitment to the assumptions involved.

While the serial testing of the hypotheses generated by a theory forms a kind of continual evaluative commentary on the theory, in each experiment it is specifically the hypotheses and not the theory which are confirmed or negated.

Yet as Kelly points out:

"The substantiation of hypotheses is really not quite as simple as this. The catch is in the design of the experiment. If the experiment is so designed that other obvious hypotheses would have expressed the same prediction, the question arises as to which hypothesis was verified. As a matter of fact, in scientific research, one never finds the ultimate proof of a given hypothesis. About the time he thinks he has such proof within his grasp, another scientist comes along with another hypothesis that provides just as plausible an explanation of the experimental results." (pp. 31–2)

This point is emphasized to underline the contention central to constructive alternativism, that events can be reconstrued. Even within the controlled rigour of the most efficiently devised experimental design where the claims of the null hypothesis have been pitted against the experimental hypothesis, there is still room for some uncertainty about what has been confirmed.

"The relevant point for the purposes of this discussion is that even the precise hypotheses which one derives from a good scientific theory are never substantiated with absolute finality, no matter how many experiments are performed. For one thing, we are always dependent upon the second-hand proof that the unlikelihood of the null hypothesis provides; for another, the null hypothesis never wholly relinquishes its claim on the data; and finally, some other plausible hypothesis may turn up unexpectedly at any time." (p. 32)

UP TO THE STARTING LINE

The theory of personal constructs was presented formally by Kelly as a fundamental postulate and eleven corollaries which are consistent with the position expressed in the central postulate, and embody various attempts at extending or defining implications of that postulate.

If one central statement is to contain the essence of a theory, it is clear that the statement must be framed with great care, because after it has been made, the implications of the concepts, points of emphasis and areas of interest become more fixed and the experimentalist will sooner or later find himself torturing his data with elaborate statistics in attempts to surmount problems inherent in the fundamental postulate. Kelly was careful in wording the central statement of his theory to surmount or avoid three of the most persistently knotty problems in psychology – namely, why people do anything at all; why over a period of time, or at any choice point, they do certain things rather than others; and how people who are so obviously different in so many ways can yet be compared within some consistent conceptual framework.

First, comes the motivational problem which, Kelly argues, was imported into psychology from physics, where the concept of "energy" worked pretty well.

"The construct of 'energy' is really an outgrowth of certain fundamental assumptions that physicists have found it convenient to make. By assuming that matter is composed basically of static units it became immediately necessary to account for the obvious fact that what was observed was not always static but often thoroughly active. What made the units active? Why 'energy' of course! Psychologists, therefore, by buying the notion of 'energy,' had implicitly bought the same assumption of static units which had first made 'energy' a necessary construct for the physicists.

For a time psychologists had trouble deciding what it was that was propelled by 'energy.' Was it ideas or people? At last, most psychologists agreed that it was people. But what were the vehicles for the energy which prodded these obviously inert objects into action? On the verbal level it was a simple matter to ascribe energetic properties to the elements of one's personal environment by calling them 'stimuli'. Or, if one preferred, he could ascribe energetic properties to aspects of the person himself; these were called 'needs.' Thus psychology developed *push* theories based on 'stimuli' and *pull* theories based on 'needs.' But both approaches tended to be animistic, in that it was the 'stimuli' or the 'needs,' rather than the person, which accounted for all the work that was done." (pp. 35–6)

As an alternative to the vision of man as essentially inert until "motivated" in some way, Kelly began by assuming that men and other living creatures are, by definition, active.

"Instead of buying the prior assumption of an inert object, either on an implicit or explicit basis, we propose to postulate a process as the point of departure for the formulation of a psychological theory. Thus the whole controversy as to what prods an inert organism into action becomes a dead issue. Instead, the organism is delivered fresh into the psychological world alive and struggling." (p. 37)

Secondly, comes the problem of finding some principle which will facilitate predictions about the general direction a man will take in the decisions which face him in life, or about the turnings he will take at the various choice points which confront him. Behaviourists have tended to use the same "motivational" constructs introduced to account for the fact that men move at all, to subsume also their direction of movement. Thus the push psychologists seem to assume that each stimulus, or some conglomeration of past stimuli, accounts for direction of movement, while the pull psychologists seem to suppose that each need or motive carries its own directional signal with it. While Kelly is happier with the directional principle used by the Gestalt psychologist, than he is with the uncertain compromise between the reality and pleasure principles favoured by the psychoanalysts, he is satisfied with neither. A psychological theory which is concerned to explain how people turn at points of choice should be reflexive enough to subsume also the direction in which the theorist moved in proposing the theory itself. In the fundamental postulate and more particularly in the *choice corollary*, Kelly specifies the directional principle he has favoured, namely, that each man moves in the direction of increased *meaning* in his own individual terms.

Thirdly, Kelly wanted to be able to describe differences between individuals in some lawful manner, so that in comparisons between individuals the unique features and organization of each individual were not completely submerged. In choosing his fundamental postulate he wanted to establish a framework within which the study of individual differences would not simply degenerate into the study of group differences. In line with this, both his theory and practical methods start by paying particular attention to the personal constructions of the individual, but higher order abstractions are proposed which allow idiographic data to be viewed within a nomothetic framework.

THE FORMAL CONTENT OF PERSONAL CONSTRUCT THEORY

Kelly proposes, as the Fundamental Postulate of his theory, that *a person's processes are psychologically channelized by the ways in which he anticipates events.* Each word in this statement expresses some aspect of Kelly's basic assumptions about the nature of man. In making this statement, he does not claim that it is true, but that it can only retain the status of a fundamental postulate when it is regarded, while its implications are being worked out, *as if* it were true.

Kelly highlights in his fundamental postulate that it is *persons* he wished to understand, not rats, earthworms or cybermen, and not parts of persons, groups of people or specific processes manifested in a person's behaviour. In concerning himself with *processes* he obviates the need for any subsequent concepts about mental energy, motives, needs or drives. He refuses to make the assumption that a person is an object which at various times is impelled into action, but starts by acknowledging that a person is essentially *a form of motion.*

This is explicitly a *psychological* theory and by stating this in his fundamental postulate Kelly indicates that no commitment to the terms or methods of other disciplines such as physiology or biochemistry need be made. His philosophical position led him to assume that events themselves do not imply their own meanings or classifications, but that events can be appreciated, appear meaningful and be classified only in so far as a person has erected constructions to subsume them. There are, then, no physiological or chemical *events* but simply events which are at present more adequately construed within one subsystem of ideas rather than another. Just as events can be construed in a physiological mode (or in a sociological or physical or political mode) they can be construed psychologically – and this is what Kelly has set out to do. All such systems of construction are man-made, and the psychologist need not accept any as final, or trim his psychological statements so that they are consistent with statements deriving from another system.

It is assumed from the start that a person's processes are psychologically *channelized* by means of a network of pathways and do not float about in an uncharted emptiness. The network of channels is presumed to be flexible and modifiable, but it is structured and both facilitates and restricts a person's range of action. These channels are erected as *ways*, or means to an end, that end being the *anticipation* of *events.* Kelly is not concerned primarily with any ideal ways of anticipating events but the ways in which individual men choose and devise, to anticipate the events of which they are aware. Different people may anticipate different events and formulate different modes for anticipating similar events.

By focusing attention on anticipation rather than responding, Kelly seeks to free his theory from the stimulus-response paradigm, and at the same time builds into it its predictive and motivational features. "Like the prototype of the scientist that he is, man seeks prediction. His structured network of pathways leads towards the future so that he may anticipate it. This is the function it serves. Anticipation is both the push and pull of the psychology of personal constructs" (p. 49). Anticipation is not an encapsulated process. Man is trying to predict in a real world and the events with which he deals are real events, even though they cannot be absolutely apprehended but only construed. Since Kelly sees the purpose of setting up structures within which anticipations can be made as the *better* understanding and prediction of future events, the evidence derived from committing oneself to specific anticipations will be incorporated in various ways within the system, which may be modified in the light of outcomes.

"In our present undertaking the psychological initiative always remains a property of the person – never the property of anything else. What is more, neither past nor future events are themselves ever regarded as basic determinants of the course of human action – not even the events of childhood. But one's way of anticipating them, whether in the short range or in the long view – this is the basic theme in the human process of living. Moreover, it is that events are anticipated, not merely that man gravitates toward more and more comfortable organic states. Confirmation and disconfirmation of one's predictions are accorded greater psychological significance than rewards, punishments, or the drive reduction that reinforcements produce.

There are, of course, some predictions we would like to see disconfirmed, as well as some we hope will indeed materialize. We should not make the mistake of translating personal construct theory back into stimulus-response theory and saying to ourselves that confirmation is the same as a positive reinforcement, and that disconfirmation nullifies the meaning of an experience. Disconfirmation, even in those cases where it is disconcerting, provides grounds for reconstruction – or of repentance, in the proper sense of that term – and it may be used to improve the accuracy and significance of further anticipations. Thus we envision the nature of life in its outreach for the future, and not in its perpetuation of its prior conditions or in its incessant reverberation of past events." (Kelly, 1966)

Man is a form of perpetual motion with the direction of the motion controlled by the ways in which events are anticipated. The ways in which a person anticipates events are defined by his personal constructs. A construct is a way in which some things are interpreted as being alike and at the same time different from other things. Various aspects of the use, organization and modification of constructs are described by Kelly in the eleven corollaries elaborated from the fundamental postulate. These will be considered briefly before further comments are made about the nature of constructs.

CONSTRUCTION COROLLARY

A person anticipates events by construing their replications

Since the events of today are never the same events as those which occurred yesterday, repetitive themes can only be appreciated in so far as a person is able to abstract similarities and differences in the continuous onrush of daily happenings. In the construing or interpreting of events a person notes features of a series of events which characterize some and are particularly uncharacteristic of others. In so doing he erects constructs involving similarity and contrast, and both similarity *and* contrast are inherent features in any construct.

"A construct which implied similarity without contrast would represent just as much of a chaotic undifferentiated homogeneity as a construct which implied contrast without similarity would represent a chaotic particularized heterogeneity. The former would leave the person engulfed in a sea with no landmarks to relieve the monotony; the latter would confront him with an interminable series of kaleidoscopic changes in which nothing would ever appear familiar." (p. 51)

Put in another way, all constructs are necessarily bi-polar in that, for example, a person cannot be seen as *intelligent* without this implying some construed similarity between this person and others who show similar characteristics *and* some contrast with characteristics shown by *stupid* people.

Kelly emphasizes that

"The substance that a person construes is itself a process – just as the living person is a process. It presents itself from the beginning as an unending and undifferentiated process. Only when man attunes his ear to recurrent themes in the monotonous flow does his universe begin to make sense to him. Like a musician, he must phrase his experience in order to make sense out of it. The phrases are distinguished events. The separation of events is what man produces for himself when he decides to chop up time into manageable lengths. Within these limited segments, which are based on recurrent themes, man begins to discover the bases for likenesses and differences." (p. 52)

Once events have been distinguished more or less arbitrarily and given beginnings and endings, it becomes possible to try to predict them. Man attempts to anticipate events in terms of the replicated themes which he has detected.

INDIVIDUALITY COROLLARY

Persons differ from each other in their construction of events

In the fundamental postulate emphasis was placed on the individual person and the particular ways in which *he* anticipated events. Different *individuality*

individuals are likely to place rather different interpretations on the same events and to set up rather different constructions to subsume the different sets of events which impinge on them. In his most recent writing on this point Kelly extends his original position

"Having assumed that construction is a personal affair, it seems unlikely that any two persons would ever happen to concoct identical systems. I would go further now than when I originally proposed this corollary and suggest that even particular constructions are never identical events. And I would extend it the other way too, and say that I doubt that two persons ever put their construction systems together in terms of the same logical relationships." (Kelly, 1966)

ORGANIZATION COROLLARY

Each person characteristically evolves, for his convenience in anticipating events, a construction system embracing ordinal relationships between constructs

If a person is concerned to anticipate events and sets up a multitude of constructs to aid his predictive efforts, he is bound to find that unless some organization is brought into the collection of constructs evolved, he will be trapped in repeated confusion and uncertainty because different subsets of constructs yield contradictory or unrelated predictions. Kelly here suggests that each person sets up a characteristically personal *hierarchical* system of constructs where some constructs are more important than others. Different individuals will vary in the degree to which inconsistencies are eliminated, and few, if any, will attain completely watertight systems. Although a construct system is considered more stable than the single constructs which constitute it, it is not static but evolves and takes new shapes over time. Personality, conceptualized in this way, is seen as continuously taking new shapes. In these terms, a man's "personality" is his way of viewing himself and the world around him; thus it is his invention and he may invent anew.

Just as constructs are seen as bi-polar and personal, they must be understood as interrelated. A single construct by itself would allow no predictions, since it is along the line of interrelationships *between* constructs that predictions are made. Only when constructs are interrelated and organized into some kind of system can they form the bases for consistent or useful anticipations.

This corollary involves a similar notion to the idea of class inclusion in traditional logic (e.g. the class of "furniture" subsumes chair, table, sofa etc.) but since constructs are bi-polar, it is not identical to that proposed in traditional logic.

DICHOTOMY COROLLARY

A person's construction system is composed of a finite number of dichotomous constructs

A construct system is made up of nothing but constructs, and its organization is based on constructs about constructs, which may be set up in concretistic pyramids or abstractly cross-referenced in a hierarchical set of relationships. No man's thinking is, however, completely fluid and none experiences infinite possibilities of manoeuvre. The pathways along which a man's thoughts and actions are channelled are limited in number. So far, so good! But can constructs be usefully considered as dichotomous – black-or-white affairs? Kelly was well aware that many of those who might be ready to agree with his claims up to this point, here begin to have doubts. Surely to assume that constructs are black or white without any shade of grey, condemns their user to categorical or absolutistic thinking and denies that relativism which the sophisticated and the liberal demand. While admitting that on the face of it this looks bad, Kelly insists that there is nothing categorical about a construct.

"When we look closely the initial point of difficulty in following personal construct theory usually turns out to lie in certain unrecognized assumptions made earlier while reading the exposition, or even carried over from previous habits of thought. Let us see if we can get the matter straightened out before any irreparable damage is done.

Neither our constructs nor our construing systems come to us from nature, except, of course, from our own nature. It must be noted that this philosophical position of constructive alternativism has much more powerful epistemological implications than one might at first suppose. We cannot say that constructs are essences distilled by the mind out of available reality. They are imposed *upon* events, not abstracted *from* them. There is only one place they come from; that is from the person who is to use them. He devises them. Moreover, they do not stand for anything or represent anything, as a symbol, for example, is supposed to do.

So what are they? They are reference axes, upon which one may project events in an effort to make some sense out of what is going on. In this sense they are like cartesian coordinates, the x, y and z axes of analytic geometry. Events correspond to the points plotted within cartesian space. We can locate the points and express relations between points by specifying x, y and z distances. The cartesian axes *do not represent* the points projected upon them, but serve as guidelines for locating those points. That, also, is what constructs do for events, including ones that have not yet occurred. They help us locate them, understand them, and anticipate them.

But we must not take the cartesian analogy too literally. Descartes' axes were lines or scales, each containing in order an infinite number of imaginary points. Certainly his x or y axis embodied well enough the notion of shadings or a succession of grays. Yet a construct is not quite such an axis.

A construct is the basic contrast between two groups. When it is imposed it serves both to distinguish between its elements and to group them. Thus the construct refers to the nature of the distinction one attempts to make between events, not to the array in which his events appear to stand when he gets through applying the distinction between each of them and all the others.

Suppose one is dealing with the construct of good versus bad. Such a construct is not a representation of all things that are good, and an implicit exclusion of all that are bad. Nor is it a representation of all that are bad. It is not even a representation of all things that can be called either good or bad. The construct, of itself, is the kind of contrast one perceives and not in any way a representation of objects. As far as the construct is concerned there is no good-better-best scale, or any bad-worse-worst array.

But, while constructs do not represent or symbolize events, they do enable us to cope with events, which is a statement of quite a different order. They also enable us to put events into arrays or scales, if we wish. Suppose, for example, we apply our construct to elements, say persons, or to their acts. Consider three persons. One may make a good-bad distinction between them which will say that two of them are good in relation to the third, and the third is bad in relation to the two good ones. Then he may, in turn, apply his construct between the two good ones and say one of them is good with respect to the other formerly 'good' one and the one already labeled 'bad.'

This, of course, makes one of the persons, or acts, good in terms of one cleavage that has been made and bad in relation to the other. But this relativism applies only to the objects; the constructs of good versus bad is itself absolute. It may not be accurate, and it may not be stable from time to time, but, as a construct, it has to be absolute. Still, by its successive application to events one may create a scale with a great number of points differentiated along its length. Now a person who likes grays can have them – as many as he likes.

But let us make no mistake; a scale, in comparison to a construct, is a pretty concrete affair. Yet one can scarcely have himself a scale unless he has a construct working for him. Only if he has some basis for discrimination and association can he get on with the job of marking off a scale.

Now note something else. We have really had to fall back on our philosophical position of constructive alternativism in order to come up with this kind of an abstraction. If we had not first disabused ourselves of the idea that events are the source of our construct, we would have had a hard time coming around to the point where we could envision the underlying basis of discrimination and association we call the construct." (Kelly, 1966)

CHOICE COROLLARY

A person chooses for himself that alternative in a dichotomized construct through which he anticipates the greater possibility for the elaboration of his system

(The 1955 version referred to "the extension and definition" of the system, but in the 1966 Introduction the term "elaboration" is used to cover both.)

It is in this statement that Kelly makes his central assumption about the directionality of man's behaviour. The statement also contains the only idea in construct theory which seems at all like a value judgment. We have already noted that for Kelly, the psychologist, perhaps the most important feature of a good psychological theory is its fertility – the degree to which it encourages adventurous experimentation and inventive thought. Here he is suggesting that men in general will tend to place greater value on the alternatives in their construct system which seem to offer them a clearer sight of the things they know, or a base from which to strike out towards unexplored possibilities. In either instance, whether a man is choosing to *define* or to *extend* his system, Kelly assumes he will tend to make a choice, when the necessity arises, in favour of the alternative in the dichotomies which confront him, which seems to provide the best basis for anticipating ensuing events.

Note that each person does not necessarily or consistently choose the alternative which in any "objective" sense will lead to the clearest definition or the most extensive elaboration of his system. His choice – and this corollary does not presuppose that choices are merely or primarily intellectual – is governed by his own *awareness* of the possibilities involved. Note also, that the choice is between alternatives expressed in the construct, not between the objects separated out by means of the construct. The point here is that personal construct theory is a psychological theory and concerns itself with the behaviours of man, not the nature of objects. A construct then governs what a man does, not what an object does.

"In a strict sense, therefore, man makes decisions which initially affect himself, and which affect other objects only subsequently – and then only if he manages to take some effective action." . . . "Men change things by changing themselves first, and they accomplish their objectives, if at all, only by paying the price of altering themselves – as some have found to their sorrow and others to their salvation." (Kelly, 1966)

"Under the Choice Corollary we are able to reconstrue some of the issues for which hedonism and motivational theory provide awkward answers. Stimulus-response theory requires some sorts of assumptions to explain why certain responses become linked to certain stimuli. In certain theoretical structures this is managed by some supplementary theorizing about the nature of motives or need satisfactions. But in our assumptive structure we do not specify nor do we imply, that a person seeks 'pleasure,' that he has special 'needs,' that there are 'rewards,' or even that there are 'satisfactions.' In this sense, ours is not a commercial theory. To our way of thinking, there is a continuing movement toward the anticipation of events, rather than a series of barters for temporal satisfactions and this movement is the essence of human life itself." (p. 68)

RANGE COROLLARY

A construct is convenient for the anticipation of a finite range of events only

Just as we noted earlier that a construct system includes only a finite number of constructs, so also a construct system, sub-system or specific construct dimension has only a limited range of utility or applicability. The classical idea of a *concept* is that it embraces all elements which are similar in some particular respect and it excludes all other elements. This is not how a *construct* is defined. A construct is a personal invention, whereas a concept usually has reference to a category thought to exist *in* nature. More important, a construct includes a basis for assessing similarity *and* contrast *and* the exclusion of events irrelevant to the distinction being drawn. To say that a man is tall is to do more than just exclude all objects that are not tall. You are also denying that the man is short *and* asserting that there are other events, like the weather, artistic ability or what you will, that are *neither* tall *nor* short.

"Psychologically, the only point in commenting on the man's being tall is to deny some alternative that needed denying. What is excluded, therefore, includes some pretty important considerations, as well as some irrelevancies.

If we are to understand a person's statement we had better take into account just what it was he felt he must negate, as well as what he used as the subject or the predicate of his sentence. This, again, is a way of saying that the construct is a basis of making a distinction and, by the same act, creating an association, as one does when saying that a man is tall and implying thereby that he is like some other objects in that respect. Especially, one must keep in mind that a construct is not a class of objects, or an abstraction of a class, but a dichotomous reference axis." (Kelly, 1966)

A construct then has its *focus of convenience* (a set of events which its user finds can be most conveniently ordered within its context) and its *range of convenience* (a broader set of events which the construct can deal with, if sometimes less effectively) and a further set of events in relation to which it is useless. The words used to specify the poles of a construct must not be confused with the underlying constructive distinction being employed. Thus two people may use the same words where a rather different similarity-contrast dimension is being operated, and perhaps differing foci and ranges of convenience are involved.

EXPERIENCE COROLLARY

A person's construction system varies as he successively construes the replication of events

Since the fundamental postulate argues that man is concerned essentially with the anticipation of events, it becomes necessary to suppose that as events unfold and his predictions turn out for better or worse, his construct system will vary to incorporate some aspects of the new evidence. If this were not so, predictions would become progressively less realistic and the system would become less useful. Among the many forms of construct change which may occur are the following. The construct may be used to deal with a different set of events from the usual one, resulting in changes in the position of elements. For instance, the countryman coming to live in the town continues to use his construct *friendly-aloof*, but in the new situation begins to see some actions he would previously have called *aloof* as relatively *friendly* in the different social context. The kind of distinction implied by the construct may be changed somewhat. Thus in Kelly's example, the countryman in town may gradually come to regard *aloofness* as one aspect of a neighbourly respect for privacy, rather than necessarily a wholly unneighbourly action. The construct's relations to other constructs may be altered as, for example, when *aloofness* is seen as implying respect rather than disrespect, and respect comes to imply empathy and consideration rather than subservience or adulation.

Events do not repeat themselves – the person sees aspects of similarity between events, in terms of the constructions he has available for dealing with them. Thus, Kelly argues that experience refers to the constructions and revisions of constructions placed upon events, rather than to the repeated confrontation with events which are always viewed in exactly the same way. If a person does not modify his constructions as a result of the outcomes of his predictions, he gains no *new* experience, rather he has the *same* experience many times repeated. When he becomes aware of some inconsistencies between what he anticipated and the outcome, he places himself in a position where he may have to change some aspect of himself in order to accommodate the new evidence. For Kelly, the amount of a man's experience is measured not by the number of events with which he collides, but by the investments he has made in his anticipations and the revisions of his constructions that have followed upon his facing up to consequences.

Kelly assumes that learning takes place all the time and is so general that it need not be elevated into an area of study in its own right. In arguing that a person's construction system varies as he successively construes the replication of events, and assuming that all psychological processes are channelled by one's construction of events, he sought to build the notion of learning into the assumptive structure of his theory, rather than deal with it as a particular category of events. Thus he suggests that the questions of whether or not learning takes place, or of what is learned and what is not, need no longer be important debating topics *within his system*. "The burden of our assumption is that learning is not a special class of psychological processes; it is synonymous with any and all psychological processes. It is not something that happens to a person on occasion; it is what makes him a person in the first place." (p. 75)

The idea of an individual varying aspects of his construction system as he construes the regularities and repetitive themes he appreciates in the events which confront him can radically alter our view of the subject even in the traditional learning experiment.

"He too directs his psychological processes by seeking the recurrent theme in the experiment. If he segments the experience into separate 'trials' and then further separates the 'trials' into 'reinforced trials' and 'unreinforced trials,' he may hear the same repetitive theme which the experimenter hears. On the other hand, he may not be so conventional. He may listen for other kinds of themes he has heard before. He may not even segment his experience into the kinds of trials or events the experimenter expects. In the language of music, he may employ another way of phrasing. Viewed in this manner, the problem of learning is not merely one of determining how *many* or what kinds of reinforcements fix a response, or how *many* nonreinforcements extinguish it, but rather, how does the subject phrase the experience, what recurrent themes does he hear, what movements does he define, and what validation of his predictions does he reap? When a subject fails to meet the experimenter's expectations, it may be inappropriate to say that 'he has not learned'; rather, one might say that what the subject learned was not what the experimenter expected him to learn. If we are to have a productive science of psychology, let us put the burden of discovery on the experimenter rather than on the subject. Let the experimenter find out what the subject is thinking about, rather than asking the subject to find out what the experimenter is thinking about." (pp. 76–7)

One important point concerning the reconstruction of events is that confirmation of a prediction may, just as readily as disconfirmation, lead to reorganization of some aspect of one's outlook. Disconfirmation of a prediction can show up the relative inadequacy of one's present bases for anticipating the events in question and so lead to adjustments to allow greater accuracy in the future. Confirmation can provide a basis of security or certainty in one area, which can allow the person to be more adventurous and ready to try out unusual constructions in an adjacent part of his system.

MODULATION COROLLARY

The variation in a person's construction system is limited by the permeability of the constructs within whose range of convenience the variants lie

We all know that people do not always change their ideas when evidence to support them is not forthcoming. Kelly introduces the notion of permeable and impermeable constructs to account for the limitations of change occurring within any person's construct system. A permeable construct is one which is open to the inclusion of new events, while an impermeable construct is one which cannot allow new elements or events to be subsumed within its range of convenience. By permeability, Kelly does not mean plasticity or undue readiness to be changed, implying instability, but rather he is talking about the construct's capacity to be used as a reference axis for new events and to accept new subordinate constructions within its range of convenience.

Aspects of a person's construct system will vary to take account of a new construction only if the person has some construct or constructs within that section of the system relevant to the events on hand, which can incorporate the old and the new constructions (the variants) and make sense of them by allowing the person to view them from a higher, more superordinate level.

If, for example, a person has been accustomed to distinguish between people in terms of those he *fears* and those he *frightens*, then after meeting a new set of friends he may begin to sort out people he *respects* from those he *holds in contempt*. Kelly argues that such a shift would be possible only if he had available a superordinate construct to subsume both the construct *fear-frighten* and the construct *respect-despise*; such a construct might be that of *maturity-childishness*, with the dimension of *fear-frighten* being subsumed as *childish* and the other as *mature*. If such a superordinate construction, permeable enough to incorporate the old and new constructions, is not available, the new construction is likely to stand as an isolated reference axis, which will be difficult for the person to use in a consistent manner so that it makes sense in relation to the rest of his system.

FRAGMENTATION COROLLARY

A person may successively employ a variety of construction
subsystems which are inferentially incompatible with each other

Although the presence of permeable constructs may allow the variation of aspects of a person's construct system to accommodate new evidence, this does not mean that a person's system will be completely logically related, with every construct being implied by every other one. The way a person will behave today cannot necessarily be inferred from the way he behaved yesterday. A parent may kiss and hug a child at one moment, smack him a little later and shortly afterwards ignore him when he insists on showing off by excessive chattering. To the casual observer, it may seem that one response could not be anticipated from the previous one and that grossly inconsistent behaviour and constructions were being adopted by the parent. This may be the case, but need not be so. Just because different constructions do not seem consistent with each other and one cannot be inferred from the other directly, it does not mean that no consistency exists for the person involved or for some other observer of the scene. When, for example, the parent's *superordinate* constructs concerning love and training are considered, some thread of consistency in the various actions may be noted.

On the one hand, a person may use a number of apparently incompatible constructions to structure similar sets of events and behave in diverse ways to test out his constructions, but still see himself as acting consistently within the context of some superordinate construct. On the other hand, a person may move from an act of love to one of possessiveness and on to one of vindictiveness, without realizing that his last construction cannot be inferred from his first. Both of these ideas concerning aspects of logical consistency and inconsistency are important in Kelly's conception of construct systems, the one indicating that certain incompatibilities may be more apparent than real, and the other, that people are not aware of the blind spots and contradictions within their own systems.

COMMONALITY COROLLARY

To the extent that one person employs a construction of experience which is similar to that employed by another, his processes are psychologically similar to those of the other person

(In his original writing Kelly (1955) used the word "psychologically" to modify "processes," but in his most recent introduction to his theory (1966) he apologizes for this mistake and makes it modify "similar".)

This statement brings the focus of attention back from the individual in his system building and modifying efforts, to a basis for making comparisons *between* individuals. Kelly indicates here that two "similar" people need not have experienced "the same" events, or even "similar" events, nor need the ways in which they have tested out their constructions of these events have been the same or similar. What has to be similar, in order for their processes to be psychologically akin, is their construction of experience. In common language, the point here is that having bumped into different sets of circumstances, and worked out their ideas about what these circumstances were all about, they have come to similar conclusions.

SOCIALITY COROLLARY

To the extent that one person construes the construction processes of another, he may play a role in a social process involving the other person

Finally, Kelly moves from a basis for comparing individuals, and their interpretation of events, to the one elaboration of his fundamental postulate concerned directly with interpersonal understanding and interaction. Kelly here attempts to formulate a truly psychological rather than sociological or economic definition of role. He illustrates his conception of role by suggesting two ways in which you, the reader, can be described. Firstly, we can see you as an object, a bent figure, with finger alternately skimming the lines of print and raised to scratch the head. A second possibility is to view you as trying to make some sense of what you are reading; to think of you scanning the pages seeking some clear expression to lift the fog of confusion generated by reading the last few pages, trying to fit what is being said into the framework of what you already know, to see what is worth thinking about further and what seems meaningless. These two views of you in action are very different – the first is a strictly behaviourist view which treats you as a "behaving organism"; the second attempts to see you as an active interpreter, seeking to make sense of what you are reading, and depicts the kind of activity important for understanding Kelly's concept of role.

This example may highlight the contrast Kelly wishes to draw between construing the construction process of another person and construing only his behaviour. As Kelly points out

"In the first instance, I construed only your behavior. There is nothing wrong with that, as far as it goes. In the second case I went further and placed a construction upon the way in which I imagined you might be thinking. The chances are that I was more or less mistaken in both instances, particularly the second. But the point I want to make lies in the difference in my mode of construing you. In both formulations I was indeed concerned with your behavior, but only in the second did I strive for some notion of the construction which might be giving your behavior its form, or your future behavior its form. If immediate accuracy is what I must preserve at all costs, then I had better stick to the first level of construction. But if I am to anticipate you I must take some chances and try to sense what you are up to." (Kelly, 1966)

A person, then, plays a role in relation to another when he makes an interpretation about what the other thinks about him or about the particular problem on hand. The person's interpretation need not be accurate, and may be a grossly inaccurate representation of the other person's position, but when he attempts to make some sense of what the other is about, he plays a role in relation to him. Just as one's construction of the construction processes of another need not be accurate to allow one to play a role in relation to him, neither need the attempt to understand the other make one a compliant or accepting companion. Indeed, one may use one's construction of the other to impede his progress rather than aid it.

Kelly's concept of role can be readily exemplified in terms of two individuals with sharply contrasted construct systems confronting each other – say, an adult talking to or playing with a child. The adult does not rest content with a simple mental tabulation of the child's overt behaviour, since (unlike the behaviourist psychologist) he recognizes that the same significance cannot be attached to behaviour by a child as could be attached to "equivalent" behaviour by an adult (e.g. tears) and he insists on seeing behaviour in terms of its *significance*. Additionally, the adult will not usually talk and behave in his customary manner, and leave the child to make what he can of it. Rather he will construe the construction processes of the child and *in terms of this construction* he will enact a role in relation to the child. The child will undertake a similar venture. However well or badly this construing of others' construction processes is carried out, it is in the attempt that the role relationship subsists.

Because this is a psychological definition of role deriving from an understanding of the individual's attempts to interpret the interpretative system of others, it makes no initial commitments to the language of any other discipline. There are no reasons, however, why the implications of this definition for the sociologist or the economist should not be explored.

"When one construes another person's outlook, and proceeds to build an experiential cycle of his own upon that construction, he involves himself, willy nilly, in an interesting way. He can test his construction only by activating in himself the version of the other person's outlook it offers. This subtly places a demand upon him, one he cannot lightly reject if his own experience is to be completed. He must put himself tentatively in the other person's shoes. Only by enacting that role can he sense the impact of what happens as a result of taking the point of view he thinks his friend must have.

This means making a behavioral investment of his own, following the hypothesized lines and experiencing the consequences. The enactment by which he pursues this experiential venture comes close to what is popularly regarded as role-taking. While not all enactments constitute roles in the personal construct sense, and not all role enactments culminate in completed experiential cycles, these brief comments may serve to suggest why the term *role* has been given such a salient part in the development of this theory." (Kelly, 1966)

The concept of role is equally central to the methodology (Role Construct Repertory Test and grid) and the therapeutic technique (Fixed-Role therapy) associated with the theory.

THE NATURE OF CONSTRUCTS

Enough has perhaps already been said about constructs to provide the reader with a general idea of what Kelly had in mind. Some more direct consideration of the nature and characteristics of constructs might now be useful. At one point Kelly likened constructs to sets of goggles through which a person could view sections of the world. Sometimes the goggles present distorted images of the world, which may lead the person to act in inappropriate ways. When the person becomes aware that he is not "seeing" things correctly, he may adjust the lenses to provide a better approximation to the realities involved.

More generally, a construct is a way in which some things are seen as being alike and yet different from others. A construct is therefore essentially a two-ended affair, involving a particular basis for considering likenesses *and* differences *and* at the same time for excluding certain things as irrelevant to the contrast involved. Accordingly, a construct is very different from the logician's notion of a concept. In formal logic, a concept is usually described as a basis for grouping together certain things and distinguishing them from everything else. Thus *black* and *white* would be considered as two concepts and not as aspects of one distinction. *Black* would only be contrasted with *not black*, and *white*, with *not white*. Thus, *dress shoes* might be considered as being just as *not white* as a *good joke* or *a sense of well being*. The idea of relevant contrast and of limited range of applicability or convenience is not involved in the notion of a concept, but is essential to the definition of a construct. The positive statement that a person is *kind* would be meaningless and useless if something were not being negated at the same time. For different people, different contrasts may be involved, (thus one may contrast *kind* with *cruel*, another *kind* with *tough*, or *kind* with *critical*) but for each person the basis of discrimination can only be understood when the nature of the contrast is appreciated. Knowledge of the range of usefulness of the construct is also necessary if it is to be understood adequately. Two people may use the distinction *kind-cruel*, but one may limit its use to describing characteristics of people's behaviour in relation to himself, while the other uses it more broadly to include also natural phenomena like the sea, the weather and his fortunes in life. They may use a similar discrimination, but employ it with very different ranges of convenience.

Sometimes concepts are also regarded as ways in which certain things are *naturally* alike and *really* different from all other things. This use suggests that a concept is being considered as a feature of the nature of things, an inherent categorization of reality. The idea of a construct does not carry with it any such assumption, but rather is seen as an interpretation *imposed upon* events, not carried in the events themselves. The reality of a construct is in its use by a person as a device for making sense of the world and so anticipating it more fully. It must be stressed that all invented dichotomies, however widely agreed (*large-small*), specifically annotated (*bass-treble*), or scientifically approved (*acid-alkali*) are constructs – useful inventions, not facts of nature. The relative predictive value of constructs can be meaningfully explored, but none are absolute truths of nature.

A construct is thus explicitly a tool to allow not only discrimination and organization of events but also the anticipation of future possibilities. The suggestion that every construction involves a number of explicit or implicit predictions may at first seem a little improbable. However, the use of the construct *kind-cruel* to order certain experiences with people, does not merely allow person A to be categorized as *kind* and person B to be classed as *cruel*. By describing A as *kind*, we immediately imply a number of predictions about his future behaviour in relation to ourselves or others. We may expect A to lend us money, to look after a sick relative and be likely to consider other people's feelings, whereas B may be expected to disregard other people's needs, kick us in the teeth when he gets the opportunity and leave old ladies in the middle of the street. All these additional subordinate constructions are anticipations deriving from the original construction of the subject on the one dimension *kind-cruel*. These anticipations do not come out of the blue, however, but reflect the interlinkages between constructs in the *construct system* operated by our observer. Constructs do not exist in isolation; they are, as the organization corollary indicates, linked to other constructs in a more or less coherent and orderly manner. Not only are single constructs personal affairs; but also the way constructs are interrelated with each other differs as between individuals. A person can be understood to the extent that his *system* of constructs for ordering and anticipating events is understood.

By suggesting that a person can be understood by understanding his construct system, Kelly implies, not that a person's constructs are just optional and rather luxurious extras which may sometimes elaborate our understanding of a person's observable behaviours, but that *behaviour* cannot be seen in any meaningful perspective unless the constructions which are being tested by it are appreciated. Kelly sees each man's behaviour as essentially experimental and question-posing, in the man's own terms.

The system of constructs which a person establishes for himself represents the network of pathways along which he is free to move. Each path can be viewed as a two-way street, and while the individual may choose either of these directions, he cannot, so to speak, strike out across country without building new constructions, new routes to follow.

When a person must move, he is confronted by a series of dichotomous choices – each choice being channelled by a construct. Each construct represents a pair of rival hypotheses, either of which may be applied to a new element which the person seeks to construe. Thus, just as the experimental scientist designs his experiments around rival hypotheses, so each person is seen as designing his daily explorations of life around the rival hypotheses which are yielded by the constructs within his system. Moreover, just as the scientist cannot foresee possibilities that he has not, in some manner, conceptualized in terms of hypotheses, so any individual can prove or disprove only that which his construction system allows him to see in terms of possible alternatives. The construct system sets the limits beyond which it is impossible for a person to perceive, and in this way constructs are seen as controls on a person's outlook and also, in an ultimate sense, as controls on his behaviour.

Kelly suggests that the controlling influence of constructs becomes particularly interesting when a person begins to use himself as an event in the context of the constructs he is developing or operating. When a person uses himself as a datum in forming new constructs, he finds that the constructs formed operate as a tight control on his own behaviour. In forming a set of constructs which include the self as an element within their range of convenience, the person plots the dimensions along which it will be possible to organize his own behaviour in relation to others. Thus a person who includes himself in the context of the construct, say, *powerful-weak*, binds himself to assess his own behaviour in relation to that dimension. Whether he sees himself as *powerful* or *weak* is of interest to a psychologist, but it is secondary to the fact that the person has ordered his world and himself *with respect to* the *powerful-weak* dimension.

From the point of view of personal construct theory, any person, when viewed by another, is regarded as the point of intersection of a number of personal constructs used by the observer. Just as the North pole is defined as the point of intersection of a number of geographical constructions, so also the viewed person is to be identified as the meeting point of a series of dichotomized, categorical and personal intepretations.

THEORY AND METHODS OF MEASUREMENT

Kelly developed various methods for eliciting and measuring personal construct systems. The most elaborate and fully developed of these practical inventions is the grid form of his Role Construct Repertory Test. This technique will be described fully in the next chapter and examined in some detail in later sections, but it may be useful to note at this point some of the assumed features of constructs and ideas derived from a personal construct theory view of man, which are reflected in the technique of measurement.

Almost all the points mentioned in the preceding section concerning the nature of constructs are explicitly built into the measurement method. The ideas that constructs are personal, bipolar abstractions with limited ranges of conveniences, used to structure aspects of a person's world (for example his interpersonal world) are acknowledged in the procedure for eliciting constructs from the person being tested. The importance of exploring and understanding a person's *system* of constructs, rather than single isolated dimensions, is acknowledged by requiring the elicitation of a number of constructs and by providing statistical techniques which allow assessment of associations or links between the constructs involved.

Since Kelly was a practising psychotherapist, he was concerned to provide a practical method for estimating aspects of his patients' ways of ordering their lives – a method which would have important implications for how they organized their view of the world and their own place and actions in relation to it, and how they could change. He chose to focus his attention on eliciting primarily role-governing constructs and exploring the systematic organization of these. He was concerned to understand the dimensions along which his patients understood themselves and others, not just to know dimensions along which they could describe themselves or others as moving objects. His method focuses attention on just this kind of construct, and by allowing examination of the interweave of these role constructs with, say figure constructs, (father, mother, friend, self etc.) the nature of the intersects by which the patient defines himself or any of the other figures can be made explicit and public.

GENERAL FEATURES OF CONSTRUCTS

The discussion to date may have suggested that constructs come in un-differentiated masses. Kelly, however, supplied a number of "professional" constructs to describe different kinds and features of constructs. One important point about constructs which is frequently misunderstood is that many, perhaps most, constructs are *not* highly intellectualized with precise dimensions of discrimination, clearly and adequately expressed in words. Often a construct may be acted out in a tentative manner rather than consciously appreciated and conceptualized by its user. The nature of the contrasts involved may be blurred and confused by contrasts involved in separate but closely related constructs. Even where word labels are available and used by a person to specify the poles of a construct, they may ill define the nature of the contrast forming the basis of the construct, and the words used to describe a construct should not be mistaken for the underlying discrimination involved. Although the psychology of personal constructs is presented in a highly intellectualized form, Kelly emphasizes that this does *not* mean that all or most of the constructs any individual uses are of this form. Many constructs have no word labels and represent *nonverbal* and *preverbal* bases of discrimination and organization, and these may occupy important and even central places in the economy of a person's orientation towards himself and the world.

Sometimes, only one pole of a construct may have acquired a verbal label. In such a case the other pole is said to be *submerged*. When a person describes two people as *generous* and says another is not, he *may* not be aware of the nature of the contrast he is invoking and using. In psychotherapy, one important task may be to help such a person to clarify and make explicit, for himself and others, the implicit kinds of discriminations he is making.

The organization corollary made it clear that Kelly envisaged a system of constructs as structured in a series of ordinal relationships. Some constructs are more important or more general than others. *Superordinate constructs* are ones which include others as elements within their context. Thus a construct like *good-bad* occupies a relatively superordinate position within many people's systems and it subsumes many other constructs, ranging variously through actions, intentions, foods, clothes, paintings and so on. Constructs which are included as elements within the context of another are called *subordinate constructs*. Each construct in any person's system (except perhaps those at the very top and bottom of the system) is subordinate to many other constructs and at the same time occupies superordinate positions in relation to others. In order to understand something of the long-term commitments of a man's life, the relatively superordinate constructions in his system need to be examined, and such constructions are likely to be more stable and more resistant to change, than the lower-order, more specific, and less organizing constructs dealing with day-to-day or minute-to-minute events.

One particular grouping of superordinate constructs is of particular importance for organizing a person's approach to life and the roles he plays. These Kelly calls *core constructs*. He defines them as those constructs which govern a person's maintenance processes; they enable him to maintain his identity and sense of continuing existence. These may or may not be verbalized, but they cannot be changed in any way without disturbing the very roots of a person's existence. In contrast to these are *peripheral constructs*, which are likely to be subordinate in the system, and these can be altered without serious modification of core structures. Kelly indicates that the reformulation of a peripheral construct is a much less complicated affair than the reformulation of a core construct. He suggests that, for the most part, formal education may deal with what are probably peripheral constructions, while therapy deals more often with core structures or at least with constructs which start by being core structures.

Some constructs are more *comprehensive*, subsuming a wide variety of events, while others are described as *incidental* and subsume a narrow range of events. As the modulation corollary indicated, some constructs are *permeable*, readily admitting newly perceived elements into their context, while others are relatively *impermeable*. Some constructs are very exclusive or *preemptive*, or rather are used in a preemptive manner, alloting the elements within their context in such a way as to indicate, for example, that "this book is *nothing but* rubbish." Alternatively, some constructions allot their elements in a *constellatory* fashion, in the form – "if this is a book on psychology *it must also* be vague *and* fascinating *and* expensive etc." A *propositional* construct is different again; it does not exclude other possible ways of viewing its elements, as happens with the preemptive construct, nor limit the number of possible alternative constructions appropriate to it, as does the constellatory construct, but rather it leaves all other possibilities open. This is construing of the "as if" type – "we can look on this *as if* it were, among other things, (e.g. an emergency toilet roll, a sedative) a book on psychology."

Some constructs are very closely interrelated with other constructs and lead to unvarying predictions (this is a *table*, therefore it is *solid*). These are called *tight* constructs. Others, *loose* constructs, lead to more varying predictions while still retaining enough structure to maintain their identity. As constructs are tested out in action and the predictions implied by them validated or otherwise, their relationships with other constructs may go through successive phases of tightening and loosening. Neither tightness nor looseness is in itself a "good" or a "bad" thing; to achieve different ends, looseness or tightness in construct relationships may be the more appropriate or useful posture. A system which is too loose, however, will not allow any accurate predictions or realistic assessment of outcomes, and a system too tightly organized may be too restricted and too readily made obsolete by the march of events.

Just as relations between constructs may vary in terms of tightness and looseness, so also specific constructs or construct subsystems may undergo *dilation* or *constriction*. When, following a series of alternating uses of incompatible systems, a person broadens the field construed in order to reorganize it on a more comprehensive level, this stratagem is called dilation. When, on the other hand, a person minimizes the apparent incompatibility of his construction systems by drawing in the outer boundaries of the field construed, the relatively restricted mental process that ensues is described as constriction.

None of these constructs about constructs represent an all-or-none classification.

"These professional constructs do not refer to disease entities, or to types of people, or to traits. They are proposed as universal axes with respect to which it is possible to plot any person's behavior, at any time or at any place. They are also axes with respect to which it is possible to plot the changes that occur in a person's psychological processes. In themselves, they are neither good nor bad, healthy nor unhealthy, adaptive nor maladaptive. They are like the points of the compass; they are simply assumed in order to enable one to plot relative positions and chart courses of movement." (pp. 452–3)

CONSTRUCTS CONCERNING CHANGE

In addition to the central ideas which constitute personal construct theory, Kelly appended a variety of constructions which he used to structure various aspects of psychological change. Some of these concern disruptions or dislodgments within a person's system, while others describe various sequences of reconstruing which may lead to new or precipitate action and reconstruction.

Kelly intended that these constructs concerning change should be of particular relevance to the clinician. He attempted new definitions of *guilt, anxiety, threat, fear, aggression* and *hostility*. As might be anticipated, these terms are defined within the context of personal construct theory as experiential or psychological phenomena. He acknowledges that the definitions he has suggested limit the meanings of the concepts to the confines of his psychological system, and this limitation is alternative to the current and common meanings attributed to the terms. He aims for a unified reinterpretation of these important ideas consistent with the language of his theoretical position.

Rather than interpreting *guilt* as a derivative of punishment, he suggests that a person will experience guilt when he is aware of some dislodgment of the self from his core role structures. In other words, when a person begins to realize that he is acting in a way discrepant from his essential view of his role in relation to his fellow men; he finds that, in some important respect, he is doing that which he did not anticipate of himself. Thus a man who has built his role around the idea of his own wickedness may just as readily experience guilt, when he finds himself doing good deeds, as a self-styled paragon of virtues when he has been trapped in sin.

Anxiety loses its physiological trappings and is seen as a structural limitation within a person's construct system; the awareness that one's constructs, as so far elaborated, are inadequate to deal with new events on hand. "Anxiety is the recognition that the events with which one is confronted lie outside the range of convenience of one's construct system." If the events were completely outside the range of convenience of one's constructs they would not be perceived at all and no anxiety would ensue. Kelly suggests, instead, that anxiety is experienced when there is just enough structure available to appreciate that events are not being adequately grasped. Personal construct theory has as its central motivational construct the idea that man is constantly seeking to elaborate his system of meaning, to extend or clarify his areas of understanding. If the theory were to be posed in a defensive rather than a positive form, man's endeavours could rather have been viewed as an avoidance of anxiety – that is the avoidance of a state of lack of adequate understanding.

Threat is regarded as an interpretation which a person places on some of the events which confront him, and does not necessarily refer to events which someone else would consider dangerous for the person. "Threat is the awareness of imminent comprehensive change in one's core structure." Death, for example, is threatening to most people. It is threatening because it is seen as likely to happen and likely to cause drastic changes in one's core structures. It is less threatening when it is thought to be far away or when the fundamental meaning of a person's life is not affected by it (as when he believes that life substantially continues in the hereafter).

Fear is like threat, but less completely disrupting. "Fear is the awareness of an imminent incidental change in one's core structures." "One tends to be threatened by that which he construes comprehensively and is only made fearful by that which he construes simply. What threatens us is that which we are likely to know a good deal about. What makes us fearful is that which we know less about. We are threatened by hauntingly familiar things and frightened by unexpectedly strange things. But whether the disturbance is seen as comprehensive or incidental , it is the imminent likelihood of a sudden reconstruction of the *core* of our personalities that makes it a disturbance." (p. 494)

The notions of *aggression* and *hostility* no longer imply simply criticism or anger or attack. "Aggressiveness is the active elaboration of one's perceptual field" while "hostility is the continued effort to extort validational evidence in favour of a type of social prediction which has already been recognized as a failure." Of course the person who is actively elaborating his outlook (being aggressive) may also show hostility. Thus the timid man who tries to play the part of the debonair man-about-town, may begin to insist that people regard him as something of a wit, even though nobody laughs at his jokes and people avoid him. His insistence that outcomes are other than they are involves hostility, while his attempt to extend his social activities is an aggressive act. These terms, like guilt, have long carried a connotation of judgment and criticism. Within Kelly's system they are redefined to refer to psychological processes without carrying moral overtones.

These constructs about construct systems in states of transition are particularly interesting in that traditionally the terms refer to "emotional states," and the whole concept of "emotion" in its conventional sense (as a mysterious hydraulic pressure within the person) has no place in personal construct theory. Instead Kelly is proposing one psychology (not two psychologies, one of "cognition" and one of "affect") with an integral language. Within this scheme "emotions" lose much of their mystery. There are occasions when the acceptance of incoming evidence would disrupt vast areas of our personal construct system and threaten us with chaos. We are then likely to become *hostile*, to cook the books, to bully others into providing confirmation, however spurious, that we are right, until a gradual re-ordering of the system permits us to accept the evidence without leaving us in a senseless world. Hostility is thus defined within the theoretical terms used throughout the psychology of personal constructs, and, given an adequate grasp of a person's construct system, we should be able to predict its occurrence and (particularly important in Kelly's view) possibly limit the degree to which we arouse it in psychotherapy. Hostility, like the other constructs discussed in these paragraphs, is a defineable dimension and parameter of change in the person.

Since this is intended as a short introduction to personal construct theory and not a comprehensive statement of the ideas it contains or a full discussion of its terms, little more will be said about these or further constructs concerning change. The reader may refer to the original text for a fuller discussion of these clinical constructs and other terms not mentioned here. A summary of the formal structure of the theory and a glossary of construct theory terms is contained in the Appendix to this volume.

SOME COMMENTS ON THE THEORY

Our concern has not been to deal exhaustively with personal construct theory but simply to outline some of its main contentions, so that the methods which are described and examined in the next and subsequent chapters can be viewed in their proper context and in the perspective of the theoretical position they exemplify. Because of this, no detailed critique or appreciation of the theory will be attempted here. However, since the theory is an unusual one in modern psychology, on a number of counts, a few evaluative comments seem appropriate.

An outline of the theory has been given without reference to any experimental or clinical evidence. Bonarius (1965) has provided a useful summary of research findings which relate to the viability of the assumptions underlying a number of the corollaries; and later in this volume there is a discussion of a substantial amount of experimental work, which tests the validity of various hypotheses derived from the theory. While many of the studies reported are generally encouraging and support further use and application of the theory, in whole or part, it is still true that the evidence available is scanty and disproportionately small in relation to the size of the theoretical structure which has been erected.

Such is the imbalance between theory and evidence that many empirically minded psychologists may be inclined to dismiss the theory as yet another unwanted and unnecessary host of speculations in a field already overburdened with ideas and starved of facts. An argument for this view could readily be countered by the contrasting view that in psychology there has been too little theorizing at a high level of abstraction, concerning a broad view of man in relation to his world. Too often theories have been concerned to account for limited sections of man's activities. Facts relevant to isolated notions about small subsections of behaviour or experience may provide an *ad hoc* basis for a sort of psychological technology but no basis for any coherent view of man's psychological processes. These arguments, of course, will never be conclusive on either side, since they derive from different assumptions about the nature of scientific enquiry and psychological functioning.

One important feature of personal construct theory, which distinguishes it from most other psychological theories, is that it is an explicit expression and elaboration of a particular point of view about the nature of human functioning. Theories which are based on a less coherent point of view and which fail to state their philosophical bases may require a great deal of experimentation simply to disentangle their unstated assumptions.

What kind of theory is personal construct theory? Kelly commented on answers which have been given to this question.

"Some have suggested that personal construct theory not be called a psychological theory at all, but a metatheory. That is all right with me. It suggests that it is a theory about theories, and that is pretty much what I have in mind. But I hope that it is clear that it is not limited to being a metatheory of formal theories, or even of articulate ones.

There is also the question of whether or not it is a cognitive theory. Some have said that it was; others have classed it as existential. Quite an accomplishment; not many theories have been accused of being both cognitive and existential! But this, too, is all right with me. As a matter of fact, I am delighted. There are categorical systems in which I think the greater amount of ambiguity I stir up, the better. Cognition, for example, strikes me as a particularly misleading category, and, since it is one designed to distinguish itself from affect and conation, those terms, too, might well be discarded as inappropriately restrictive.

Personal construct theory has also been categorized by responsible scholars as an emotional theory, a learning theory, a psychoanalytic theory (Freudian, Adlerian, and Jungian – all three), a typically American theory, a Marxist theory, a humanistic theory, a logical positivistic theory, a Zen Buddhistic theory, a Thomistic theory, a behavioristic theory, an Apollonian theory, a pragmatistic theory, a reflexive theory, and no theory at all. It has also been classified as nonsense, which indeed, by its own admission, it will likely some day turn out to be. In each case there were some convincing arguments offered for the categorization, but I have forgotten what most of them were. I fear that no one of these categorizations will be of much help to the reader in understanding personal construct theory, but perhaps having a whole lap full of them all at once will suggest what might be done with them." (Kelly, 1966)

Some may think it an over-intellectualized theory, but again Kelly can best speak for himself.

"In order to make the point, I have had to talk about constructs in such an explicit manner that I have probably given the impression that a construct is as highly articulate and cognitive as my discussion has had to be. If I had been able to say what I have said in metaphor or hyperbole I might have left the impression that a construct had something to do with feeling or with formless urges too fluid to be pinned down by labels. But personal construct theory is no more a cognitive theory than it is an affective or a conative one. There are grounds for distinction that operate in one's life that seem to elude verbal expression. We see them in infants, as well as in our own spontaneous aversions and infatuations. These discriminative bases are no less constructs than those the reader may have been imagining during the reading of the preceding paragraphs. Certainly it is important not to consider a construct as another term for a concept, else a major sector of the arena in which constructs function will be obscured from view." (Kelly, 1966)

While personal construct theory should not and need not be regarded as concerned primarily with verbalized constructions, it is still true that the bulk of the experimental work reported so far has concentrated more on the measurement of such constructs, than on the other varieties mentioned in this quotation.

The fact that different people see construct theory as being *essentially* similar to so many different and even incompatible viewpoints may derive from its novelty as a psychological theory and from the difficulty psychologists have experienced in subsuming it adequately within preexisting frameworks. Although the exercise has not been attempted in detail, it seems probable that other existing theories might more readily be subsumed within the context of personal construct theory than *vice versa*.

Be this as it may, its construed similarities to so many different orientations results in large part from the fact that it is a theory stated at an unusually high level of abstraction. This will be considered as a weak point by some, in that it presents the reader with what some have described as a content-free theory – there are no things or events which the theory preempts as of particular importance in all people's lives. On the other hand, this very quality of being concerned to make generalizations about the structure of people's functional approach to life, rather than focusing down on specifics which do not have general applicability, may be one of the theory's strongest advantages in the struggle for scientific survival. Since the theory is not concerned with segments of people's lives or with particular subgroups of people, but with conceptualizing the ways in which people organize their experience and anticipate events, it frees itself from the built-in obsolescence of theories which refer specifically to the peculiar anomalies of some period of time which cultural change may outdate, or some subcultural factors which cannot be generalized to studies where other cultural organizations and influences exist. At the same time, the content-free nature of the assumptive structure of the theory in no way prevents the experimental gathering of information to flesh out problems from a construct theory viewpoint, and work reported later illustrates the almost limitless possibilities of extension in this manner.

At the beginning of this chapter we noted that perhaps one of the most significant and definitive features of the subject matter of psychology – people – is that they can and do try to make sense (or nonsense) of the experimenter who tries to predict their behaviour. No theories in psychology deal very adequately with this feature of human behaviour, and many do not even acknowledge it. There are probably no theories which, at one and the same time, attempt to provide a framework within which people's behaviour in general can be explained and understood *and* attempt an explanation and understanding of the behaviour which led to the elaboration and exposition of the theory itself. In physics or chemistry or any of the natural sciences, this *reflexive* quality of a theory is not required, but in psychology it would seem ultimately essential – and if ultimately essential, why not presently attempted? Kelly makes such an attempt in seeking to use the same concepts and language to structure man's approach to the understanding of events and the scientist's approach to understanding himself and man. The language of personal construct theory can be used to describe the characteristics and functions of the theory, the theory builder and his purpose in building the theory. The general relevance of the reflexivity issue to psychology is discussed by Oliver and Landfield (1963), Landfield (1961) and Lynn (1957).

Another feature of the theory relates to the level of abstraction at which the theory is stated, but emphasizes a slightly different aspect. Personal construct theory was erected with a specified focus of convenience (those events in relation to which it should prove particularly effective) and an *intentionally* broad range of convenience (those events in relation to which it may prove useful). Neither time nor completed research work can yet allow any conclusions to be drawn about the eventual usefulness of this characteristic of the theory builder's intentions. It is arguable, however, that the theory may prove useful over a very broad range of events without drastic alteration of its structure, to a degree not evidenced by other psychological theories.

Unlike almost every other theoretical approach in psychology, personal construct theory carries with it a number of techniques of investigation and measurement, which are closely tied to many of the assumptions in the main body of the theory. They allow, if not a "royal road," then at least a "custom-built route" from the abstractions of the theory to the practicalities of investigation and research.

The importance of this specific linking of theoretical concepts and operational definitions cannot yet be assessed; but, on logical grounds, a theory which is explored and tested through methods which objectify its basic constructs and which are consistent with its central assumptions, should allow sensitive and stringent assessment of its usefulness and worth. Such potential rigour in theory testing is not possible when measures are employed which are logically divorced from the postulates of the favoured theory, and conceptually alien to the assumptions the theory involves.

The introductory chapters of Kelly (1955) are available in separate form in Kelly (1963). Elaborations of aspects of the theory are given in Kelly (1958, 1961a, 1962, 1963a, 1963b, 1964 and 1965). Summaries of the theory have been made by Sechrest (1963) and Bannister (1962a). A discussion of the psychological validity of the idea of constructs is provided by Mischel (1964), and counter comments to this are made by Warren (1964).

CHAPTER 2

An Introduction to Grid Methods

IN THIS SECTION a broad picture of various grid forms is given. Technical details of administration and analysis are illustrated *en passant*; but the discussion centres on the main characteristics of different grid forms, the demands made on experimenter and subject during the administration of grids and the reasons underlying various modifications of Kelly's original grid method.

FUNCTIONS AND REQUIREMENTS OF CLINICAL TESTS

Grid method, like any other attempt to find practical expressions for theoretical notions, needs to be viewed in the perspective of the ideas which generated it. Some links between personal construct theory and the Role Construct Repertory Test and grid have already been indicated, but a more elaborate discussion, arising out of Kelly's ideas about tests and the functions of testing, is relevant.

Kelly developed his theory in the context of his interest in the psychological problems of patients and a concern with the idea of developing useful therapeutic procedures. The focus of convenience of this theory was explicitly and intentionally clinical. Although the present writers would contend that personal construct theory is likely to prove useful in a much wider field than that which is usually dubbed "clinical," Kelly's avowed intention was to develop a theory which had relevance, first and foremost, to clinical problems. His comments on the functions and characteristics of useful psychological tests are made in terms of his conception of clinical requirements, and it should be noted that in the context of American clinical psychology "clinical" often implies "psychotherapeutic," in addition to the more limited "testing" connotations of British clinical psychology.

"There are two ways in which one can look at psychological measurement and clinical diagnosis. On the one hand, he can seek to fix the position of the subject with respect to certain dimensions or coordinates – such as intelligence, extraversion, and so on – or to classify him as a clinical type – such as schizoid, neurotic, and the like. On the other hand, he can concern himself with the subject's freedom of movement, his potentialities, the resources which can be mobilized, and what is to become of him. From the point of view of the psychology of personal constructs, in which the emphasis is upon process rather than upon fixed position, the latter represents the more enlightened approach. Let us say, then, that the primary purpose of psychological measurement in a clinical setting is to survey the pathways along which the subject is free to move, and the primary purpose of clinical diagnosis is the plotting of the most feasible course of movement." (p. 203)

Kelly goes on to define more specifically the purposes which a good test should serve.

"The first function of a test which is to be used in a clinical setting is to define the client's problem in usable terms."

Kelly here argues that a test which does not define a client's problem in a way which helps the clinician to deal effectively with him is not valid for clinical usage, no matter how highly it correlates with certain "external criteria." Usability, rather than accuracy, he holds to be the minimum requirement of a good clinical test, and he is prepared to consider usability as a good operational definition of accuracy.

"The second function of a test which is to be used in a clinical setting is to reveal the pathways or channels along which the client is free to move."

Kelly, of course, sees these pathways as defined by the personal construct dimensions that the person uses to organize his life experience. Since constructs are bipolar dimensions, the contrast or implicit pole of any construct (in terms of which the person sees himself as an element at the emergent pole) may serve to specify one alternative in that person's repertory of choices, if he is forced to abandon his present view of himself. Thus, a person who uses the dimension *broadminded – narrowminded*, and sees himself as *broadminded*, has made available for himself the possibility (or the danger) of shifting to a *narrowminded* position, if the alternative hypothesis is invalidated. A good test should reveal such pathways of possible movement; it should reveal the available choices *in the subject's terms*.

"The third function of a test which is to be used in a clinical setting is to furnish clinical hypotheses which may subsequently be tested and put to use."

In Kelly's view, it is not always necessary in a clinical setting for a test to present the clinician with *conclusive* findings; instead it may serve a therapist well if it provides him with a variety of hypotheses regarding his patient. The verification or negation of the hypotheses is part of subsequent therapeutic experience with the patient.

"The fourth function of a test which is to be used in a clinical setting is to reveal those resources of the client which might otherwise be overlooked by the therapist."

Kelly argues that a great deal can be "wrong" with a person, without these defects necessarily impairing his ability to get along in the world. He considers that a good test should help ascertain a person's resources and untapped potential.

"The fifth function of a psychological test which is to be used in a clinical setting is to reveal those problems of the client which might otherwise be overlooked by the therapist."

Sometimes a patient may attempt to delimit the area within which he seeks help, and may wish to conceal from the clinician personal information which might be relevant to the treatment strategy. A useful test, according to Kelly, should reveal as many as possible of a person's vulnerable psychological commitments.

EVALUATING TESTS

A construct theory approach crystallizes these general requirements into a series of specific issues for clinicians, which Kelly posed as follows.

Firstly, the clinician must be concerned with the question – *whose yardstick does the test represent*? Is the test one of the "objective" variety, in which the patient is required to guess what the clinician is getting at by the test items, or is it a "projective" assessment, in which the patient is credited with having a private world of his own, and the clinician is presented with the problem of guessing what this world is all about? As a result of "objective" testing, the patient is plotted in relation to the axes chosen by the psychologist, and the patient's axes are largely ignored. Here, the patient stands still and is measured; he is treated as an object, rather than understood as a measurer in his own right.

Kelly clearly favours the "projective" approach, because it credits the patient with having some personal vision of the universe, a vision which constitutes the basis of his actions. In using projective tests, the clinician admits that his initial concern is with the yardsticks used by his patient. He admits, however, that the clinician cannot use the patient's yardsticks as if they were his own. He himself is only human and must depend on the yardsticks he has himself accumulated during his life and professional training. Kelly contends that it makes a great difference whether the clinician uses his yardsticks to measure the patient as a simple object, or whether he tries to measure the yardsticks used by the patient. Within the psychology of personal constructs, each psychologist is invited to examine the patient's performance as a projection of his outlook.

"This does not mean that the clinician cannot also be objective. Indeed, we see this approach to the client as being *more objective* than that of the old-fashioned psychometrician. It is more objective, not because it is more legalistic – a feature which is often confounded with objectivity – but because it is more object-orientated. It recognizes that it is the client who is the primary object of the psychologist's investigation and not the test. Thus we would argue that the psychology of personal constructs *is more objective because it is more projective*." (pp. 207–8)

Clearly, a test which does not allow the client to reveal something of the dimensional structure of his own view of the world, and does not allow the psychologist the opportunity of erecting professional dimensions to subsume features of his client's system of thought, will not be a clinically useful tool, as viewed from the standpoint of the psychology of personal constructs.

Psychology, in this sense, is not a science concerned with erecting constructs about people, in the way that physics erects constructs about objects. It becomes a science concerned with erecting constructs which can subsume the construct systems of people at a higher level of abstraction.

Secondly, in assessing the utility of a test, Kelly is concerned with its *ability to elicit permeable constructs*. As noted earlier, a permeable construct is one to whose context new elements can be added; it is still being developed by a person as a means of organizing and summarizing new evidence or events. It is one "which can be used to embrace the future as well as to pigeon-hole the past." An impermeable construct is defined as one which has been closed off, and does not allow entry to any present or future elements the person may meet – it may be useful for organizing past experience, but not for anticipating future possibilities. Kelly, in underlining the need to elicit permeable constructs, is arguing that the constructs elicited by a test should have some continuing and teleological relevance to the person's life.

Many approaches to the psychological understanding of the individual place considerable emphasis on uncovering those events in the patient's past life which might be viewed as determinants of his present and future actions. Kelly's emphasis is placed elsewhere.

"From the standpoint of the psychology of personal constructs, the events of the past are not the primary basis for predicting the future; rather it is the structure that one places upon the past that determines how he will let it influence his future. We say it another way too; we say that a person is not the victim of his biography but that he may be enslaved by his interpretation of it." (p. 208)

Kelly here stresses that not all interpretations of the past may be useful for explaining or understanding a person's present or future choices. It is better to spend time examining constructs which are sufficiently permeable to be of continuing use and relevance. A good test is one which points to constructs which have continuing usefulness for the subject, not to those which have been relegated to the archives as historical relics.

Thirdly, Kelly asks whether the elements included in the test are *representative of life's events*. He insists that the items in the test should be representative of the items the patient is likely to face in building some structure for his life. Inkblots (as in the Rorschach) and ambiguous pictures (as in the Object Relations Test or the TAT) are unlikely to form a major portion of a person's life experience, and inferences *from* responses to such circumscribed elements *to* real life situations are dubious at best. From a construct theory viewpoint (within which attention is focused on problems of interpersonal relationships) the inclusion of *people* as the central elements in a test increases its utility even though, for specific purposes, elements other than people can be used.

Fourthly, since construct theory is centrally concerned with the inter-personal problems presented by patients, Kelly asks whether the prospective test elicits *role constructs*. We have already noted that he defines a role as a course of activity which is played out in the light of one's understanding of the outlook of at least one other person. Role constructs thus have other people as elements in their contexts, or, more precisely, they have the presumed constructs of other persons as elements in their contexts. In this respect, Kelly suggests that reliance might be placed more on a test like the TAT as a means of finding out how a person structures his role in relation to others, than on one like the Rorschach, where the elements are abstract rather than personal. Again, from the point of view of his own theory, he suggests that a maximally useful test might go further than either of these, incorporating as elements the very people who were and are important to the person in his daily life.

He does not deny the possible usefulness of existing projective techniques, but suggests that the clinician should beware of assuming that a test which is concerned with the perception of ambiguous forms or the sorting of objects will reveal all that he needs to know about how the person manages his life in a social setting.

His fifth question concerns *stability versus sensitivity* as characteristics of tests. Kelly does not offer any detailed guidelines concerning the most appropriate balance that should be struck between sensitivity and stability. His theory, however, is one which acknowledges the possibility of changes within an individual at a variety of levels. Within some parts of a person's construct system, minute-to-minute or day-to-day fluctuations and changes may be common, while other constructions may remain stable over longer spans, and some may show little fluctuation across a period of years. From the point of view of the clinician, the most transient constructs may be of little importance. Kelly suggests that the clinician usually wants a test that will "measure those constructs which tend to continue in operation for protracted periods of time, but which are not so 'reality-bound' and so conventional that there would be no point in trying to revise them". (p. 212)

Whether the psychologist seeks to assess change or stability within either his professional constructs or within the personal system operated by his patient, Kelly seems to discourage too great an adherence to the notion of the value of test stability. He sees the problem as one of psychological concep-tualization rather than as simply one of test technology. It is the kind of dimensional structure, within which the psychologist chooses to examine his patient, which governs the type of picture which emerges. His test measures, whether showing stable or variable results, are governed as much by these prior conceptualizations as by features of the person.

Finally, Kelly asks whether the test will reveal constructs which are *communicable* to other clinicians. Again, he is concerned here with both the clinician's dimensions and the personal constructs of the patient. He accepts that clinical psychologists working in a psychiatric team may often find difficulty in communicating their test findings in a way which remains faithful to the test limitations and proves useful to the needs of the patient.

"To some extent this is a problem of words and syntax. Somewhat more fundamentally it is a problem arising out of the differences in the construct systems employed by psychologists on the one hand and psychiatrists and social workers on the other. Most fundamentally of all it is a problem arising out of the inadequacy of current psychological and psychiatric theories which are either laid out with an eye to the client's immobility or which presume, as in the case of psychoanalytic theory, that there is only one acceptable kind of psychotherapeutic procedure for producing mobility." (pp. 212–3)

Although Kelly lays stress on the importance of *revealing* a person's constructs, rather than on *testing* the efficiency with which the person can use the examiner's constructs, he recognizes that it is only in so far as a framework can be evolved which can subsume the patient's personal system and allow some understanding of the dynamic interactions and functions of different parts of that system, that a useful contribution can be made to solving problems of psychological change.

"If the psychologist attempts to communicate his hypotheses regarding the client, as he has inferred them from test data, he may find that the systematic frame in which he is making his presentation has no parallel axes among the frames used by his colleagues who represent other disciplines. It then becomes necessary for him to consider whether or not he can rotate the axes of his data in such a way as to bring them within the ken of his colleagues. If he cannot, he may decide that it is more practical to change his test and operate more nearly within their system from the outset.

The system implied by any test may be checked from time to time. We have proposed that one of the criteria for evaluation of various clinical tests is their capacity to define the client's problem in *usable* terms. By 'usable' we mean helpful in planning therapy, in determining client management, or perhaps even for statistical records. If a test does not meet this criterion, it can be abandoned, altered, or a new type of scoring system may be developed for it." (pp. 214–5)

Here, Kelly indicates his relative lack of concern for the concrete permanence of a particular test form and his emphasis on the usefulness of the basic methodological conception. This attitude has already led other workers to modify and extend Kelly's original test forms. Such developments are likely to continue at an increasing rate, perhaps leading to the abandonment and replacement of most existing grid forms.

AN OVERVIEW OF GRID METHOD

Before embarking on a discussion of particular grid forms, one further description of the grid approach is offered in the form of a quotation from Kelly (1961). Here, he links some of the theoretical issues already discussed in the first chapter and practical points which will be the focus of later sections.

"Personality itself is, then, our abstraction of the activity of a person and our subsequent generalization of this abstraction to all matters of his relationship to other persons, known and unknown, as well as to anything else that may seem particularly valuable. Thus there are three points to be kept in mind in dealing with personality: (1) It is a venture in abstract thinking undertaken by psychologists who examine the processes of the individual person, and not an object simply to be discovered by them; (2) it cannot ignore the person's relationship to other persons; and (3) it is bound to be value-laden.

But abstraction and generalization of human activity are not the exclusive prerogatives of professional psychologists. What they do any person may do. Indeed every person does! Each individual the psychologists study abstracts and generalizes on his own, for he is even more vitally interested than they can ever be in the task of understanding himself and his relationship to other persons and values. Thus the psychology of personality is not simply a matter of disinterested psychologists assessing a disinterested organism, but of psychologists, who happen to be professionally and casually interested in their chosen subject matter, assessing a non-professional psychologist who, on his part, is intimately and urgently involved with the job of making sense out of the life upon which his existence depends. Moreover, this non-professional psychologist – who is any person we assess – does much of his abstracting and generalizing in precipitate ways he cannot easily depict for us in words or gestures.

For the person who assesses his own behaviour, no less than for the scientists who examine it from the outside, the abstractions he makes enable him to see where he is going. At the personal level this is science too. But there is a special redundancy in the scientific determinism one applies to himself, for the same abstractions that enable one to forecast what he is about to do may serve also to determine how to act in order to fulfil or forestall his predictions.

Now we have four points to be kept in mind. Not only, as we have said before, is assessment of personality based on the abstraction of a person's known activity so it can be generalized to his unknown activity, not only is it particularly concerned with a person's relationship to other persons, not only is it bound up with values, but also assessment must take into account the person's own abstractions and generalizations about himself, even when they are imperfectly symbolized. These four considerations call for a psychology of personal constructs and for the development of techniques for appraising personal constructs.

THE NATURE OF ABSTRACTION

In order to develop a psychology of personal constructs for assessing personality it is necessary to concern ourselves with the psychological nature of the abstraction process itself. Whatever we may already understand abstraction to be from the standpoint of classical logic, it is necessary in addition to ask what it is from the standpoint of psychology.

Do persons indeed do their abstracting in classical form? Apparently not. Probably the most important deviation of psychological logic from classical logic is in its use of contrasts. For example, two women with whom one is acquainted may be abstracted as similar not only because they are feminine but just as much because their femininity contrasts with the masculinity of men. Thus speaking of femininity makes psychological sense only if one also implies the masculinity with which it stands in meaningful contrast.

This principle holds true for all the other abstractions with which human beings ● psychologically structure their world. To sum it up, then, we may say that each of us finds meaning in his life not only by identifying things for what they are, but also by noting what they are not. Moreover, in noting what they are not we clarify the alternatives that are open to us, thus establishing the psychological basis of what is most important of all – human freedom.

There are other features which seem to distinguish psychological logic from classical logic, and the study of all of them would probably be a lifetime undertaking. But perhaps I have said enough to trace the general line of inquiry I have been following and to suggest the basis for the methods of personality assessment I am about to describe.

METHODS OF ASSESSING PERSONAL CONSTRUCTS

Perhaps the best place to start the discussion of methodology is with the description of a particular technique. Then later I can attempt to describe the broader methodology of which this technique is a particular example.

Suppose I were to give one of you a card and ask you to write on it the name of your mother. Then I would give you another and ask you to write the name of your father. On a third you might write the name of your wife, and on a fourth the name of the girl you almost married – but didn't! We could continue until you had as many as twenty or thirty cards, each showing the name of a person important in your life.

Then suppose I should select three of these cards, perhaps the ones of your father, your mother, and your boss or supervisor. Suppose I should ask you to think of some important way in which any two of them seem to be alike and in contrast to the third. What will you say? Perhaps you will say that your mother and your boss have always seemed to know the answers to the questions you asked but that your father hesitated or told you to seek out your own answers.

Now if this is a distinction you can apply to your father, your mother, and your boss, can you extend it also to the other persons you have named? You probably can. The important fact is that as you apply it to person after person you are not only characterizing those persons but you are also providing an operational definition of what you have in mind. Applied to enough persons this operational definition provides a more extensive definition of a particular channel of your thought than do words you may use to symbolize it.

Now suppose I select another three cards, perhaps the ones with the names of your mother, your wife, and the girl you did not marry. What about them? Is there an important way in which two of them – any two – differ from the third? Perhaps you will respond immediately by saying that your wife and your mother are loving but that the girl you did not marry turned out to be harsh.

And how will you extend this personal construct to the other persons who are important in your life? Now let me suppose – for the sake of this discussion – something which I doubt would be true of anyone in this audience. Let me suppose that each person you characterize as 'loving' is a person you have previously characterized as ready to answer your questions, and each person you characterize as 'harsh' is one you previously characterized as sending you off to look for your own answers. Suppose this were true in case after case, on out to infinity. What could we say then? Would we then be ready to say that the two constructs were identical in everything but name?

Not quite! In our illustration the two constructs have been applied only to persons as whole entities. There is still the question of whether the constructs are applied identically to the separate acts of persons. To go even further, this suggests that, in general, the equivalence of constructs is determined by their similar application to all types of events, not merely to human events alone.

Moreover, we need also to make sure that both constructs occupy exactly the same range of convenience. That is to say, can the first construct in my illustration – the response-rejection construct – be applied to all the events to which the second construct – the loving-harsh construct – can be applied; and, of course vice versa? If there are some events that can be classified by the person as responsive or rejecting but which he cannot treat in terms of lovingness or harshness, then the range of convenience of the two constructs are different and the constructs themselves are therefore not quite the same.

All of this is a mathematical or logical problem and it leads to the formulation of one of the theorems underlying personal construct theory. Since, however, this paper is more concerned with the methodology of personal construct theory than with its mathematics, I shall limit myself to pointing out merely that such propositions exist.

Let us return to our deck of cards. We can represent the data produced so far in a flat matrix with events – in this case the names appearing on the cards – ranged along the top from left to right, and with the constructs ranged along the side from top to bottom. The entries in the matrix are single digit binary numbers, indicating simply whether the event is regarded one way or the other in terms of the construct. For example, if you regarded your mother as loving, this particular datum would be represented in the matrix by the numeral '1' in the first cell of the second row – below 'mother' and opposite 'loving-harsh.' If you regarded your father as harsh the numeral '0' would be entered in the next cell, etc.

Now we may go on to expand the matrix until it is large enough to give us a stable idea of how the person construes his world. Starting with different triads of cards we can successively produce row after row of matrix entries.

This is not an interminable undertaking. Experience shows that only persons with the most complex or schizoid outlooks require more than twenty or thirty rows to express their repertory of constructs. Repertoires used in everyday affairs are generally quite limited, and, especially so it appears, among those who prefer to act rather than reflect.

As you can see, the matrix can be factor-analyzed to see to what extent the person is employing a variety of constructs, or only a few constructs masquerading under different names. We can examine the columns in the matrix to see which figures in his life are viewed as similar to others, or whether, indeed, there is any great variety perceived among them. For example, does the subject see himself as like his father, or does he see his psychotherapist as like his father – as psychoanalytic theory suggests he should at certain stages of his treatment?

Incidentally, with regard to this particular psychoanalytic hypothesis, the research does not confirm psychoanalytic thinking. Patients entering into long-term psychotherapy seem rather to view their therapists as more and more like their family physicians.

Again, there are some men who can see complex differences among men, but only one-dimensional differences among women. There are some who have attempted to reduce all their interpersonal relations to the simple structure of one dimension – some military men, for example, and there are some who have done this in an effort to control the multi-dimensional confusion of their anxiety.

Research seems to indicate that there are advantages in having complex repertory of personal constructs, but there are disadvantages, too, particularly in decision-making. It appears that schizoid persons have a complex repertory, but their constructs lack sufficient ranges of convenience to enable the person to relate one of them to another. Thus the system fails to function as a whole and we find erratic sequences in the matrix.

But let us turn away from the particular kind of matrix we have described – which, after all, is only one example of the application of the methodology – and look at other kinds of personal construct matrices. Suppose, instead of asking you to write the name of a person on each of the cards I gave you, I would ask you to list an important experience you had had. Suppose, for example, I asked you to think of your wedding and make a note of it on the first card. On the second card you might note the occasion when you had a serious quarrel with your parents, on the third the time when you believed you were near death, on the fourth the ceremony at which you were awarded your university degree, then the meeting when a paper you presented was most severely criticized, and so on. Then suppose you were to construe these events, three at a time as you did the persons in your life, and then extended the constructs to all the other events you had mentioned. This would generate another kind of matrix whose columns and rows, as well as its verbal content, could be analyzed.

Or you might list only the catastrophes in your life and then ask yourself which of the persons you had named could, if they had been available at the time, have been helpful to you in meeting each emergency. Such a matrix provides information about one's allocation of his interpersonal dependencies – whether he has faced difficulties in which he feels no one could be of help, whether he turns to one or two persons only for all kinds of help, or whether he is indiscriminate in his selection of persons upon whom to depend.

Some researchers have used the methodology to come to an understanding of how a young person confronted with making a vocational choice views the different occupations and professions open to him. Others have used it to analyze personal factors in job dissatisfaction. Some have studied changes in the construing process during a year of university training, and others have studied similar changes during psychotherapy.

THEORETICAL IMPLICATIONS OF PERSONAL CONSTRUCT METHODOLOGY

Let us return now to some of the theoretical implications of this kind of methodology. As you see, our inquiry takes us into the field of personal constructs, their operations in relation to events as well as to words, and their interrelations with each other. While the constructs are personal and each individual has his own repertory of them, they are not so inaccessibly private that we human beings must despair of ever understanding each other. On the contrary, the methodology of matrices enables us to comprehend the complexities of differing personalities without having to reduce them to single-dimensional behavioural formulas, to physiological terms, to historical determinisms, to autonomous motives, or to any of the other reductionistic schemes that psychologists commonly employ. The psychology of personal constructs is then essentially a methodological psychology rather than the usual content psychology, though, of course, it yields content as a secondary product."

After outlining his ideas about the functions of psychological tests in relation to clinical problems, Kelly went on to present his various attempts to meet the criteria he had erected. He described two rather different approaches to the measurement of construct systems – the Rep test (with the grid form as an extension of this approach), and a Self Characterization approach in which constructs are elicited and their functions examined within the context of a brief autobiographical character sketch. Although attention here is focused on the grid form of the Rep test, the authors do not wish to imply that the grid is always the most useful test form to use, or that it can provide all the types of information that the Self Characterization method offers. Particular attention is given to the grid because it represents the most elaborate model of construct theory, and it is this technique which has received most research attention.

Kelly seemed to allot the simple form of the Rep test pride of place in his armamentarium of clinical tools, and apparently viewed the grid extension of this technique as a piece of methodological flamboyance which would intrigue the research worker rather than aid the hard-pressed clinician. In Britain, where clinical psychologists have less opportunity to control or even participate in treatment programmes, the grid method has received almost exclusive attention both inside and outside the clinical field.

Since the administrative procedure for the Rep test is very similar to that for the grid method generally, a brief description of this simpler form is given, so that the relationship between the two methods can be clearly seen.

The Rep test was designed specifically as a test to be used in a clinical setting. According to Kelly, it was intended primarily to provide material on which to form clinical hypotheses. Since in this setting great importance is attributed to role constructs, the test was structured to elicit such constructs. The Rep test is methodologically similar to many previous forms of concept formation procedures – to quote Kelly:

"Unlike the traditional concept formation test, the Rep Test is concerned with how the particular items are dealt with, not merely the level of abstraction involved. Unlike the picture sorting tests, the Rep Test is concerned with the subject's relations to particular people." (p. 220)

ADMINISTRATION OF THE REP TEST

Full details of administration can be found in Kelly (1955), and only a simplified outline is presented here.

Each subject is given a list of role titles, which are chosen to sample a wide range of the people and relationships which may have been important in any person's life. In the original form, Kelly included 24 role titles. Special role titles could be selected for any particular person, but Kelly included the following among his suggestions: a teacher you like, a teacher you dislike, wife (or girl friend), husband (or boy friend), father, mother, a person of your own sex you would enjoy having as a companion on a trip, a person with whom you have been closely associated recently who appears to dislike you, the most intelligent person you know personally, the most successful person you know personally, the most interesting person you know personally. The subject is required to supply a different person to fit each role, and when he cannot supply a suitable name he is asked to nominate some other important person he has not previously included, and to describe the role played by that person in relation to himself. The names of each person suggested by the subject to fit the role titles are written on separate cards.

The examiner now picks out three of the cards and lays them in front of the subject, asking him to suggest some *important* way in which two of them are alike and thereby different from the third. The subject may say that two of the people, perhaps his sister and his best friend, are *friendly*. Often the subject will indicate spontaneously which two people are being judged alike, but if not, the examiner should ask him. The examiner then points to the third card, perhaps a disliked teacher, and asks how this person is different from the other two. The subject may suggest that he has a *cold nature*. The examiner records this similarity and contrast, noting which elements represented each, as the construct dimension resulting from the first sort, and proceeds to the second and subsequent sorts using different triads of cards.

Just as role titles may be chosen to fit the person being investigated, so also sorts may be selected which incorporate juxtapositions of figures whom the clinician may consider particularly important for that person. No set number of sorts need be made, but between 10 and 25 seems a common range.

Following Hunt (1951), Kelly suggests a variety of constructs which may warrant further questioning. If the subject provides some of the following, he may be asked to provide alternative constructs or to give clearer specifications of those he is using. *Situational Constructs:* sometimes a subject will say that two people both come from the same town, or he met both in the same pub, and so forth. Kelly suggests that such a person be asked how their coming from the same town or being in the same pub makes them alike.

Alternatively, he may be asked if he can suggest some *other* way in which the people are alike. *Excessively Permeable Constructs:* e.g. the construction that both are women. Although such a construction may be useful, it may sometimes be profitable for the examiner to follow a similar procedure to that suggested previously. *Excessively Impermeable Constructs*: e.g. the comment that these two lost a leg in the war, this one lost an arm. *Superficial Constructs*: e.g. a subject may say that two people have small ears; it is perhaps important to keep in mind that a construct which may seem superficial to the examiner, may represent something very important within the subject's system. *Vague Constructs:* e.g. the remark that both of these people are O.K.; here the subject should be encouraged to explain further and cite possible examples. *Constructs which are a Direct Product of the Role Title*: e.g. the statement that both of these teach children; in such an instance, the subject may be asked whether there is something about teaching children which makes them alike.

Throughout the test, the subject should be encouraged to produce different constructs from those already elicited, and Kelly suggests ways of testing whether two construct labels seem to mean the same to any subject, or whether they seem to apply to different things.

DIFFERING ELICITATION METHODS

The procedure described above is termed the Minimum Context Card Form, in which three elements are selected for the subject's consideration and the relevant cards separated from the pack and laid before him. Kelly has suggested that the minimum context within which a construct can be formed consists of three elements. This he considered to be the smallest number of elements from which a generalization could be made regarding similarity and relevant difference. In this Minimum Context Form, he tried to translate this theoretical consideration into test routine.

In the Full Context Form, Kelly suggested that the subject be confronted with all the elements at once and be asked to consider important ways in which groups of these people are alike. All the cards are spread before the subject, and the examiner says, "I want you to consider the important ways in which groups of these people are alike. Will you arrange these cards so that the people who are alike in some important way are together?" When the subject selects two or more cards to be put together, the examiner asks how they are alike. When subsequent cards are added, the examiner says "Are these still the . . . ones?" When a card is taken away from any group, the examiner asks "Why did you take that one away? Are you still thinking of that pile as the . . . ones now?"

The examiner should record the way in which piles are built up in sequence, by using numbers to indicate cards which are added or removed from groups.

When the subject indicates that his sorting is complete, the examiner re-checks the constructs which identify the groups and checks the constructs which identify the cards left in isolation, if any. A record is kept of the final classification of all cards, whether grouped or not, as well as a running record of intermediate constructs and their elements.

Another possible variation in the process of eliciting constructs, called the Sequential Form, is perhaps more exacting and exhaustive than the forms already described. This again requires the use of cards, and, as in the Minimum Context Card Form, three elements are presented together at any one time for the subject's consideration. Thus, cards 1, 2 and 3 might be presented first, in the manner described previously. In the second sort, the examiner removes *one* of the cards and inserts another, saying "*Now* what would you say is an important way in which two of these people are alike but different from the third?". This second sort could consist of cards 2, 3 and 4. The third might include 3, 4 and 5, and so on.

Kelly suggests one other variation on this form, called the Self-Identification Form. Here, the subject is offered the possibility of providing the constructs he verbalizes to identify himself in contrast to others. The card presentation is similar to that for the Minimum Context Card Form, except that two cards bearing other people's names and the card showing the subject's *own* name are presented. The administration is like that for the Sequential Form, except that the card showing the subject's own name is retained as one of the three in each sort.

By a further modification, the test may become one which more specifically encourages the production of role-governing constructs. In this version, called the Personal Role Form, the mode of presentation is the same as in the Self-Identification Form. Here, the examiner, however, gives the following instructions: "Now suppose that the three of you were all together by yourselves for an evening. What kind of place might it be? What would happen? How would you yourself be likely to be acting? How would each of the others be likely to be acting?" Many other situations and conditions could be suggested here, depending on the area of interest under investigation.

One further suggestion is made by Kelly – superimposing the Personal Role feature on the Full Context Form. After the subject has made his sorts in the Full Context Form, the examiner lays the *myself* card beside one of the groups, and says "Suppose that you were to spend an evening with this group, what would be likely to happen? What kind of place might it be? How would you all get along together? What would you talk about? How would you yourself be likely to be acting? How would each of the others be likely to be acting?" After this the *myself* card would be laid beside each of the groups in turn (including the isolated cards), and the same questions asked.

Since the range for further modifications of elicitation procedures seems virtually unlimited, any simple attempts to standardize these methods would seem futile. However, some study of the characteristics of constructs tapped by the different methods (in terms of superordinancy, permeability, role regnancy, and so forth) could be practically and theoretically fruitful.

ANALYSES OF REP TEST RESULTS

No attempt will be made here to describe all the kinds of information that can be derived from Rep test protocols, or to indicate the various formal and clinical tabulations and analyses of Rep test data suggested and discussed by Kelly (pp. 232–66). Since our primary interest is in the grid form of the Rep test, Kelly's introductory summary of scoring possibilities will suffice.

"Rep Test results can be subjected both to formal analysis and, in case the examiner is a skilled clinician, to a clinical analysis. The constructs themselves can be analyzed as to content or tone and as to more abstract features, such as permeability and communicability. The figures also can be taken into account – that is, the kinds of people they are construed to be. From such an analysis one can get some insight into the facets of the subject's role – what he sees himself called upon to do in certain types of situations: at home, at work, and so on. Some judgment of the extent and flexibility of the subject's constructs can be made; also of the difficulties the subject has in construing some figures within his construct system." (pp. 232–3)

GRID FORM OF THE ROLE CONSTRUCT REPERTORY TEST

The focus of this presentation is on the repertory grid rather than on the original Rep test, because the grid incorporates all aspects of the Rep test, and adds a number of developments which give it greater scope, more elaborate links with personal construct theory and considerable methodological elegance. In spite of a number of important limitations, which are discussed later, repertory grid method seems to be an important and fertile innovation in the field of psychological measurement.

The repertory grid is not a test (though any particular grid could be made into a test) but a methodology which, for practical purposes, is extremely variable. It allows for the use of many different types of elements, constructs and scoring systems.

Kelly points out that a construct is not to be confused with the verbal label which may be used to identify it. Some constructs may not be verbally symbolized, some may be very inadequately indexed by words and some, though clearly represented by words in the common language of the culture, may involve some dimension of discrimination and prediction which is completely idiosyncratic and cannot be inferred by consulting the standard cultural dictionary. In the Rep test, the examiner elicits construct labels which are frequently used by the subject to organize some aspect of his life. Both the Rep test and the repertory grid have been used mainly to deal with constructs which have articulated verbal labels though it should be possible to design grids to incorporate non-verbalized constructions (e.g. Scott, 1962 and 1963).

In Rep tests, the validity of analyzing results leans heavily on the assumption that the examiner will correctly interpret the meanings of the verbal labels used by the subject. In a clinical situation where the procedure is being used to generate hypotheses which will be tested out during therapy, such a procedure may not be too misleading for the sensitive clinician. When viewed in relation to the demands of construct theory and in connection with measurements where subsequent intimate knowledge of the subject's ways of thinking may not be so readily available, the assumption of commonality of construction underlying similar verbal labels may be less easy to justify. Grid methods, in contrast with Rep test protocols, offer at least a crude means whereby similarities and differences in constructions underlying similar labels can be ascertained.

Construct theory lays considerable stress on the idea that each person erects for himself a hierarchically organized system of interrelated constructs. The Rep test, in its basic form, cannot readily specify types or degrees of relationships between constructs as used by any person, or facilitate other than a subjective estimate of the hierarchical importance of constructs. The repertory grid, on the other hand, takes at least the first step towards allowing investigation of both construct relationships and hierarchical status.

ADMINISTRATION OF REPERTORY GRID

The grid is an extension of the Rep test, and all that has already been said about the administration of the basic Rep test applies here. Most published work on the grid has involved some form of Minimum Context approach to the elicitation of constructs, though any of the methods of construct elicitation already described could be called into service.

As with the Rep test, Kelly suggested that each subject should supply names to fit various role titles. In the example given by Kelly, 19 role titles were used: Self, Mother, Father, Brother, Sister, Spouse, Ex-flame, Best Friend, Ex-Friend, Rejecting Person, Pitied Person, Threatening Person, Attractive Person, Accepted Teacher, Rejected Teacher, Boss, Successful Person, Happy Person, Ethical Person. Obviously the number of role titles can be varied, and in most of the examples given here 20 have been used. The subject is required to supply names of the people, from his own acquaintances, who most closely fit these or other appropriate roles. In instances where the subject may not have, for example, a brother or sister, he would be asked to provide the name of someone else who has most nearly filled that role in his life. No person should be chosen, at this point, to exemplify more than one role title. These names may be written either on separate cards or in a list beside the appropriate role title. A grid form is prepared, on squared paper, with numbers along the top, representing the numbers on each of the role title cards (see Fig. 1).

FIG. 1. Role Construct Repertory Test Form

Role Titles

Self	Mother	Father	Brother	Sister	Spouse	Ex-flame	Best Friend	Ex-friend	Rejecting Person	Pitied Person	Threatening Person	Attractive Person	Accepted Teacher	Rejected Teacher	Boss	Successful Person	Happy Person	Ethical Person	Neighbour	Constructs
1	2	3	4	5	6	7	8	9	10	11	12	13	14	15	16	17	18	19	20	
																O	O	O		1
					O	O	O													2
O					O		O													3
	O				O	O														4

Circles indicate triads of figures for eliciting constructs. The two poles of each construct are written in alongside the row and ticks entered in the row to indicate which of the figures are allotted to the first (emergent) pole of the construct. Blanks indicate that the figures are seen as characterized by the contrast pole. In the grid form of the test the array of ticks and blanks can be scanned vertically to examine relationships between constructs and horizontally to examine relationships between role figures.

All the role title cards, bearing the names of relevant people selected by the subject, are laid out before him. The examiner selects a group of three cards, e.g. Father, Mother and Sister, and asks the subject to suggest some important way in which two of these people are alike and different from the third. The elicitation procedure here is the same as that described for the Rep test.

Although the examiner has freedom to choose the cards which will constitute each sort, (just as he can choose any role titles he thinks appropriate for any particular subject), Kelly suggests a variety of sorts which might help the beginner. These include triads involving *Value Sorts* (e.g. representatives of

Success, Happiness and Ethics) *Authority Sorts* (these may include teachers, boss, etc.) *Intimacy Sorts* (e.g. Spouse, Ex-flame, Best-Friend), *Family Sorts* (Mother, Father, Brother), *Mating Sorts* (e.g. Mother, Spouse, Ex-flame), and *Identification Sorts* (e.g. Self, Spouse and Best Friend).

Sometimes a subject will provide the same word to specify one pole or another of constructs derived from different sorts. The examiner should attempt to assess whether the same word covers a slightly different construct, or whether the same total dimension is being repeated. In the former instance, the construct (including both emergent and implicit poles) would be retained; while in the latter instance, the subject would be asked to think of some other dimension of discrimination between the figures involved.

"When the clinician suspects that two constructs are functionally equivalent in the mind of the subject he performs four tests for equivalence. For example, suppose that in one sort a subject gives 'honest' as the construct and 'dishonest' as the contrasting [pole]. In another sort the gives 'trustworthy' as the construct and 'not trustworthy' as the contrasting [pole] perhaps involving the same person in the 'honest' and 'trustworthy' categories. The examiner then re-presents the figures which elicited the construct of 'honest' and asks, 'which two of these are the most trustworthy?.' Next the examiner re-presents the figures which originally elicited the construct of 'trustworthy' and asks, 'Which two of these are the more honest?.' Next the examiner asks, 'Is a person who is honest almost always trustworthy?.' Finally he asks, 'Is the person who is trustworthy almost always honest?'" (p. 233)

Although Kelly suggests this procedure in relation to the basic Rep test, the same or similar questions and instructions would be appropriate for other forms of grid.

At this point in the administration, the first construct has been elicited. Let us suppose that in a sorting involving Father, Mother and Sister, the first two were called *kind* and the other *cruel*. Up to this point, the procedure has been identical with that for the Rep test, but the next step is different.

When the subject provides his discrimination between the elements in the first sort, the examiner puts ticks in the appropriate grid cells for Father and Mother (which are subsumed by the emergent pole of the construct) and leaves the cell for Sister blank. He then asks the subject to look at the other people named on the other cards, and say which of them he would also call *kind* rather than *cruel*. The subject is asked to think about each person involved and call out the number representing that figure. The examiner then records further ticks in the appropriate cells (see Fig. 2).

The same process is then repeated for another group of three figures. This time, two figures (for example, under the titles of Rejecting Person and Threatening Person) might be described as *frightening*, while the other (e.g. Best Friend) may be contrasted as *gentle*. The examiner records the appropriate ticks, and the subject is again asked to say which of the other people indicated on the role title cards he considers *frightening* as opposed to *gentle*.

Fig. 2. Completed and Analyzed Section of R.C.R.T. (Grid Form)

Role figures

1	2	3	4	5	6	7	8	9	10	11	12	13	14	15	16	17	18	19	20	Constructs
	⊗	⊗			○	×		×		×		×	×			×	×	×	×	1. *kind—cruel*
						×	○	×	⊗		⊗			×	×	×				2. *frightening—gentle*
		×	×	×		×						×	×		×	⊗	⊗	○		3. *carefree— conscientious*
	×		×		⊗	○	⊗					×	×			×	×	×	×	4. *understands me— unsympathetic*
○		×	×	×	⊗		⊗		×			×	×		×	×	×			5. *confident—anxious*
×	⊗	×		×	⊗	○		×		×				×	×		×		×	6. *simple—intellectual*

Matching scores

1–2 4	2–3 8	3–4 13	4–5 13	5–6 8
1–3 12	2–4 5	3–5 18	4–6 7	
1–4 17	2–5 8	3–6 8		
1–5 12	2–6 8			
1–6 10				

The matching scores matrix is akin to a correlation matrix in which low scores represent negative associations (e.g. 1–2, the construct *kind—cruel* as related to *frightening—gentle*), high scores represent positive associations (e.g. 3–5, the construct *carefree—conscientious* as related to *confident—anxious*) and median scores indicate no association (e.g. 1–6, the construct *kind—cruel*, as related to *simple—intellectual*).

Given an extension of the number of constructs, role figures could be compared with each other or individually examined for say, contradiction i.e. the degree to which they combine characteristics which are incompatible in terms of construct matching score patterns.

A largely median set of scores indicates little structure for the area of construing examined, whereas 'all extreme scores' suggest a very simple structure largely explicable in terms of one dimension. There are no heavily lopsided constructs in this sample section of a grid except that construct 2 has only 7 ticks (or crosses) to 13 blanks which may, in itself, affect matching scores. Note that what are here referred to in concrete terms as "ticks" and "blanks" are termed, by Kelly, incidents and voids and should represent the *two poles* of a construct, *not* the presence or absence of a quality.

These further choices are recorded in a similar fashion on the prepared grid matrix.

This whole process is then repeated a further 15 or 20 times, with groupings of three figures being used as contexts for the elicitation of constructs – constructs from the repertoire (hence the term *repertory* grid) which the subject uses to structure his interpersonal world. The examiner then has before him a grid of ticks and blanks which formalizes and represents the intersection of various bipolar construct dimensions with various external events (in this instance people) in the subject's life.

In this description, the examiner has filled in the grid form with the various ticks representing the subject's choices. This degree of personal involvement by the examiner is not always necessary, though it may sometimes be important if the subject seems unwilling or unable to work on his own, and may be especially useful for a variety of clinical or research purposes, where it may be instructive for the examiner to know how the subject goes about his task. Kelly does, however, provide a sample form which is designed to make the test procedure suitable for self administration.

The most convenient way of calculating matching scores (in this test, the measure of relationship between constructs) is to make a copy of row 1 (construct 1) on a slip of paper, place this underneath row 2 and count the number of times that tick matches tick and blank matches blank, repeating this comparison of row 1 with rows 3, 4, and so on. Then row 2 is copied and scanned against the remaining rows. Subsequent rows are dealt with similarly.

. RATIONALE OF THE GRID METHOD

If a subject describes one of the figures in his role title list as *enterprising* and later as *intelligent*, these responses may be of considerable interest to someone else who also knows this figure, or to someone who wants to know what our subject thinks of this figure. However, in itself the information seems of only limited use, since we do not know what the subject means by these terms or how he uses them to organize his experiences of other people. If, however, we ask him to extend his application of each of these labels to a large group of other people known to him, we set up a situation in which we can examine how he uses these words in the context of a broader population.

Once the subject has used his constructs to categorize a number of figures, we can begin to understand something about the relationship (degree of similarity or difference) *between the constructs* as they function in his system. If each person who has been described as *enterprising* is also described as *intelligent*, and those described as *timid* have been designated *stupid*, this not only tells us something about this subject's view of these people, but, more importantly, it also suggests that for this subject the constructs represented by these terms are very similar (they *match* highly). In the context of the people (figures) involved, this may mean virtual equivalence in spite of the difference in verbal labels. Again, if none of those described as *intelligent* were classified as *enterprising*, this would suggest a negative relationship between the constructs involved. If roughly half of those described as *intelligent* were also described as *enterprising*, then the dimensions thus represented may be unrelated for the subject. For any intermediate degree of congruence in element choices, the degree of association between the constructs could be calculated and the statistical significance estimated by use of the binomial expansion formula.

Where there is either complete positive or complete negative agreement in element selection for two dimensions, some caution is needed in interpreting the relationship involved. If there are events which can be classified by the person as *enterprising* or *timid*, but which he cannot categorize in terms of *intelligent* or *stupid*, then the ranges of convenience of the two constructs are different and the two constructs are in this respect not equivalent.

FACTOR ANALYSIS OF REPERTORY GRIDS

A grid with, say, 18 constructs and 20 elements would yield an 18 by 20 matrix (20 elements represented along one axis and 18 constructs along the other axis). Such a grid contains 360 cells, either ticked or left blank in the manner of a two-point (one-zero) rating scale. This parallels, *in an individual subject*, the situation which is common in group studies where, say, 20 subjects have provided scores on 18 tests. In such a situation, psychologists have sought to simplify the array of data so that it can be more easily conceptualized and the main trends more economically expressed. Various factor-analytic procedures have been developed for this purpose, and Kelly devised a non-parametric, factorial method specifically for grid data.

Levy and Dugan (1956) in an early factor analytic attack on repertory grid data, made use of conventional procedures. More recent cluster analysis developments are discussed later. The Levy and Dugan exploratory study indicated that, regardless of the wide variety of words used in grids, subjects protocols were in some cases reducible to two factors. The amount of labour involved in factor analyzing each individual's grid matrix is prohibitive for clinical purposes, where computer facilities are not readily available. Kelly's simpler procedure is less time consuming. He argued that the results obtained (the factors emerging) were very similar to those found by more conventional methods of analysis, though results provided by Arthur (1963) suggest that, while similarities are clear for the first factor extracted, variations in the factor picture are noticeable with lower-order factors.

Commenting on his non-parametric method of factor analysis, Kelly makes the following point.

"The method of factor analysis of Rep Test protocol which we have devised does not involve the computation of tetrachoric r's. Since the sum of the intersects in any two rows is always the same, we may simply count matchings of incidents and voids between any two rows. The number of matched pairs of intersects gives us a measure of the relationship (not a correlation coefficient) between the two variables represented by the rows. Moreover, the significance of the matching can be computed by a *p*-value (level of statistical significance) determined even more appropriately than in the case of a correlation coefficient." (p. 281)

Kelly provides a worked example involving his method of factorial analysis and suggests a number of uses and interpretations of results obtained in this fashion.

Grid data can be subjected as readily to analysis of *element* relationships and clusters, as to analysis of relationships between constructs; and Kelly makes a number of suggestions about how a variety of clinically relevant analyses in terms of figures may be conducted and interpreted. Thus, the examiner may be able to analyze the subject's responses in terms of his identification with other figures; he may explore the subject's sex identification, or his relationship with figures in authority.

VARIATIONS IN METHODS OF ELEMENT ALLOTMENT

Some of the possible variations in methods of eliciting constructs have been outlined and variations in choice and form of role titles indicated, depending

FIG. 3. Lopsidedness

Elements

1	2	3	4	5	6	7	8	9	10	11	12	13	14	15	16	17	18	19	20	Constructs
		×										×								1. *clergymen—laymen*
				×																2. *sex-maniacs—normal*

Matching score between construct 1–2 = 17 (out of 20)

on the problem under study. In recent years, a number of modifications of the format within which grid data are collected have been brought into use. Kelly suggested that, when a construct dimension had been elicited from a subject, the person should then be allowed freedom to classify as many or as few of the other elements involved, as he saw fit, under each pole of the construct. This procedure permits the appearance of very lopsided constructs – constructs where very few elements are subsumed by one pole and many by the other. Thus, a situation like that shown in Fig. 3 may arise, where two constructs may show a high matching with each other (matchings calculated by counting the numbers of ticks coinciding with ticks and blanks with blanks in a comparison involving any two rows) suggesting a positive association between the two constructs.

However, this matching may be misleading, since, in our example, none of those who were classed as clergymen were also described as sex maniacs. The high matching results simply from the preponderance of blanks in both rows, enforcing statistically significant relationships, and may wrongly be taken to imply psychological association.

Because of the possibility of deriving distorted estimates of construct relationships when the subject is allowed complete freedom in his choice of elements to fit one or other pole of any construct, and because of the mathematical difficulties involved in correcting these biases, Bannister (1959) suggested an alternative form for element allotment, in which the subject is required to place half the element sample at the emergent pole of each construct. This was proposed as an alternative to Kelly's suggestion that heavily lopsided constructs be "scanned out" of the grid. Later, Bannister (1963) introduced another form (suggested by Salmon), in which the elements were placed in rank order, from those which were most readily subsumed by the emergent pole of a construct to those where the implicit pole was most appropriate. This problem can also be tackled by having every element rated on every construct dimension, and this method will be described later.

One, as yet untried, counter to lopsidedness was suggested in Bannister (1959) and designated the "free range" method. Here, it was suggested that for every pair of uneven rows the highest possible and lowest possible matching scores be calculated, e.g. for the two rows in Fig. 3 which are heavily lopsided, the highest possible matching score is 19 and the lowest possible matching score is 17. The difference between these two scores is the "free range," and it was argued that the actual number of matchings within this free range (in this case 0/1) be regarded as the true matching. Converted to a binomial probability, this could be used as the substantive measure of association. Tables for all possible combinations, with the related binomial probabilities, could be constructed to facilitate scoring. This method will inevitably tend to yield "chance" relationships where heavily lopsided lines are compared; but it will avoid throwing up spurious association scores.

SPLIT-HALF FORM

In the split-half form, the subject is required to place half of the elements at the emergent pole of each construct, and those which are left are supposedly allotted to the implicit pole. Thus, constructs, which Kelly assumes to be basically dichotomous, must be used in a scalar fashion, since the subject is required to grade his elements to achieve an equal apportionment. He must decide which elements (people) show the various characteristics specified by each construct *most markedly*. When the constructs are being elicited, this procedure for element allotment necessitates that some constructs be discarded, since some cannot be used readily in scalar fashion (e.g. male-female). This procedure is likely to eliminate grossly lopsided constructs. This prior selection of constructs seems beneficial from the point of view of gaining less distorted estimates of construct relationship, but may well rule out the possibility of exploring the various features of construct systems which may be associated with lopsided constructs.

The split-half method is illustrated in Fig. 4.

FIG. 4. Split-half format

Elements

1	2	3	4	5	6	7	8	9	10	11	12	13	14	15	16	17	18	19	20	Constructs
	×		×	×	×			×		×			×	×		×		×		1. *generous—mean*
×		×	×		×			×	×		×		×		×		×			2. *lazy—energetic*
	×		×	×		×		×	×		×			×		×		×		3. *musical—tone deaf*
	×			×	×	×	×	×			×			×			×		×	4. *going places—stick-in-the-muds*

etc.

Deviation Scores

Chance expectancy is 10 and the matchings can therefore, for convenience, be recorded as positive or negative deviations from chance level, e.g. $16 = +6$, $8 = -2$, $10 = 0$

1–2	−4	2–3	−2	3–4	0
1–3	+4	2–4	−6		
1–4	+4				

One immediate effect of the split-half method (with 20 elements) is to restrict the range of matching scores to 11 points (as opposed to 21 in the original form) going up by steps of 2, from 0 to 20.

In a split-half grid with 20 elements, matching scores of 4 and 16 are significant at the 1 per cent level, while matchings of 6 and 14 have a probability of association at the 12 per cent level. For most practical purposes, matching scores between 8 and 12 can be regarded as within the chance range.

RANK ORDER FORM

The introduction of the rank order method of element allotment greatly increases the available range of scores in any matching between element selections. Here, the subject is asked to use his constructs in a more overtly scalar fashion, and to rank the elements from the one which he considers shows the particular characteristic (indicated by the emergent pole label) *most markedly* to the one which shows it least (i.e. that which is most clearly characterized by the contrast pole). For example, he might rank the elements from the most *intelligent* to the most *stupid*.

Any rank order correlational method can then be used to estimate the degree of similarity in element placement on any two constructs. Since correlations are not linearly related, the raw correlation estimates cannot serve as scores. Construct *relationship* scores are calculated by squaring the correlations and multiplying by 100, to provide an estimate of percentage variance in common between the two constructs represented by two grid rows. With this method, the theoretical range of relationship scores between any two constructs is 201 points (from -100 through 0 to $+100$). Here, significance levels are calculated in the usual manner for rank order correlations, and, again, the same significance limits (degrees of freedom equalling number of elements minus one) can be set to apply to the whole grid.

Figure 5 provides an example of the rank order method.

FIG. 5. Rank order form

Elements

1	2	3	4	5	6	7	8	9	10	Constructs
10	9	8	7	6	5	4	3	2	1	1. *artistic—philistine*
1	2	3	4	5	6	7	8	9	10	2. *intelligent—stupid*
1	2	8	7	6	5	4	3	9	10	3. *keep promises—let you down*

Here rank positions are entered in the body of the table. The resulting correlations (Spearman's rho) and relationship scores (variance in common — $rho^2 \times 100$ retaining sign) are shown below.

$$
\begin{array}{lll}
 & \text{rho} & \text{relationship score} \\
1\text{–}2 & -1{\cdot}0 = & -100 \\
1\text{–}3 & -0{\cdot}58 = & -34 \\
2\text{–}3 & +0{\cdot}58 = & +34
\end{array}
$$

Where $n = 10$, the 5% level of statistical significance (one-tail) is reached with a correlation of rho $= +$ or $- 0{\cdot}564$. However, in grid work, there seems no good reason why the conventionally sacred levels of significance should be given particular importance, since it seems unlikely that people, when using their construct systems, only make decisions when the probabilities of error are 5 in 100 or less. Indeed, it might be interesting to explore what mathematical levels of relationship between constructs are required for people to venture decisions based on inference from such relationships.

This variation has been less used to date than either the split-half or rank order forms. Any size of rating scale may be acceptable, though five or seven point scales may be most satisfactory.

When this method is used for element allotment, the subject is asked to rate each element on each construct dimension. The subject may be asked to rate each element from "extremely" *kind* to "extremely" *cruel*. If a seven-point scale is used, the numbers 1 to 7 may arbitrarily index the amount of

FIG. 6. Rating form

Elements

1	2	3	4	5	6	7	8	9	10	11	12	13	14	15	16	17	18	19	20	Constructs
5	3	6	2	2	2	7	1	7	6	5	4	5	3	5	5	5	6	4	3	1. *Kind*
5	3	6	2	2	2	7	1	7	6	5	4	4	2	4	5	5	5	2	3	2. *Generous*
6	1	6	6	3	3	6	5	5	6	5	3	4	5	3	4	6	5	5	3	3. *Energetic*
3	5	5	4	4	3	4	6	4	6	5	6	4	4	4	4	6	4	4	2	4. *Intelligent* etc.

Fig. 6A

1. In this instance element ratings on 7-point scales have been obtained using single poles of constructs. The extreme and mid-point of the scale were named as follows.

Not at all		Average		Extremely	
1	2	3	4	5	6	7

2. The midpoint (4) was used here as an intermediate rating since the subject was first asked if he *could* meaningfully describe each figure (element) in terms of each construct. The ever present range of convenience problem could also be tackled by encouraging the subject to use the middle rating for elements which, for him, lie outside the range of convenience of the construct in question.

3. Relationships between constructs can be calculated in a number of ways.

(a) The highest ratings in each row can be noted and converted into ticks, the other cells being left blank. If, in each row nearly half of the cells are ticked, a grid like that shown in Fig. 6B may be obtained. The scoring procedure is then identical with that for Kelly's free method (see Fig. 2) and the split-half form.

the characteristic attributed to each element. Alternatively, if only one pole of the construct is presented, the subject may be required to rate each element on a scale ranging from most *kind* to least *kind*. The mid-point rating can be used either as an average position, or (if appropriate instructions are

FIG. 6B

1	2	3	4	5	6	7	8	9	10	11	12	13	14	15	16	17	18	19	20	
×		×			×		×	×	×		×		×	×	×	×				1. *Kind*
×		×			×		×	×	×					×	×	×				2. *Generous*
×		×	×			×	×	×	×	×			×		×	×	×			3. *Energetic*
	×	×				×		×	×	×					×					4. *Intelligent*

Matching Scores:

1–2	18	2–3	15	3–4	11
1–3	13	2–4	12		
1–4	10				

(*b*) The ratings in each row can be ranked and Spearman's rho calculated between each pair, as for the rank order method.

Relationship scores (rho$^2 \times 100$):

1–2	+91	2–3	+24	3–4	+8
1–3	+24	2–5	+5		
1–4	+3				

(*c*) Other methods may be developed for comparing rating patterns in successive rows. For example, in comparing any two rows, the ratings for each element could be subtracted and the differences for the row totalled to provide a Difference score in which low numbers indicate close relationships between the constructs and high scores indicate negative relationships. The actual range of possible Difference scores would depend on the number of elements and the size of the rating scales used. In this instance the possible range of Difference scores is 0 to 120.

Difference Scores:

1–2	6	2–3	26	3–4	23
1–3	26	2–4	31		
1–4	31				

4. As in the other forms, examination can be made of figures rather than constructs. This can be achieved by totalling the ratings in each column to give some estimate of the degree of clarity (in terms of extremity of ratings) with which each figure is construed, in terms of the constructs involved. Some estimate of variation in ratings for any figure (e.g. standard deviation) could indicate something of the subject's differential perception of each figure.
5. Further features of the subject's use of single constructs could also be estimated. Figure 6C shows the distributions of elements across the 7-point scale for each construct. The body of the table shows the number of elements receiving the particular rating on the specified construct.

given) as a rating to be given in cases where the construct dimension does not properly subsume the element – i.e. the element may be outside the range of convenience of that construct. The rating method is illustrated in Fig. 6.

The rating method, on logical grounds at least, would seem to offer a number of advantages. The subject is allowed much of the freedom of Kelly's original method, in that he can nominate any number of elements he chooses for either pole of any construct. He is given the opportunity of making distinctions between people who, in the original methods, might receive only

FIG. 6c

Ratings

1	2	3	4	5	6	7	
1	3	3	2	6	3	2	1. *Kind*
1	5	2	3	5	2	2	2. *Generous*
1	0	5	2	6	6	0	3. *Energetic*
0	1	2	10	3	4	0	4. *Intelligent*

Estimates of lopsidedness or maldistribution of element allotment on any construct could be obtained by comparing the numbers of elements placed on each side of the mid-point. Here, for example, elements are almost equally distributed at either side of the middle position (scale point 4) for construct 2 (8/9), but not for constructs 3 (6/12) and 4 (3/7), which show more lopsided distributions. Differentiation in the use of a construct might be indicated by some measure of spread of elements across the rating positions for each construct.

a uniform tick or an equally undifferentiated blank. Although some fineness of grading is thus introduced, if five- or seven-point scales are used, the amount of differentiation required of the subject is not as great as that demanded by the ranking method. Furthermore, the subject may give the same rating to elements which might be artificially separated by the ranking method, where generally no ties are allowed, though there seems no good reason why the ranking method should be limited in this way. These two features together make it possible for a subject to place all the elements at one pole of a construct and yet differentiate between them.

As we have seen, the problem of range of convenience can be specifically acknowledged and partially solved within this type of format. Further, lopsided constructs need not be excluded from the grid examination. Although the range of possible scoring methods has not been explored for this grid form, it is almost certainly greater than for any of the other forms already discussed. Matching scores of the type obtained in Kelly's original method can still be derived, and most correlational techniques can be used to provide relationship scores of the type obtained with the rank order method. The aim throughout is to give the subject as much freedom as possible to express his judgments and to throw the onus of formalizing and quantifying on to post-test statistical processing.

FURTHER VARIATION IN REPERTORY GRIDS

When Bannister introduced the split-half method, he also proposed and incorporated a number of other modifications which, while appropriate to the particular studies in hand, remained to influence grid procedures in other contexts.

Instead of using a specified set of role titles, he simply asked his subjects to write on slips of paper the names of 36 people whom they knew well enough to have formed some idea of what they were like in character. Since he demanded a large element sample, it could be argued that most important figures in the subject's life would be included. The procedure has now become common, and subjects are usually instructed to include a wide range of people in their element list, including their immediate family, friends, colleagues at work, people of both sexes and people they dislike as well as people they like. The people selected as elements in this manner have specifically been adults, since for most grid applications the focus of interest is not on constructs spanning adult and child elements. It has seemed best to limit the element sample in this way, because many constructs which can readily be applied to adults cannot be used very meaningfully on children, or may mean something different when used in the context of children. This generalizing of the element population abandons the safeguards provided by the role title system.

Bannister (1962a) introduced another change when he used sets of passport-type photographs as elements, instead of people familiar to the subjects. This further step away from the original grid requirements could, again, be readily justified in the *particular* studies involved, but again, the use of photographs of people unknown to the subject as grid elements has become common since then in situations where the use of familiar people as elements might well have been more appropriate.

Additionally, since Bannister's original studies were concerned with thought disorder in schizophrenics, the primary focus was on certain structural features of the organization of constructs, and not on the meaning of the particular constructs in individual use. Because of this, he supplied the same adjectives (*good, mean, likeable* and so forth) to subjects in the experimental groups (normals and various psychiatric samples). The assumption was that they would all share *some* common understanding of these terms, and that such commonalities would provide a fair basis for comparisons of *structural* features in construing. Again, the procedure of *supplying* adjective labels has become more widely favoured than can be theoretically or experimentally justified.

Although it seems quite legitimate to supply constructs, or rather labels which, for the subjects, may represent constructs (after all we do it every day when we hold a conversation), exclusive use of supplied words seems to negate the important ideas in construct theory noted in the individuality corollary. The supplying assumes that the experimenter knows best what is and is not important for the subject. However, it must be granted that, in both experimental and clinical investigations, some use of supplied construct labels may be useful and necessary. The examiner may be particularly interested in how the subject uses constructs in the general areas of sex or aggression or ethics, and in how such constructs relate to others within his system. If the subject himself does not supply constructs in the appropriate area, then the examiner may suggest some labels which seem likely to tap the relevant subsystems. In the grid form of the Rep test, some understanding of the meaning ascribed to the construct labels supplied by the examiner, in terms of the subject's system, can be gained from examining the mathematical relationships *between* supplied and elicited constructs.

ASSESSMENT OF CONSTRUCT RELATIONSHIP SCORES

In all forms of repertory grid, the unique measures provided by this technique take the form of numerical assessments of relationships between two or more construct dimensions. In grids of the type at present in use, only one type of relationship between constructs is indexed, a simple reciprocal relationship represented by a correlational or chi-squared type of association measure. The limitations of this type of scoring procedure, and the other types of measures which might prove useful, are discussed later.

In standard grids, the relationship between constructs is always *inferred* from the congruence of element placements on the construct dimensions. In this situation, the examiner assumes that a *statistical* relationship in sorting (revealed by the similarity of two or more sets of discrete choices) reflects a *conceptual* relationship for the subject. The subject here is not usually asked *directly* to say which constructs relate to which others.

This indirect method, which requires inference rather than elicitation from the subject of the links between his constructs, has both advantages and disadvantages. On the one hand, the subject himself need not be asked to make a very abstract or highly generalized statement about the links between his constructs (which for many people might be an unnatural and unusual task), and he may thus demonstrate links whose existence he could not articulate. On the other hand, the direct method (i.e. asking a person directly to say how his various constructs relate to each other) allows investigation of the degree to which a person has construed aspects of his own construct system.

Many types of scores have been derived from grids as further extensions of basic matching or relationship measures. A convention has been established which distinguishes between measures of *structure* and those concerning *content* of construct systems. Structural measures represent various mathematical characteristics of construct systems derived from grid scores. All these are based on counts of one kind or another, regardless of (or at least without primary regard for) the particular constructs involved. Measures of content usually direct attention to the actual constructs, and fall into the area which usually comes under the heading of "meaning." Instead of paying primary attention to the degree and kinds of links between constructs in a grid, note is taken of the actual verbal labels used to define the construct dimensions, so that some understanding can be gained of the things which interest a person, or of the meaning he attributes to events in the area of, say, interpersonal relationships.

In talking of structure and content, we are not concerned with a dichotomy, since concern with the actual constructs involved underlies the interpretation and use of many structural measures. Similarly, interpretation of construct labels is often aided by reference to certain mathematical features of construct links demonstrated in the grid. The distinction between content and structure refers to the level of abstraction at which the grid data are to be discussed, that is, to the degree of superordinancy of the constructs used to subsume grid material.

A danger inherent in the use of the distinction between structure and content arises from the picture it suggests of some stable mechanical apparatus existing within the individual, through whose convoluted tubes meaning flows. This type of concrete notion may encourage investigators to look for *things* rather than *processes* within the individual.

A person living in terms of his construct system may ponder aspects of its structure. Statements such as "I have a vague feeling that . . ." or "the issues involved are absolutely clear cut" or "nothing makes any sense" are essentially structural comments on aspects of construct systems, even though they relate to the construing of particular events. However, men are primarily concerned with *using* their construct systems rather than analyzing them, and they focus on *what* the system deals with and what it predicts, rather than on *how* it predicts. A psychologist is professionally committed to the analysis of construct systems *as* systems, and may therefore seek mathematically to subsume aspects of their structure, while still needing to subordinate structure to content when he is cornered by the need to understand particular individuals in particular situations. It may be that the functional importance of differences in structure will be one of the main areas opened up for detailed investigation by grid technique.

CLUSTER ANALYSIS OF GRID DATA

All the "cluster" approaches to the analysis of grid data have as a main aim, the extraction of the more simple formal structure which is obscured by the detail of the original matrix – they yield a simpler picture, with the inherent virtues and vices of simplicity. A number of computer programmes are available which allow for the factorial analyses of the grids of individuals or the averaged grids of groups. J. Kelly (1963) prepared a computer programme for the original non-parametric form of factor analysis proposed by Kelly (1955); and other developments in programmed cluster analysis have been described by Fager (1962) and summarized by Bonarius (1965). Slater (1965 and 1967) has prepared what is perhaps the most elaborate programme. It accepts grids cast in *any* of the forms of element allotment described earlier, and is a form of principal component analysis. This analysis delineates significant orthogonal structure *both* of constructs in relation to elements, and of elements in relation to constructs. Thus a fairly detailed overview can be obtained in mathematical terms, and this can be examined visually in terms of a hypersphere which represents a person's psychological space as subsumed by grid method.

A simpler, cruder, but sometimes more convenient method of extracting the main construct dimensions in grids has been described by Bannister (1965a). Here, no computer, other than the experimenter himself, is required. Each construct's relationship scores (or matching scores expressed as a deviation from chance level) with every other construct in the grid are totalled, regardless of sign. The construct with the highest total of such relationships (i.e. the construct accounting for most of the variance in the matrix) is accepted as the first axis of a graph (calibrated from $+100$ to -100, or from the highest possible to the lowest possible deviation score). The second axis is the construct with the next highest total of relationship scores, which is *not* significantly related to the construct chosen as the first axis. This axis is drawn on graph paper at right angles to the first axis, intersecting at zero; all other constructs are plotted in relation to these, by reference to the basic matrix of construct relationships. Alternative dimensions with high totals can be selected as further axes in attempts to gain, through visual representation, further psychological insights. This procedure is termed the Anchor method, because the "factors" are anchored into the specific constructs used as axes.

THE SIGNIFICANCE OF "FACTORS"

The solutions and summaries resulting from these various factorial procedures constitute *empirical* statements about the mathematical features of construct systems (e.g. statements concerning the number of significant factors or components summarizing the grids, the numbers of constructs with significant loadings on the first factor, the amount of variance taken up by the first factor, and so forth). They can also be used as bases for more theoretical statements within the context of personal construct theory. This latter use has perhaps been as common as, if not more common than, the former, though the links between the mathematical and psychological models are not always wholly convincing. Kelly suggests that the constructs defining major factors emerging from his analysis might be considered relatively superordinate within the section of the individual's construct system under study. This argument suggests that the more "generalized" the construct in factorial terms, the more superordinate it is in psychological terms. Doubts will later be cast on this assumption.

Both Levy (1954 and 1956) and Bennion (1959) used similar measures as mathematical definitions of constellatory and propositional constructs. Constellatory constructs were defined operationally as the five constructs with the highest loadings on the first Rep test factor. Propositional constructs were defined as the five constructs *not* loaded on this factor and emerging as isolated residual factors in themselves.

Perhaps the most extensive use of Rep test and grid measures of structure outside the theoretical system suggested by Kelly is in the field of study concerning the postulated dimension of cognitive complexity-simplicity. This work was initiated by Jones (1954, journal report 1961), and has been continued by Bieri (1955) and many others, to form what is now virtually a self-contained research area. The wide variety of different measures of cognitive complexity-simplicity (including estimates of variance accounted for by the first factor) that have been used to date have been summarized by Bonarius (1965) and discussed in some detail by Crockett (1965). Untested assumptions and loose argument abound in this area of study; and the work will be cited later in connection with various distortions which the original notion of personal construct systems has undergone.

VARIETIES OF STRUCTURAL MEASURES

Among the other structural measures so far developed which have an arguable relationship to construct theory are some suggested by Bannister (1960 and

1962a). His measure of Intensity of construct relationships has been used in a number of studies (Warren, 1966 and Mair, 1964), and was intended as an overall measure of the amount of construct linkage within any grid. Bannister considered that a high Intensity score might indicate a high degree of organization in the segment of the subject's construct system under investigation, and thereby represent what Kelly termed "tight" construing. Low Intensity of construct relationships might indicate a relative lack of clear-cut conceptual structure. This measure has been used both in this form (as a general statement about construct links in a grid) and also as an index (Bridges, 1965 and Mair, 1967) of the intensity of the network linking into specific constructs.

Bannister (1960 and 1962a) also introduced a measure of Consistency in construct relationships. This was another general measure involving all constructs in the grids under study, and in its original form is similar, in conventional test terms, to that obtained from the completion of a test *and* a parallel, though not identical, form. In the original form of this measure, two similar sets of grid elements, and the same set of adjectival labels to indicate the construct dimensions under consideration, were used. The subject completed the element sorting on the various dimensions on the first set of elements, and then proceeded immediately to carry out the same procedure on the second set. Consistency scores were calculated by estimating the agreement, in correlational terms, between construct matching or relationship scores on the first grid and the equivalent scores on the second grid. High scores were taken to imply a relatively high degree of stability and generalizability in the construct links under study, and low scores, the converse.

There are apparent similarities between some measures of cognitive complexity and Bannister's measure of Intensity. High Intensity scores might operationally be equated with relatively simple cognitive structure, while low Intensity might indicate greater Complexity (since many factors might be required to explain the set of low construct links obtained). However, the measure of Intensity was developed as part of an investigation of schizophrenic thought disorder, and in a series of studies it was shown that thought-disorder schizophrenics yield low Intensity scores. Does this mean (by simple application of Bieri's concept) that thought-disordered schizophrenics are cognitively complex? Hardly, since it was simultaneously shown that thought-disordered schizophrenics are markedly low on Consistency. Thus, their construct relationships are better described as random, since while (mathematically) random sorts are inevitably "complex," we can reasonably reserve the term complex for patterns of interrelationship which, while of low order correlational value, are stable over different element samplings – this latter state of affairs being frequently manifest in normals. Quite apart from a number of challenges to the adequacy of the ideas underlying the proposed complexity-simplicity dimension to be discussed, and others raised by

Crockett (1965), these findings raise the problem, for Bieri and others, of distinguishing between complexity and confusion.

Binner (1958) and Gottesman (1962), in studying Kelly's notion of construct permeability, encouraged subjects to mark a zero in the Rep test if neither emergent nor contrast pole could be applied to a figure. They used the sum of all zeros in a grid as a measure of the permeability of the constructs involved. This method of element allotment is similar to that used by Fjeld and Landfield (1961) and Landfield (1967), but these writers like Hess (1959), thought that the measures derived were more relevant to Kelly's concept of range of convenience than to permeability.

Among the many other measures which have been derived from Rep test and grid data are some which lie somewhere between the realms of content and those of structure. Various measures of identification have been proposed (Jones, 1954 and 1961; Lederman, 1957; Giles, 1961; Salmon, 1967), and also of transference (Sechrest, 1962 and Crisp, 1964) though these are measures derived from studies which are, in conception, outside the framework of personal construct theory.

THE GENERALITY OF GRID METHODOLOGY

In this discussion, we have presented grids with only one type of element – namely, people. This limitation was accepted for the sake of simplicity in presentation. We cannot too strongly emphazise that the content of grids (the constructs and elements) is, for practical purposes, very variable.

Apart from those using people as elements, grids have been constructed to subsume elements such as films (Carver, 1967), paintings (Mair, 1966a), inanimate objects (Bannister and Salmon, 1966), emotions (Fransella and Adams, 1965), problem situations in a person's life (Kelly, 1955) and types of bread (Jones, 1963).

Kelly's Situational Resources grid is an interesting example of an alternative grid focus. Here, there are two title lists. The first concerns situations of different types (the time you were most hard up financially, the time you made the most serious mistakes in your life, the time you were most lonely, the time you had most serious trouble with your parents, and so forth), which the patient might be expected to have experienced as stressful. He is asked to say where and when these situations were experienced. The other title list includes role titles designed to elicit the kind of people upon whom one might lean at some time in one's life. The intersects in the grid are marked in terms of whether or not the subject feels that the person nominated to represent the role title would be helpful in the particular stress situation denoted. In this way, it is possible to use the grid method to uncover systematically those areas of stress in which the person feels he has few human resources, and to indicate the people on whom he primarily depends for various types of succour. Factorial analysis here could show how he groups his stressful experiences, and how he groups his human resources. Such grids are designed to analyze dependencies which have relevance in psychotherapy.

THE NATURE AND PURPOSE OF GRIDS

Kelly extensively discussed the nature of grid method, and from his evaluation the following passages are quoted as particularly definitive.

"What we have been saying about the construing of persons can be generalized. Basically, construing is simply the erection and application of a system of grids, whereon the intersects between events may be plotted.

We have been talking about one type of grid, the Rep Test Grid. This particular grid is composed of the intersects between certain personal constructs of the person who takes the test and certain representative persons whom he knows. Both his constructs and the persons whom he construes are real events. But they are of somewhat different orders. The person-events are presumably reflections on real events, events which would take place even if the examinee were not alive; but, as far as the grid is concerned, they are themselves really the examinee's own acts of perception. On the other hand, the personal constructs which the examinees weaves through these person-events are also events; but, presumably, neither they nor their possible counterparts would exist if the examinee were not alive. Thus two different orders of events constitute the warp and weft out of which the pattern of the person's social life is woven.

We need only to extend this notion in order to arrive at a view of conceptualization in general. Our conceptualization of *poverty*, of *freedom*, or of *evil*, for example, may be viewed in the same manner. Certain events in our lives may be interwoven with the construct of *poverty*. This and this are *poverty*, while that and that are *not poverty*! These events are represented by *freedom*, while these events are represented by *enslavement*. Here and there we find the *good* which stands out in contrast to the intervening *evil*. It is by such interweaving that both the events of our lives and the constructs we use for dealing with them take on meaning. Each provides operational referrents for the other.

In this chapter we have suggested a type of analysis of Rep Test protocol which transcends both the subject's verbiage and the particular individuals who make up his personal-social milieu. The test protocol can be meaningfully analyzed even if one clips off the names from the top of the test blank and the constructs from the side. What we have left is exclusively a geometric or a mathematical structure of the person's psychological space. The grid of intersects is speckled with incidents and voids. Some of the rows tend to match each other and some of the columns are almost alike. Moreover, certain rows are somewhat representative of all the rows, that is, all the constructs, – and some of the columns are representative of all the columns – that is, all the figures.

Not only can the grid notion be generalized to all conceptualization, but this mathematical notion can also be generalized. The incidents and voids which populate a grid of intersects provide the binary numerical basis for a mathematics of psychological space. This cybernetic model permits us to scan any grid with a hypothetical scanning pattern and note the concurrences of incidents and voids, row by row or column by column. Thus we may have a mathematical basis for expressing and measuring the perceptual relationships between the events which are uniquely interwoven in any person's psychological space." (pp. 301–2)

This statement about the generality of usefulness of the original grid idea has encouraged a number of workers to formulate a variety of applications beyond those implied by the original people-sorting form. However, it is already apparent that the original binary grid and its more recent variations cannot adequately subsume all the ingenious, and sometimes contorted forms of construing which men have undertaken. Not least among its limitations is its fixity in expressing only one type of linkage between constructs (the reciprocal linkage represented by a unitary index of association), and its failure to incorporate some important aspects of construct theory.

ASSUMPTIONS INVOLVED IN THE USE OF GRID METHOD

In presenting the outlines of the Role Construct Repertory Test and the repertory grid form, Kelly recognized that the use of any practical methodology which might allow the elicitation and organization of role-related constructs involved the examiner in making a number of more or less adventurous bets or assumptions. All measurement methods involve assumptions, and the Rep test and grid, no less than others. One unusual feature in Kelly's presentation of his methods is the attention he gives to specifying, in some detail, the various assumptions made by him in their development, and made by any investigator in applying them to particular problems. Many of the assumptions underlying the Rep test and those underlying the grid form are similar, and only those relevant to the repertory grid methods are discussed here.

(i) *Representative Figures*. In using grid methods to examine aspects of the content and structure of a section of a person's construct system, it must be assumed that the sample of elements (people, things, or what you will) is an adequate representation of the total population of the relevant elements in the person's world. Representativeness in sampling presents both theoretical and practical difficulties. As Kelly indicates, "it is not enough to say that the sample must be representative – it must be representative with respect to certain dimensions. It is only as the sample is representative along essential dimensional lines that it can be called representative of a population." (p. 270) This statement serves to move the problem of definition to the word "essential"; and no completely satisfactory means of assessing which dimensions are essential within any element sample has yet been devised. Kelly sought to justify the legitimacy of making this assumption of representativeness of element sample, by the use of his carefully selected role title list. "What we must assume here is simply that the figures elicited by the Role Title List are representative of those with whom the client must interact and that the dimensions of their representation are relevant to those lines along which he has chosen to structure his life role." (pp. 270–1)

In some of the more recent modifications of the grid form described above, the assumption of element sample representativeness may be less justified, since either the element selection has been left to the discretion of the subject (with the experimenter hoping that, if a large enough sample is used, it may tend in some unspecified ways to be fairly representative of the person's interpersonal world), or it has been chosen by the experimenter without regard at all to the importance or otherwise of the elements chosen for the subject involved. With some rank order grid forms, where the elements (e.g. photographs of unknown faces) are chosen by the experimenter, and only a very small sample (perhaps eight elements) is used, any assumption about the representativeness of the sample, as regards important figures in the subject's life, may not be at all justified.

(ii) *Representative Sorts.* "Here again," Kelly suggests, "one must assume that the sorting problems proposed for the client are representative of those with which he must deal in structuring his life role. This does not necessarily mean that he must meet all three figures in the same social situation at the same time; it means, rather, that the trio calls for the kind of discrimination which invokes one of the personal dimensions in terms of which his psychological space is structured." (p. 271)

Again, in more recent grid uses involving the supplying of construct labels to the subjects, this assumption is ignored completely. No such thing as *general* representativeness can be achieved (just as there is no such thing as the general reliability or general validity of a test). The problems of representativeness in constructs and elements needs to be faced and made explicit in relation to the hypotheses under test in each investigation.

(iii) *Stability of Conception.* During the process of eliciting constructs, or in using them in the grid sorting task, it is necessary to assume that the person being tested does not shift ground between giving or using the emergent pole of a construct, and giving or using its implicit pole. If he does blur the distinction he is making, and shift ground, he may give the examiner what are essentially the emergent poles of two different constructs.

(iv) *Range of Convenience.* This assumption is not required in the use of the Rep test, but becomes of considerable importance in the grid form. As Kelly says "this assumption is implied when we insist on interpreting a void as specifying the implicit pole of the personal construct. This may not be a good assumption in all cases; it may be that the client has left a void at a certain intersect simply because the construct does not seem to apply, one way or the other, to this particular figure." (p. 271) Some attempts have been made by different investigators to control for this possibility, by, for example, allowing the subject to indicate on a rating scale whether or not the elements can meaningfully be grouped, scaled or rated in terms of each construct dimension used in the grid. Alternatively the subject may be encouraged to indicate for each element whether it belongs to the emergent *or* the contrast pole, *or* that the construct does not apply, *or* that he is "undecided." This makes for greater difficulties in statistical analysis, but it allows the subject greater freedom to express his personal constructions (cf. Landfield, 1967).

(v) *Word Labels.* In the Rep test, the examiner must assume that the words used by the subject, to describe the construct discriminations he is making, mean much the same to the subject as they do to him. This is an assumption underlying all questionnaire and rating scale approaches to psychological measurement, but is slightly *less* important in the repertory grid than it is elsewhere. "The use of the grid permits the psychologist to make a rather extensive analysis of the protocol without once looking at the terms which the client has employed. It is this advantage that argues strongly for the use of the grid, both in clinical settings and in research." (p. 272)

In addition to these assumptions outlined by Kelly, a number of others seem to be involved, and to underlie the use of recent grid modifications. Kelly's grid method involves the assumption that, in obtaining matching or relationship scores, congruence of element choices, or ratings on different construct dimensions, represents functional linkage between these construct dimensions. The essence of a grid is that conceptual linkages are inferred from statistical relationships in sorting. Further, the application of one or other of the statistical factorial procedures is assumed to yield a picture of aspects of total structure which represents features of the subject's personal economy in the organization of his view of life.

Other assumptions made in using recent forms are : (i) that the various grid forms (split-half, rank order, etc.) will provide essentially equivalent data concerning the relationships between the constructs involved, and that similar relationships would have emerged had Kelly's original free allotment method been used: (ii) that supplied construct labels are relevant to important constructs of the individuals tested (although no attempts have been made to check on this possibility): (iii) that when construct labels are supplied to groups of subjects, a high degree of commonality will exist in terms of their usage of the words (any differences in meanings for different individuals, showing up in differences in the relationships between the various supplied constructs).

Additionally, in a number of investigations, whole-figure constructs (e.g. Like Father, Like Myself, Like the Doctor, etc.) have been used and subjects asked, for example, to sort the elements in terms of how like or unlike their own *father* are the figures in the element list. From the matchings between these whole-figure constructs and more specific construct dimensions, the examiner hopes to gain some information about how the subject sees the figure represented by the whole figure construct. The purpose seems partly to avoid asking directly for specific information about the key figures. Such an approach seems potentially useful, but a risky assumption is made, in that the information emerging from such analyses may not tally with the subject's overt claims (cf. Mair, 1967a) and we do not know what the discrepancy implies.

In using different types of elements within the same general area (e.g. people known to the subject, or photographs of unknown people) it is assumed that they will each provide similar results, and that selection of one or other element set may be guided by various marginal advantages in economy or ease of administration.

Pending points of advantage and disadvantage raised later, this outline of grid method is meant to imply that the potential of grids is only equalled by our ignorance of many of their psychological significates.

CHAPTER 3

Developments in Personal Construct
Theory and Method

TEN YEARS after Kelly described his conception of the psychology of personal constructs, the first major elaboration and definition of some aspects of that theory was attempted by Hinkle (1965). Prior to this, a number of other investigators had utilized aspects of the theory and method within specific areas of psychological interest without undertaking any major restatement of the theory. Thus Landfield (1954 and 1955) and Landfield and Fjeld (1960) concentrated on the nature of *threat* and the means whereby it could be investigated experimentally; Bieri (1955 and 1961) and others focused their interest on the complexity-simplicity of conceptual structures inferred from variations of the Rep test and rep grid procedures; and Bannister (1960 *et seq.*) concentrated on using measures of construct interrelatedness, deriving from modifications of grid technique, to distinguish between the structual properties of the construct systems of thought disordered schizophrenics and those of other clinical groups.

CONSTRUCT SYSTEMS AS IMPLICATIVE NETWORKS

While working within the framework of construct theory, Hinkle chose to emphasize certain aspects of the theory and define them more rigorously as a basis for his experimental work. He began his thesis with the contention that "construct definitions must involve a statement of the *location* of a construct dimension in the context of a hierarchical *network* of construct implications. Here 'implication,' 'prediction,' 'anticipation,' and 'expectation' are regarded as being synonymous terms. From this viewpoint, constructs will be regarded as having only one characteristic, quality, or property; namely, a construct has differential *implications* in a given hierarchical *context*."

The differential implications of the two poles of a construct can run up or down the construct system; that is, they can be superordinate or subordinate implications. Kelly originally defined a superordinate construct as one which includes another as one of the elements in its context, and he defined a subordinate construct as one which is included as an element in the context of another. Hinkle sees as one possible operational definition of a superordinate implication that the construct is likely to be produced in answer to the question "why?" If we ask a man why he prefers to be a *white collar worker* (as contrasted with a *manual worker*) and he replies that it is because he wants to be a member of the *upper classes* (as contrasted with the *lower classes*), then it can be argued that *upper class* is one of the superordinate implications of the construct *white collar worker* and that thereby *upper class* is the more superordinate of the two constructs within the system as a whole. Conversely, we might argue that subordinate implications are likely to be elicited by questions such as "how do you know that?" or "what is your evidence for that?" For example, if we ask a man on what basis he sees himself as *white collar* and he points out that he *works in an office* (as contrasted with *working in a factory*) then *working in an office* is one of the subordinate implications of *white collar worker* and is the more subordinate of the two constructs. Only constructs which have a line of implication between them can stand in subordinate or superordinate relation to each other, although these terms can be used as generally descriptive of contrasts within a hierarchical system. Another way of defining the relationship is to say that what implies a construct is its subordinate constructions and what is implied by a construct is its superordinate constructions. In devoting a considerable amount of attention to a discussion of subordinate as contrasted with superordinate implications, Hinkle is emphasizing a prime difference between construct theory and earlier ideas and experimental work on concept formation. Earlier work on concept formation tended to treat all concepts as "equal" and to investigate them as if they were simply adjacent categories. Construct theory stresses the hierarchical nature of construct networks.

From this argument Hinkle draws the conclusion that superordinate constructs carry a greater number of implications than subordinate constructs. This becomes clear if we note that the line of implication between subordinate and superordinate constructs is not always reciprocal. We cannot argue that *upper class* directly implies *white collar worker*, because it implies the possibility of *many* subordinate constructions (in addition to *white collar*) which *together* constitute the superordinate construct. This is to say that many constructions concerned with income, education, parentage and so on might together imply *upper class*, but for none of them as a single construct does the reverse implication necessarily and inevitably hold good. In this sense construct hierarchies are rather like categories in traditional logic, which include their sub-categories but do not conversely imply them. The traditional logical point – that all books are paper but not all paper is books – exemplifies this.

Hinkle deals in some detail with the various forms of implication which may hold good between two constructs. The passage dealing with this question is quoted in full below. It is useful, in that it draws attention to the complexity of construct interrelationships, although in his actual experimental work, Hinkle restricts his attention to parallel and reciprocal forms of relationship.

"Let us now turn our attention briefly to the various forms of implication between two constructs; for example, construct A-B and construct X-Y. A wide variety of specific implicative combinations are possible, but four commonly observed patterns are the parallel, orthogonal, reciprocal, and ambiguous forms, which are described as follows:

1. *Parallel*: A implies X and B implies Y. (e.g., love-hate; pleasantness-unpleasantness).

2. *Orthogonal*: A implies X, but B does not imply Y; also A implies X and B implies X, but neither implies Y. (e.g., employed-unemployed; has income-has no income. Also, good-bad; evaluative-objective).

3. *Reciprocal*: A implies X and B implies Y and X implies A and Y implies B. (e.g., nervous-calm; tense-relaxed). This kind of a relationship suggests a functional equivalence of the construct labels.

4. *Ambiguous*: A and B imply X, and B implies Y; also A implies X and Y, and B implies X and Y. One subject, for example, when relating desirable-undesirable and realism-idealism, said that realism and idealism both implied desirable and undesirable aspects for him. Conflict theory and double-bind theory relate to these *implicative dilemmas.* Such situations seems to result from (1) an incomplete abstraction of the differences between the contexts in which the construct was used; or (2) in the case of the example above – the subject used one construct label for two independent constructs, e.g., realism-idealism in the sense of testing ideas-not testing ideas and realism-idealism in the sense of not having goals-having goals. When clarified, the subject could then relate each of these usages of realism-idealism to desirable-undesirable in the unambiguous parallel form. In this sense psychological movement, conflict resolution, and insight depend on the locating of such points of ambiguous implication and the resolving of them into parallel or orthogonal forms." (Hinkle, 1965)

Having thus stressed that a construct must be defined in terms of its location in a *hierarchical* network, that is, in terms of its subordinate *and* superordinate implications, Hinkle goes on to discuss the question of context. Obviously, constructs with wide ranges of convenience may be used in a number of different contexts, and the interrelationships between them may not be identical from one context to another. The construct *efficient-inefficient* may carry implications for the construct *to be scrapped-to be retained* in the context of, say, "typewriters," but the two constructs may not be related in exactly the same way in the context of, say, "people." This raises the question of the sense in which we think of constructs as being "the same" from one context to another, and highlights the need to keep in mind the distinction between the construct label (the word used to summarize and communicate) and the actual construct itself. Hinkle tentatively suggests that the *transcontextual* identity of a construct should perhaps be defined as "the points of identical subordinate and superordinate implications." He argues thus: if in context x, A, B, and C imply *honesty*, and *honesty* implies 1, 2 and 3; while in context y, A, D and E imply *honesty*, and *honesty* implies 1, 4, and 5, then the trans-contextual identity of *honesty* consists of A and 1. This at least, offers us a logical definition of equivalence between constructs in different contexts, however difficult this may be to translate into grid terms.

One of the effects of the particular definition of constructs for which Hinkle argues, is to emphasize that such theoretical constructs as permeable-impermeable, loose-tight, core-peripheral, constellatory-propositional and so forth are not properties or characteristics of constructs as such, and certainly they form no part of the *definition* of constructs. They should be viewed as ancillary dimensions used to describe characteristics of the network of implications from a structural viewpoint, and, in this sense, they are open to revision more readily than the central tenets of personal construct theory.

In terms of the central constructs of construct theory as he saw them, Hinkle chose to study *change* as a prime aspect of construing. The main question to which he sought an answer was "what determines the relative resistance to change of different personal constructs?" He accepted as a starting point Kelly's distinction between two types of change. *Shift change* is involved when a person moves from using one construct dimension to using another in a given context, e.g. the auditor who, when checking a firm's accounts, begins by seeing them in terms of the construct *careful-careless*, but eventually decides that it would be more appropriate to look at them in terms of the construct *straight-crooked*. The second form of change is termed *slot change*, when use is made of the alternative pole of the construct dimension rather than calling an alternative dimension into play, e.g. the auditor who initially construes the accounts he is examining as *straight*, but eventually decides that they would be better subsumed under the alternative pole *crooked*.

Hinkle chose to concentrate his experimental attention on slot change, although he measured this in terms of the willingness of his subjects to make a slot change on one construct *as compared* with their willingness to make it on another. Hinkle construed the choice corollary of personal construct theory as implying that a person seeks to use his dichotomous constructs in such a way as to achieve a greater number of implications for his system. That is to say, a person will resist movement in the direction of reduced implications (threat) or relative absence of implications (anxiety). Thus Hinkle suggested that slot movements might be expected to occur more on constructs having approximately equal numbers of implications for each pole, and for which each set of implications is estimated to be equally com-patible with the rest of the construct system. Conversely, there would be greater resistance to slot change in a situation where there were markedly more implications for one pole of a construct than for the other, or where acceptance of one of the sets of polar implications would involve widespread incompatibility of inference in relation to other parts of the system.

From the organization corollary he argued that the higher in the hierarchy any construct is placed, the greater the number of constructs which will be needed to define its polar implications, that is to say, it would have a greater range of subordinate and superordinate implications. From this it is argued that there will be a higher level of resistance to change on superordinate constructs, because any change at this level will necessarily involve a great number of related changes and a considerable risk of the development of inferential incompatibility within the system. For most of us, to decide that we are *unmusical* rather than *musical* is a tenable change in self construing, since it has a limited number of implications, whereas to decide that we are *bad* rather than *good* is to involve ourselves in a considerable number of related and implied changes, the extent of which cannot be easily envisaged. It is interesting to note that this argument relates to Kelly's concept of *hostility*, which he defined as "the continued effort to extort validational evidence in favour of a type of social prediction which has already been recognized as a failure." In construct theory terms, hostility occurs when we cannot accept invalidation of our expectations, because it implies a shift in our construing which would involve so many related changes as to presage chaos.

HYPOTHESES AND METHODS

Hinkle proposed four general hypotheses, and his methodology is presented in relation to these, since they were developed, in the first instance, in order to provide a structure within which these hypotheses could be tested.

Hypothesis 1: "The relative resistance to slot change of personal constructs will be directly related to the superordinate range of implications of those constructs."

Hypothesis 2: "Constructs functioning at a higher level of superordination in a hierarchical context will have a larger superordinate range of implications than constructs functioning at a low level."

Hypothesis 3: "Constructs functioning at a higher level of superordination in a hierarchical context will have a larger subordinate range of implications than constructs functioning at a low level."

Hypothesis 4: "Constructs functioning at a higher level of superordination in a hierarchical context will show a greater relative resistance to slot change than constructs functioning at a low level."

This is the central "change" hypothesis; while the second and third hypotheses define aspects of structure, the fourth focuses on change *in relation to* structure.

PROCEDURE

Twenty-eight student subjects participated in the experiment. There were 11 males and 17 females; their mean age was 20 years (ranging from 18 to 31).

1. *The introduction.* Hinkle informed each subject presenting himself for his "personality interview" that he was interested in having him explain himself in a particular fashion which could later be mathematically analyzed. Each was told that the results would be explained to him later, should he desire it. The average experimental time per subject was just under three hours, with short breaks after each major section of the interview, and at other times if the subject wished. It is of interest to note, when considering the experimental procedure, that, while it yields formalized and quantifiable data, it must have seemed to the subject like a structured interview rather than a "test."

2. *Elicitation of figures.* Each subject was asked to give the names of nine people who currently played an important role in his life and whom he knew well. Parents, nearest siblings, boy or girl friends, and such like were suggested, and the only restriction made was that the subject should have known any figure chosen for at least six months, and should regard that person as *currently* important in his life. In each case the subject's own name was used as the tenth figure.

3. *Elicitation of ten subordinate constructs.* The procedure here was similar to the triad method suggested by Kelly. However, in order to ensure that the constructs elicited referred to the subjects themselves, triads were used in which the person's own name always figured as one of the three elements. In each case the subject was asked to think of some way in which two of the three figures in the first triad were alike and different from the third. This was repeated nine further times with different triads, thus eliciting ten construct dimensions. Care was taken to ensure that no subject produced the same construct on more than one occasion, and after completion of the elicitation procedure, subjects were asked to check that no construct produced was simply a rewording of some other construct in the list. When both subject and experimenter were satisfied that ten different constructs had been produced, they proceeded to the next stage. (It should be noted that these constructs were only held to be subordinate *relative* to constructs produced by the "laddering" method later described – some of them may have been relatively superordinate in absolute terms.)

4. *Pole preference of the subordinate constructs.* The subject was then required to indicate which pole of each construct dimension listed was "*clearly* descriptive of the kind of person he prefers to be." Thus, preferred self constructions, not necessarily actual self constructions, are being sought (note: it would have been interesting to know which were actual *and* preferred,

and actual and non-preferred, since this would have shown if people identified themselves as at the pole with most implications, as Hinkle suggested they would). In any situations where no clear pole preference could be established, further constructs were elicited until the necessary criteria, noted here and in the previous section, were met. The requirement of a definite pole preference was designed to ensure that the constructs used would have clearly differentiated implications.

5. *The hierarchical technique for eliciting the superordinate constructs of the preferred self hierarchy (laddering procedure).* At this stage in the procedure, Hinkle required his subjects to construe some of the superordinate implications of at least some of the subordinate constructs elicited in Section 3 above. The subject was presented with his first subordinate construct and given the following instructions: "Now on this construct you preferred this side to that side. What I want to understand now is why you would prefer to be here rather than there (pointing). What are the advantages of this side in contrast to the disadvantages of that side as you see it?" In providing the required explanation, the subject inevitably gave a further construct dimension, which again had a preferred pole. This supposedly more superordinate construct was then used as the basis for a repetition of the same query, and the subject, in explaining the advantages he attributed to the preferred pole, provided a further construct dimension. Hinkle continued this "laddering" elicitation procedure until either the subject could no longer give further dimensions, or until he had provided ten such superordinate dimensions, which he considered as clearly different from, though related to, one another. In each case a clear side (pole) preference was elicited. Thus, for example, a subject might start from the dimension *reserved-emotional* (preferring to see himself at the *reserved* pole) and in answer to the question 'why do you prefer' to be *reserved*, might indicate that reserved people tend to be *relaxed*, while emotional people tend to be *nervous*. The dimension *relaxed-nervous* was then taken as the first superordinate construction, with the subject preferring to view himself as *relaxed*. Next (in answer to "why?") he might suggest that he preferred being *relaxed* because, in his opinion, being relaxed would lead to *getting on better with people*, while being nervous might result in *difficulties with people*. Here the second superordinate is *getting on better with people-difficulties with people*; the preferred pole is known, and a further query will lead on to the next act of superordination and so forth.

If the subject was unable to produce ten such superordinates from one original construct, then another was selected from the subordinate construct list and the same procedure repeated.

Hinkle found in a pilot study that students could usually provide about 8 to 12 superordinate constructs by this laddering procedure before reaching the top of a hierarchy. Some recent attempts at using the laddering technique in Britain have indicated that Hinkle's methods or students must have been more productive of such constructs than seems generally the case here, since most people produced considerably fewer superordinates in any ladder. In his pilot work, Hinkle also attempted hierarchical elicitation for each subject on every construct, but abandoned the procedure for the main study because it was so time-consuming. Additionally, the series of superordinates deriving from the first subordinate construct was almost always repeated in subsequent ones. As the organization corollary would lead one to expect, there was a convergence of constructions at higher levels of superordination.

In relation to the emphasis on n-Achievement and n-Affiliation made by McClelland *et al.* (1953), Atkinson (1958) and others, it is of interest to note that in the college student group of subjects used by Hinkle, the themes of achievement and affiliation were frequently observed in the hierarchies of superordinate constructs elicited.

6. *The determination of the relative resistance to slot change of the elicited constructs.* At this stage Hinkle introduced his resistance to change grid procedure. A 20 by 20 cell grid blank was prepared for each subject. The ten subordinate constructs were listed and numbered from 1 to 10, and the ten superordinate constructs, derived from the hierarchical elicitation procedure, listed and numbered from 11 to 20. A completed resistance to change grid is shown in Fig. 7.

Each construct dimension was written on a small card with the preferred pole marked. The subject was then presented with the cards two at a time, until each construct had been paired with every other one. Constructs 1 and 2 were presented to the subject, who was given the following instructions: "Look at these two constructs. The check marks indicate the sides you said you would prefer to be on. Now, let's assume for the moment that you had to change from the preferred side to the unpreferred side on one of these constructs, but would remain the same on the other. Which of these two constructs would you prefer to remain the same on? Remember, you will have to change on the other one. What we are trying to find out here is if you had to change, which of these two changes would be the more undesirable, as you see it? We would prefer you to make a choice whenever possible, but there are two circumstances in which you will find it impossible to make a choice. The first is when the two changes both appear to be undesirable to exactly the same degree. In most cases, however, you will be able to detect some difference between the two which will enable you to make a decision. The second instance is when it is not logically possible to change on one construct and at the same time remain the same on the other. This is the case where changing on one construct logically implies that you must also have changed on the other construct. Let me know when either of these two circumstances occur. Any questions?"

FIG. 7. Resistance to change grid

20	19	18	17	16	15	14	13	12	11	10	9	8	7	6	5	4	3	2	1	
																				1
																		×		2
																				3
																	×	i		4
																	×	×	×	5
																	×			6
														×			×	×		7
														×			×			8
											×	×	×	×	×	×	×	×		9
																		i		10
										×				×			×		i	11
								i	×					×	i		×		i	12
							i	i	×					×	×	×	×		i	13
							i	i	i	×				×			×		i	14
						i	×	i	i	×				×			×	i	i	15
							i	i	i					i			i		i	16
				×		×	×	×	×	i				i			i		i	17
		i	×			×	×	×	×	×		×	×	×	×	×	×	×	×	18
						i		i	i	×				×			×		i	19
			i				i		i					i			i			20

Constructs

1. *face problems—escape from problems*
2. *prefer to save money—spend it on unnecessary things*
3. *dependable—undependable*
4. *mature—immature*
5. *interested in school—disinterested*
6. *neat—sloppy*
7. *hard worker—lazy*
8. *doesn't gossip—does*
9. *plays cards—doesn't*
10. *prompt—slow in paying debts*
11. *solve problems—can't*
12. *achievements—few achievements*
13. *boost ego—tear it down*
14. *do better—do worse*
15. *gain more material things—gain few*
16. *satisfied—dissatisfied*
17. *gain respect of others—loose*
18. *wanted—unwanted*
19. *make right decisions—make wrong decisions*
20. *self interest—lack of self interest*

(i) Constructs 1–10 are subordinate (i.e. elicited by the triadic method) and constructs 11–20 are superordinate (i.e. elicited by laddering).

(ii) An " × " in a column indicates those constructs on which a subject preferred to make a slot change in order to remain the same on the given constructs indicated by the column. A blank in a column indicates, therefore, those constructs on which a subject preferred not to make a slot change, but was willing to change the column construct in order to do so. An " × " or a blank in a row, however, has just the opposite meaning. The letter "i" is used to indicate those construct pairs for which a change on one, while remaining the same on the other, is logically impossible. Construct pairs for which no choice could be made, because both changes were equally undesirable, are indicated by the letter "e" (no such construct pairs appear in this grid).

First, construct 1 was paired with all the other constructs, then removed from from the pack; next, construct 2 was paired with the others in similar fashion, and so on. Hinkle then estimated the relative resistance to slot change of the twenty constructs – rank ordering them (from high to low resistance to change) by counting the number of times each construct was nominated for "no change" during the pairing process. He omitted from the count construct pairs which the subject had judged "equal," or logically entailed.

The implication grid technique. In this procedure Hinkle attempted to provide, within the framework of a grid, a schematic representation (in matrix form) of the superordinate and subordinate implications that inter-relate a set of constructs. He stressed that he had, thus far, only considered those implicative relationships of the parallel and reciprocal form. His instruc-tions to subjects were as follows: "Consider this construct for a moment (Construct 1). Now, if you were to be changed back and forth from one side to the other – that is, if you woke up one morning and realized that you were best described by one side of this construct while the day before you had been best described by the opposite side – if you realized that you were changed in this *one* respect – what other constructs of these nineteen remain-ing ones would be *likely* to be changed by a change in yourself on this one construct alone? Changing back and forth on just this one construct will *probably cause* you to predictably change back and forth on which other constructs? Remember a change on just this one construct is the cause, while the changes on these other constructs are the effects, implied by the changes from one side to the other on this construct alone. What I'd like to find out, then, is on which of these constructs do you probably expect a change to occur as the *result of knowing* that you have changed from one side to the other of this one construct alone. A knowledge of your location on this one construct could probably be used to determine your location on which of these remaining constructs?"

Each construct was paired twice with each of the others (1 with 2, 2 with 1, etc.) and the superordinate implications of parallel or reciprocal form indexed.

Hinkle notes that when any person has completed such a grid, he has essentially indicated 21 personalities for himself, since each of the 20 columns represents a possible alternative self-construction, with the set of preferred pole choices indicating a further personality.

In such an implication grid, the pattern of ticks and blanks in the *columns* is considered by Hinkle to represent the superordinate implications of the various constructs; while the pattern of checks in the *rows* indicates some of the subordinate implications of the constructs. The row patterns do not necessarily, and in fact do not generally match or mirror the column patterns. Perhaps this point, which is important for understanding the operational definitions involved in the hypotheses and the resulting calculations, can be more readily understood with the aid of an example, and one is given from Hinkle's data, in Fig. 8.

After the experimental stage was over, almost all the subjects claimed to have no idea about the purpose of the study, three only suggesting that it might be concerned with assessing something about the logical consistency of their thinking. More interestingly, subjects did not know *why* they resisted change on certain constructs more than on others. Not one subject, it seems, was able to formulate an explanation for the basis of his decisions. The usual response was – I don't know; I just seemed to know; it just felt right.

OPERATIONAL STATEMENTS OF HYPOTHESES

Hinkle stated the four hypotheses operationally, in the following form.

1. "The rank order of the constructs as derived from the resistance to change grid should be highly positively correlated with the rank order derived from the implication grid" (rank ordered by a simple count of the number of implications in each column). In general terms – the greater the number of superordinate implications involved, the greater should be the resistance to change on a particular construct.

2. "The sum on the implication grid of the sums of *columns* 1–10 will be significantly less than the sum of the sums of *columns* 11–20 for the group." In general terms – superordinate constructs (as defined by "laddering") will have more superordinate implications (as defined by the implication grid column totals).

3. "The sum on the implication grid of the sums of *rows* 1–10 will be significantly less than the sum of the sums of *rows* 11–20 for the group." In general terms – superordinate constructs (as defined by "laddering") will have more subordinate implications (as defined by the implication grid rows).

4. "Constructs 11–20 will have a lower mean resistance to change rank order (indicating a *greater* resistance to slot movement) then constructs 1–10." In general terms – a superordinate construct (as defined by "laddering") will show greater "resistance to change," (as defined by the resistance to change grid).

RESULTS

Each of the hypotheses was supported strongly, all *p*-values being less than 0·001. A few of the formal characteristics of the theory of construct implications were thus demonstrated, and the viability of the methods in relation to the problems posed was indicated.

The methods described, however, not only provide a means of exploring such relatively formal and mathematical properties of construct interrelationship and change; they also provide a vast pool of information, concerning

FIG. 8. Implication grid

20	19	18	17	16	15	14	13	12	11	10	9	8	7	6	5	4	3	2	1	
r							r									r	r			1
r																		×		2
r	×							r				×	×						r	3
	r						×												r	4
																				5
r							r						×							6
r							r										.	×		7
r	×						r													8
																				9
r	×																r	×		10
	r						r									×		×		11
×	×	×	r		r	r	r		×			×	×	×				×		12
r	r	r	r	r	r	r		r	r	×		r	r	r					r	13
×	×	×	r		r		r	r	×			×	×	×			×	×		14
×	×	×	r			r	r	r	×			×	×	×			×	×		15
×	×	×	×		×	×	r	×	×	×		×	×	×		×	×		×	16
×	×	r			r	r	r	r	×	×		×	×	×	×	×	×		×	17
×	×		r				r					×	×			×	×		×	18
×							r		r							r		×		19
							r		r			r	r	r			r	r	r	20

specific construct linkages, which can be studied in terms of its "meaningful content." Hinkle in fact presented, with obvious relish, brief sketches of a few of his subjects. There was, for example, the "19-year old intelligent, poised, very attractive, well dressed sorority girl," recently engaged to be married and flourishing her large diamond ring, announcing in a radiant manner that she was to be married "in just two and a half years." Examination of the linkages with other dimensions of her construct dimension *wants to get married–doesn't want to get married* showed, among other relationships, reciprocal implications with the dimension *self-centred–broader outlook*. While this latter dimension was reciprocally related with many of the other constructs in the grid, the former was not. It seemed therefore that this girl had not elaborated any implications of wanting to get married. In the experimental situation, while indicating the implications of the *self-centred–broader outlook* construct, she became enuretic. Hinkle speculated on the possibility that some preverbal construct was called into play when the threat of reduced implicativeness was appreciated by the subject.

Another subject was a "23-year old, thin, unshaven, dishevelled, suspicious deliberating male." With the accompaniment of much thought and intellectualization, he produced what Hinkle described as "a remarkably symmetrically patterned implication grid." The student, himself, on looking at his grid, commented on its symmetry and interrelatedness. He admitted later that he was undergoing group therapy and had been diagnosed as a paranoid schizophrenic. For the previous five years he had withdrawn into himself to think his own thoughts and put them in order, because he felt the world could never be changed and he had given up trying. Hinkle comments that the interrelatedness of his constructs was such that invalidation of any one would probably produce a massive change of implications, resulting in great

---

FIG. 8. (contd.)

(i) The number of each of the twenty constructs is indicated along the side and bottom of the grid. An " × " indicates the parallel superordinate implications of the column construct. An "r" in a column indicates the reciprocal superordinate implications of the column construct. Row entries indicate subordinate implications of row constructs.

(ii) This Implication grid was obtained from the subject whose Resistance to Change grid was shown in Fig. 7 and the constructs are those listed for that figure. Both protocols are from Hinkle (1965).

(iii) This subject is clearly in line with Hinkle's hypothesis in that the superordinate (laddered) constructs, 11–20, show more implications than the subordinate constructs, 1–10. Implication grids can be examined in simple content terms e.g. in this grid construct 15 (*gain more material things—gain few*) is reciprocally related to construct 17 (*gain respect of others—loose*). Various orders of implications can be traced through, or the grid can be cluster analysed by the methods used for grid matrices of the original type.

threat. This man was unusual in his impgrid scores, because his superordinate and subordinate constructs did not differ significantly from each other in either their superordinate or their subordinate ranges of implications. For him, however, the threat hypothesis (concerning the relative resistance to slot change in constructs with differing ranges of superordinate implications) was very highly significant.

Concerning the outcome of the hypothesis testing, Hinkle concludes as follows:

"The results of this study have furnished substantial initial evidence for the utility of the theory of construct implications and the associated methodologies of the hierarchical method, the resistance to slot change grid, and the implication grid. The broader theoretical significance of these results is that they provide support for the Choice and Organization Corollaries of personal construct theory. In addition, the findings again highlight the importance of Kelly's First Principle 'If you don't know, ask the person; he just might tell you.' Basically the methodologies of this study were the means whereby a person could explain his outlook, in a systematic fashion, to a rather thick-headed experimenter."

Hinkle was clearly aware of the limited nature of the validation of theory and method achieved in this study, and indicated the need for "experimental cross-validation using various treatment conditions within subjects, and perhaps various non-verbal behaviour correlates as well."

In this first study Hinkle concentrated on only one type of change, namely, slot change of an all-or-none-kind. Both scalar change (change from bipolar to "more-or-less" judgments) and shift change (change to an alternative construct dimension) could also be investigated within very similar procedures. Scalar change is regarded as a slot change in the magnitude used to describe a construct alternative, and Hinkle speculates that such changes might or might not result in an absolute change of implication. Because of this, scalar changes, in some instances, may be used to stabilize or alter an implicative network. The nature of such stabilizing or alteration effects could be a useful topic for further investigation.

While the format of the resistance to change grid might not be the most satisfactory one within which to explore shift change, some aspects of shifts between construct dimensions could be investigated within it. Here, as with all investigations of construct change suggested by Hinkle, it is change as superordinately construed by the subject, *envisaged* change, that is involved – not change that results from a specific experience of invalidation or validation.

This problem leads directly into the study of a person's superordinate constructions about his own construct subsystems, his constructs about constructs. People, no doubt, differ greatly in their superordinate structure for dealing with their own construing; and the processes of education and psychotherapy are often concerned to make explicit and develop a person's ideas about himself and his strategies for organizing his life. Certainly, within the framework of personal construct theory, little work on this important area has been attempted. Hinkle, with his concern to elicit and use constructs derived from superordinate positions within a person's hierarchical structure, indicates something of the possibilities of studying such highly superordinate constructs about aspects of the process of construing and reconstruing. As he suggests, "impulsivity, rigidity, propositionality, the decision making and creativity cycles, all seem to be related to these superordinate constructs about the management of construing and the anticipated status of the resulting construct system . . . we need to know a good deal more about people's personal anticipations and constructions about the process of anticipating – their principles of 'system management,' as it were."

There are many possible uses of the implication grid method in studying psychological change. As Hinkle has suggested, the superordinate or subordinate implications of any construct dimension may be independently modified (e.g. tightened or loosened). He further suggests that change in, for example, the subordinate implications of any dimensions may be facilitated if the superordinate implications are temporarily stabilized; if the superordinate implications are to be modified, it may be necessary to keep the subordinate ones relatively constant. In line with the threat hypothesis, he therefore suggests that psychotherapeutic change or constructional reorganization can take place only from a position of relative stability.

It may be that the need for superordinate stability if subordinate change is to be undertaken (and *vice versa*) is implicitly recognized in many interpersonal strategies. The teacher who is about to attack some specific contribution by a student may begin by assuring the student that "in general" he is doing very well, and undoubtedly he has a "good basic grasp" of his subject, "*but* on the topic of X" and so on. Here the teacher may be validating the student's superordinate construing, so as to limit the reverberations of an attack on some subordinate aspect of his construing. Clearly, the impgrid approach could be used to chart relative stability and change of both superordinate and subordinate implications.

Although the statistical treatment of the resistance to change and implication grid data in these studies was of a fairly simple kind, Hinkle indicates that many more diverse and complex techniques could be applied to such material. Impgrid data, for example, could readily be subjected to the same range of factor analytic procedures already brought into service for conventional grids. No attempt has yet been made to explore the range of uses to which such measures could be put, but it seems likely that future work will extend the mathematical possibilities of the methodology. The dangers of producing mathematically sophisticated but psychologically mystifying measures by the non-theoretical elaboration of this approach have already been mentioned in relation to the repertory grid, and will be further discussed later.

As Hinkle indicates, the implication grid method was developed primarily as a way of directly assessing construct relationships. Whereas in the repertory grid method, relationships between constructs are inferred by the examiner from similarities in element allotments for two or more dimensions, they are here indicated directly by the subject himself. That is to say, Hinkle demands that his subjects themselves indicate some of the links of which they are aware or which they think exist between their constructs, rather than letting the links emerge from a more indirect approach. Perhaps this basic difference between the Kelly and Hinkle grids can be stated in the terms of the theory, in that Hinkle asks subjects to make use of any superordinate constructions they have available for defining their own system structure, while Kelly requires only a more subordinate and less self-conscious set of constructs, but hopes to identify the more superordinate constructs by later statistical analyses.

Hinkle, in his advocacy of the direct method of assessing construct relationships, used only one of many possible variations of the approach. He asked his subjects to consider their own preferred self constructions. Subjects could equally well be asked to estimate various implications for their actual, present-self constructions, their past constructions of themselves, their estimates of the construct links involved in some other person's view of the world, or to consider a particular figure (given one characteristic or dimension to describe that figure) and to elicit the polar positions implied for him by that single construction. The resulting impgrid might then show the subject's network of construct implications pertaining to such a figure. Thus some constructs might be related together in the context of certain people, as the subject viewed them, but not in that of others. Such variations could be of considerable clinical interest.

The mapping of construct implications need not be restricted to constructs of the "descriptive adjective" type. Other kinds of construction concerning interactions of place, time, feeling, intention and so on, could be explored.

IMPGRID AND REP GRID CONTRASTS

Both Kelly and Hinkle are concerned to provide methods for estimating linkages between the construct dimensions used by any individual. They differ in that Kelly approaches the problem indirectly, while Hinkle asks subjects directly to indicate certain links which they think exist between their constructs. The advantages and disadvantages of each approach remain to be explored in detail. It seems likely that neither approach supplants the other but rather supplements it. Kelly's method may uncover possible construct links of which the subject himself is unaware, while in the impgrid situation, only relationships construed by the subject can readily appear.

It should be noted that the direct questioning technique of the implication grid has one "oblique" aspect. A complete implication matrix can reveal second (third, fourth and so on) order relationships. The subject has acknowledged, say, that construct 1 implies 2, 2 implies 6; 6 implies 10. This establishes a potential link between 1 and 10 that may not be articulated, as such, by the subject. Speculatively, we may redefine concepts such as "the unconscious" or "non-verbalized constructs" in terms of a network of second-order interrelationships between constructs which affect construing but which are not articulated by the subject; they carry an implicative load, but are not part of the person's self awareness. Hinkle's method may be preferable in situations where an understanding of what the person thinks of his own system is sought, and it may partially avoid the danger, inherent in grid method, of inferring relationships between constructs where no functioning links exist for the subject.

Kelly's method allows for an indirect assessment of the *degree of probability* of association between two or more constructs, while Hinkle's approach allows only for all-or-none decisions about construct links. This is not an inherent characteristic of the method, since subjects involved in the impgrid type of procedure could equally well be asked to assess the *probability* of association, or of associated change implied by positions on, or movement along, construct dimensions.

The distinction between constructs and elements, which has become generally formalized in the repertory grid, does not arise with the implication grid approach. Kelly, of course, did not consider that elements were a category distinct from constructs – everything in a person's outlook is for him a construction, and the ideas of a *dog*, a *table*, or a *best friend* are alike in being interpretations or constructions of events. The distinction drawn between constructs and elements in a grid was made simply as a convenient way of distinguishing constructions at different levels – the elements were those *constructions* which were sorted and grouped in terms of further constructions elicited to subsume them. The nearest equivalent in Hinkle's set of methodologies is in the laddering procedure, whereby constructs, supposedly subsuming the initial constructs, are intentionally elicited.

A final contrast between the two grid forms arises from the capacity of the implication grid to reveal *contradiction*. In the resistance to change grid (which, like the implication grid, takes the form of paired comparison judgments) a number of subjects produce logical intransitivities, i.e. they prefer to stay put on construct A rather than B, they prefer to stay put on B rather than C and they prefer to stay put on *C rather than A*. This is a contradiction in terms of formal logic and obviously of great interest psychologically.

Similarly, in the implication grid, lines of implication may be indexed by the subject (in a series of discrete paired comparison judgments) which eventually cross over and run into the "wrong" poles of a later construct, e.g. construct $A+ - A-$ may imply $B+ - B-$ and $C+ - C-$, but it later transpires that $C+$ implies $Z-$ while $A+$ implies $Z+$. Psychological concepts such as "conflict" might be examined in terms of manifest implicative contradictions. The repertory method cannot reveal contradictory implications because the mathematics of grid format and analysis cannot accept it – the subject is forced into either consistency or "no relationship." This point will be discussed later in another context, but it highlights one of the potentials of implication grid method.

CONCLUSION

Although implication grid technique has already been brought into use in this country (Fransella, 1966; Mair and Crisp, 1968) its range and problems are largely unexplored. On initial inspection it represents a tightening of the links between grid method generally and construct theory, and a major development in grid method as such. Hinkle's general hypothesis that people are in business to maximize their understanding of, and capacity to predict, future events and to avoid "net implicative loss" is a cogent re-statement of the central tenet of construct theory. It underlines Kelly's abandonment of the traditional tautology of reward and punishment, a tautology which underpins not only learning theory but is implicit in many eclectic psychological approaches. As a method, impgrids meet a major requirement of psychological instruments – that they should give the subject maximum freedom to express himself, while still formalizing his contribution to the point at which it can be systematically assessed by the experimenter.

CHAPTER 4

Recent Approaches to the Measurement of Conceptual Structure

THE CONCERN with problems of conceptual function and structure which are apparent in grid and construct theory studies is not an isolated phenomenon, nor a single straw in the wind of psychological fashion. Over the last twenty years there has been a gradually increasing interest in this field, with much of the related work appearing in the mid and late 1950s, along with Kelly's original volumes. Lines of influence and cross-fertilization between the various workers in this area are often far from clear; doubtless many arguments, leading to different conclusions about who exerted most influence on whom, will be proposed by those who like to see the history of psychology as a genealogical table.

In relation to the Rep test and rep grid method, Kelly clearly recognized affinities with the earlier "object" sorting tests of various kinds. Yet one point of particular interest is that few of the writers whose work is considered in this section have specifically drawn attention to similarities between their theories and techniques and those of Kelly, and the degree of cross-referring between these workers themselves is curiously limited.

APPROACH ANALOGUES

Before turning to work on aspects of conceptual structure, a few comments on work relevant to other aspects of Kelly's approach are appropriate. The work of Strodtbeck (1951) is of interest in relation to the construct elicitation procedure favoured by Kelly. As we have seen, Kelly asks the person being tested to look at three names from the element list, and to think of some way in which two of them are alike and by the same token different from the third. This procedure gives operational form to the theoretical contention that the minimum context in which a construct can be defined or developed is three elements or events. Strodtbeck had earlier produced a method of eliciting similarities and differences in ideas and opinions held by small groups of people considering various topics. For example groups of three people could consider various topics, and the observer would note ideas or topics on which two people agreed with each other, and disagreed with the third person.

These elicited similarities and differences could then be used as the basis for a more detailed examination of aspects of intra-group communication. Here, the participants in the group essentially sort the topics under consideration into groupings which involve various kinds of agreements and disagreements between themselves. At the same time, the observer is, in a sense, using the group members as elements whose self-groupings indicate discriminating constructions. This type of situation is one which, in the light of construct theory, might profitably receive further consideration as a bridge between the present fairly static methods of construct elicitation, and the more elusive (but possibly more important) features of constructs in action. Such a situation retains many aspects of natural human groupings. It allows members to delineate the constructive dimensions which define their agreements and disagreements. It allows the observer to examine the strategies by which individuals sharing various ideas and disagreeing on others manage to deal with and elaborate or define their differences. Here is the basis of an elicitation and measurement situation merging into a social, educational or therapeutic situation.

One of Kelly's main concerns was with the importance of eliciting *personally* significant constructs. This interest has, of course, been shared by many in the field of therapy; but, in measurement terms, relatively few have given much attention to the *subject's* dimensions for viewing the specific problem area under consideration, or the world in general. The Q-sort technique (Stephenson, 1953) is certainly a useful development from the usual questionnaire form, in that the subject (in cases where the subject is his own "rater") is allowed greater freedom than usual to group statements in ways which reflect his own ideas. The method, however, does not readily allow for the examination of the personal meaning of the various statements for each person being tested. More recently, Shapiro (1961) has developed a Personal Questionnaire, which shows concern for eliciting personally phrased information from the patient, and using this as the basis for scaling procedures which allow assessment of change. The technique does not, however, require an assessment of the relative importance to the patient of different complaints, nor of interlinkages for him between complaints. Again, concern with recognizing certain aspects of the freedom and complexity of the individual person is incorporated in the method; but no means are provided which facilitate scrutiny of the subject's broader conceptual framework, within which the complaints or symptoms may have meaning. A concern with aspects of personal relevance and importance has been stressed by Brunswick (1956), in his insistence on the necessity for representative designs in psychological experimentation. Brunswick implies that, in the examination of cognitive or perceptual processes, no arbitrary list of concepts or trait names or such like should be compiled, but that elements should be representative of the universe of elements habitually used by the subject in, say, his descriptions of other people.

Todd and Rappoport (1964), commenting on Brunswick's representative design, point out that representativeness in the selection of cognitive elements, when considered in the light of the wide individual differences in person perception, requires that the description of cognitive structure be carried out for each subject individually. These writers suggest that such a condition is particularly well provided for within the representative design framework. They note that this type of study of individuals does not imply an abandonment of the search for principles which have generality over persons. Rather, it seeks to establish general principles which can subsume the content found within the unique context of each individual's cognitive system.

Brunswick's insistence on the importance of sampling aspects of experience and behaviour specifically relevant to, and meaningful for, each person in an experiment parallels a similar emphasis in Kelly's writings. The latter stresses the personal nature of constructs, and the importance of attempting to achieve representativeness in sampling elements and constructs in any area under investigation.

METHOD ANALOGUES

Various measurements of the properties of cognitive structures suggested by Zajonc (1960) are of note because he describes the whole process from the elicitation of the initial information from his subjects to the construction of a set of scores defining various features of cognitive structure; this facilitates comparison with grid method. Zajonc's methods of measurement are described in a study whose main theme need not concern us here, though it is of interest in relating aspects of cognitive structure to communicating and receiving information. Suffice it to say that the initial task for the subject was to read quickly a job application letter from a candidate to a prospective employer, and the various scores discussed below were derived from responses of subjects to this experience.

Subjects were issued with instruction booklets to which were attached stacks of 52 blank cards marked from A to ZZ. After reading the job application letter, their first task was to take the cards, and on each to write one characteristic which described their conception of the applicant. They were asked to put down whatever came to mind, and were told that no "correct" or "incorrect" responses were possible. Each was asked to write down as many characteristics as he felt necessary to describe the applicant adequately. The *number* of characteristics attributed to the applicant constituted the first measure: this was argued to be a measure of the degree of *Differentiation* shown by each subject.

Three further measures were derived, quantifying degrees of *Complexity*, *Unity*, and *Organization*, as revealed in each subject's conception of the supposed applicant.

The subject was next required to lay out all the cards, and then to look and see if they seemed to fall into some broad natural groupings. If so, he was asked to arrange his cards into such groups. After this original grouping, each subject was asked to look at each group separately to see if it could be broken down into subgroups, and if so, to separate the cards accordingly. Each of these subgroups was then scrutinized by the subject providing them and, in a similar manner, subdivided further, till no additional breakdown seemed possible to him. The resulting groupings and successive subgroupings were recorded and used to determine the levels of inclusion of the attributes, i.e. the basis for computing Complexity scores. The argument, underlying the procedure for calculating Complexity, is as follows.

"Let us denote the level of inclusion of a given class by r, such that if the class K_i does not include another subclass, $r = 1$; when K_i includes some subclasses, which in turn do not include other subdivisions, $r = 2$; when K_i includes subclasses which themselves contain other indivisible subclasses $r = 3$, etc. The degree of complexity of a given cognitive structure may be obtained by weighting each attribute by the level of inclusion of its class membership and summing the weighted scores thus obtained. Thus:

$$\text{Complexity} = \sum_{r=1}^{n} rn_r$$

where n_r is the number of attributes in the rth level of inclusion." In short, the greater the number of groupings, the higher the Complexity score.

The final task presented to the subject was based on the argument that some of the characteristics listed by him might be related to each other. They might depend on one another in such a way that, if one changed, the others would change too. Each subject was required to lay all the cards out in alphabetical order, and then to list all the characteristics which would change if characteristics A were changed, absent or untrue of the applicant. Similar lists were constructed for the eventuality of B being changed, absent or untrue, and for each of the other characteristics also. On the basis of these responses, dependency matrices were constructed which allowed measures of Unity and Organization to be calculated.

The Unity measure was based on the following argument.

"If we define the dependence of the attribute A_i on the attribute A_j as equal to 1 when a change in A_j produces a change in A_i, and as equal to 0 when a change in A_j does not produce a change in A_i, then a dependency matrix can be constructed for all attributes of a given cognitive structure, and the total dependency of each attribute may easily be obtained by summing the entries in the appropriate row. To compare the unity of structures of different degrees of differentiation the measure of unity must be normalized. Given a structure with n attributes, the maximum dependency of a given attribute dep $(A_i)^{max}$, is equal to $n - 1$, and the maximum sum of dependencies in the cognitive structure to $n(n - 1)$. Unity then can be defined as:

$$\text{Unity} = \frac{\sum_{i=1}^{n} \text{dep}(A_i)}{n(n - 1)}$$

where dep (A_i) is the total dependency of the ith attribute."

In short, the greater the number of dependent changes listed by the subject (as a proportion of the total number of adjectives), the greater the degree of unity.

The measure of Organization is derived from the same dependency matrix. The degree to which a given attribute, A_i, depends on others can be calculated, as well as the degree to which it determines others. This latter value Zajonc obtained by summing the entries in the appropriate column of the matrix. Taking the determinance of the strongest attribute, $\det(A_i)^{max}$, and dividing it by the Unity of the cognitive structure, he obtained a measure which, he considered, reflected the degree to which the interdependence among the attributes was concentrated around a single core. This he regarded as the measure of Organization, and expressed it thus:

$$\text{Organization} = \frac{\det (A_i)^{max}}{\text{Unity}}$$

In short, the greater the degree to which statements of dependency can be seen as functions of the most centrally "determining" adjective, the greater the degree of Organization.

There are clearly a number of close similarities between Zajonc's method and aspects of the methods innovated by Kelly and Hinkle. Like Kelly, Zajonc is concerned to elicit, from the subject, personally relevant and important concepts or ideas, and also to achieve some assessment of the clustering of these concepts for him. Additionally, his measures of Unity and (particularly) Organization are very similar to those derived from Hinkle's implicational definition of subordinate and superordinate constructs. There is nothing in Zajonc's method, as such, which violates any important assumptions in construct theory, and the formal differences in the actual measures, could, on occasion, prove useful for the experimenter.

Though little use has been made of Zajonc's methods for assessing conceptual structure, one interesting contribution of his approach is that it focuses the subject's attention upon a specific situation, person or problem as a starting point, in contrast to much grid usage, which directs attention to generalized relationships between constructs. Zajonc encourages subjects to elaborate and reveal the concepts and ideas relevant to a specific situation, and to indicate some of the structural links between the concepts which are involved. Conventional grid forms have sometimes been regarded as too general for the examination of construct organization relevant to *specific* figures or situations. This point of view does not represent an inevitable limitation of the grid method, but Zajonc's suggestions are useful in demonstrating concretely how some aspects of the relatively general conceptual structure relevant to a specific situation could be elicited and explored.

Another feature of Zajonc's procedure, which may sometimes be usefully incorporated into construct theory investigations, is the freedom allowed to subjects to group constructs which seem to go together, and to subdivide successive groups into more limited clusters. When an investigator wishes to examine constructs which govern other constructs, such freedom may allow him more directly to study a person's *awareness* of his conceptual organization. In grid method, one of the advantages, for some contexts, is that the subject is not directly asked to group the constructs which are interrelated in his system; but, by encouraging him to make more limited choices, it is possible to infer some aspects of the relationships existing between constructs, from the mathematical equivalences between groupings of elements. Both approaches may be useful in relation to different problems; but it should be borne in mind that the more direct method favoured by Zajonc and Hinkle, while it allows considerable flexibility and generates groupings which are psychologically meaningful to the person, may sometimes prove too difficult for some people to perform adequately.

Crockett (1965) points out that Zajonc's methods, while not involving any complex mathematical assumptions, do involve important assumptions as to the validity of very complex subjective reports. In comparing Zajonc's relatively phenomenological approach with more analytical approaches, like those of Hays (1958) and Coombs (1964) – and the comparison could equally well have included Kelly's grid methodology – Crockett points out that, while it is true that the results of any method of analysis may be rendered invalid by invalid data, still the judgments required by the analytic methods tend to be relatively simple ones. They take the form, "Of these three things, which two are more similar?" or "If you know that a person has this characteristic, what are the chances he will also have that one?" Compare this, he says, with the following instruction "Consider this construct as a standard. Then look through all the rest of the constructs and find those that would be changed if the standard construct were changed, untrue or absent in the person. Once this is completed, take a different construct as the standard and carry out the same procedure." Such a series of performances, he suggests, will take longer and is more tiring than the simpler methods. In addition to this, the exact requirements of a complex phenomenological task are often difficult to communicate to subjects, who frequently find it hard to maintain a proper instructional set during the lengthy procedure.

One further possible limitation in Zajonc's methods, and also in some of the analytical approaches (to be discussed later), is that at present they do not allow for multiple meanings to be attributed to single words. Crockett points out that such a limitation is not a necessary feature of Zajonc's approach (or perhaps of those involved in the more analytic methods). If the subjects were allowed further freedom in grouping concepts, so that any concept could be successively allotted to a number of groups and subdivisions made in relation to each grouping, this problem would be partly overcome.

There are other problems involved in Zajonc's methods, but his suggestions seem to merit further study and could profitably be extended within the context of personal construct theory research. Already it is apparent, however, that the inevitable terminological jungle is developing in this area of study, with Zajonc's Differentiation score being similar to the Cognitive Complexity score used by Mayo (1960) and Ashcroft (1963) while his Complexity score bears little obvious similarity to the many, already diverse Complexity measures suggested by Bieri (1955) and others (summarized by Bonarius 1965). Care must be taken to specify the procedures involved in defining measures, and particular caution exercised in generalizing across measures based on similar, though not identical, procedures, and across procedures with identical names but dissimilar forms.

STATISTICAL ANALOGUES

A further approach to the study of conceptual structure is that suggested by Hays (1958). He describes methods of assessing trait implication and trait similarity. Although Hays uses the term "trait" rather than concept or construct, his methods are, in many ways, similar to those produced some years later by Hinkle. Hays seems to use the term trait in a similar way to Kelly's term construct, as a basis for aiding anticipation and classification in human behaviour.

"It seems reasonable," Hays notes, "to suppose that an individual makes his inferential judgments of persons in some fairly characteristic way. That is a person must have some relatively stable scheme of expectations and anticipations about others, which is gradually built up through both direct and vicarious experience. This scheme may be thought of as a set of inferential relationships among experienced attributes and traits which exists for an individual. This set of expected relations among traits of other persons has been called the individual's 'implicit theory of personality' by Bruner and Tagiuri (1954) Cronbach (1955) and others.

There is, however, another important process which goes on in a person's judgments of other people. We, as observers, are eternally in the process of comparing individuals and judging their similarity to other individuals with respect to both their physical and their behavioral attributes. In order to make these similarity judgments, it seems reasonable to assume persons must have some scheme of the relatedness of human attributes and the weight to be given these attributes and combinations of attributes in assessing similarity. This, too, in its way, must be a kind of implicit theory of trait relatedness, or, if you will, of personality."

Thus Hays introduces his attempt to delineate two simple models for describing certain formal relations which may exist among traits for any individual in judging others. Such perceived relations, he insists, may underlie the behaviour of a person inferring one trait from another, or judging the similarity between two persons.

The Implication Model: Hays starts his argument by suggesting that when an individual infers one trait from another (consciously or unconsciously), such an inference or expectation is seldom, if ever, absolute, but rather in the form of a probability (of a certain magnitude) that given trait A, trait B will accompany it. He postulates that individuals assign "weights" to certain perceived traits in others, and that these weights are some function of the frequency with which individuals having the traits have been encountered in the past. He goes on to outline a method for deducing the weights attributable to traits from a knowledge of individual or group judgments of the probability of association between the various traits involved, or rather from judgments of the probability that one trait implies another. Not only the subjective "weights" of single traits but also those of traits in combination can then be estimated.

Of even greater concern to Hays is the problem of estimating the "centrality" or "saliency" of a trait, relative to other traits, and a similar interest was shown by Kelly and Hinkle in defining superordinancy, and by Zajonc in defining the degree of cognitive organization. Hays argues that the centrality of a trait should be a function of at least two things – the extent to which a trait has a large individual weight, and the extent to which it implies many other traits while not being implied by them. It should be noted that this is the converse of Hinkle's definition of a *superordinate* construct as *being implied by* many constructs; but this difference in definition does not necessarily dictate operational differences.

By means of a multidimensional unfolding procedure, the implicational differences for all pairs of a set of traits from a person's judgments of probabilities can be analyzed to secure a "best fit" description of the relationships which traits bear to each other for the individual judge or group.

Hays' example incorporated the following eight adjectives:

Warm	Cold
Dominant	Submissive
Intelligent	Stupid
Generous	Stingy

The subjects were asked questions in the following form. "A person is intelligent. How likely is it that he is also

1. dominant   0   0·1   0·2   0·3   0·4   0·5   0·6   0·7   0·8   0·9   1

　　　　　　　　Impossible   Certain

2. stingy?" etc.

The subject was then required to check the appropriate point on the scale from impossibility to certainty for each of the 56 pairs of adjectives presented.

The relative weights of the traits were then obtained and ordered, by comparing the differential probabilities of each occurring given the other. For the pooled scores of 20 subjects used by Hays, the obtained order of weights for the single traits was as follows: *generous dominant warm intelligent cold submissive stupid stingy*.

Similarly, the orders or weights for trait combinations were assessed, and the order of differential implications from each trait was established. Finally the eight rank orders of traits resulting from this anslysis were subjected to analysis by the unfolding procedure, to tease out the rank order dimensions which would best characterize the relations among the traits. In Hays' example, two dimensions seemed adequate. The first involved an ordering of the traits with warm and cold at the extreme positions, implying that this pair showed the greatest distance or difference from each other, and the greatest average distance from the other traits. Thus Hays indicated that what-ever factor accounted for the large judged difference between warm and cold accounted for most of the other judged differences as well – that is, the warm-cold factor was most highly related to the other traits. "Thus, in this instance warm and cold would be considered the most central traits of this set in the sense of having greatest weight and implying most while being implied least by the other traits." No absolute measures of weight or centrality can be established by this method, since the whole procedure is based on rank positioning *within* the sample of traits involved.

The second dimension emerging had the terms intelligent and stupid at the extremes. Extreme positions here should, according to Hays, indicate that the traits involved are relatively central, but maximally unrelated to the factor or factors responsible for the first dimension.

The similarity model: in the situation involving judgment of similarity, Hays suggests an instance where a person, who knows the relevant information about others, has to make comparisons between two or more complexes of traits. His method for estimating similarity in judgment is based on the use of specified trait clusters, rather than direct comparisons of known people. Hays suggests that judgments of similarity between two clusters of traits are likely to be affected by (a) the weight or functional importance of each of the traits, for the subject making the comparison, (b) the weight or importance of the trait patterns, in combinations, which each possesses and (c) the congruence of the traits and trait combinations of the two individuals.

Hays presents a limited example to illustrate his procedure. He again used the traits noted in the illustration for the implication model. Sixteen trait lists of hypothetical persons were made up, using all combinations of the four polar adjective pairs, warm-cold, intelligent-stupid, dominant-submissive, generous-stingy, e.g.

A. Warm, stingy, submissive, intelligent. B. Stingy, cold, submissive, stupid. etc.

These stimulus lists were then presented three at a time, each subject being required to make "snap judgments" for each triad, as to which pair were "most alike" and which pair "least alike". Hays provides a means of assessing the relative weights of the various traits from tabulations of the triads which differ from each other by only one trait name. When analyzed by the unfolding technique, the data involved here were adequately described by four dimensions. It thus seemed likely that subjects judged similarity between stimulus lists according to:

(i) the over-all good-bad impression given by the respective stimuli,
(ii) the presence of intelligent or cold versus the presence of stupid or warm,
(iii) the presence of dominant or generous versus the presence of submissive or stingy,
(iv) the agreement or otherwise of the first traits presented in the lists.

Comparisons: the Implication model reported by Hays is of interest because of its similarities to the Implication Grid described by Hinkle. It seems clear that Hays has developed little in the way of a theoretical context within which the methodology and variations of it can find a natural place. Furthermore, his use of the term "trait" implies a more static and "thing-measuring" approach than that favoured by either Kelly or Hinkle. Though there is some lack of clarity about the nature of "traits" in his use of the term, he seems at times to imply that traits actually exist in individuals, and are there to be seen and assessed. Such a point of view is not shared by Kelly, who takes pains to argue for the interpretative or constructive assessment of others – whereby constructions placed on others reflect something of the uniqueness of the construer, not simply that of the object construed. The basic practical methodologies do show marked similarities; but in spite of this, it is not clear that Hays' approach has any advantages over that suggested later by Hinkle, while Hays' elaborate mathematical argument (not discussed here) prevents easy understanding of his approach and may hide an essential simplicity. His use of a multidimensional unfolding procedure, for the extraction of dimensions underlying the trait implication judgments, presents the experimenter with accumulations of various trait organizations, which are cumbersome and difficult to translate into psychologically useful terms. The information derivable from the dimensions resulting from this kind of analysis is limited to crude estimates of the *relative* differences in the "distances" between traits, in terms of their implications. These dimensions indicate something of the ordering of traits, but nothing of the *degree* of importance or significance attaching to specific traits or different dimensions.

The Similarity model is somewhat akin to parts of Kelly's method of grid analysis. Here, instead of comparing complex groupings of constructs ascribed to actual individual people, (and Kelly defines an individual, as seen by another, as an intersection point of many constructs used by the perceiver), the subject compares groupings of trait *names* in terms of their similarities and differences. One problem in this model is in the assumption underlying it, that all *relevant* information is available to subjects when they make similarity judgments. Such an assumption seems artificial and unrealistic; and, indeed, one common feature of similarity/difference judgments is that people often make them without being able to state the basis of their decisions. Even when various characteristics have been specified, the basis on which certain similarity judgments are made may remain elusive.

Interest in the method is again in the *attempt* to examine similarity within a conceptual model showing some points of correspondence with Kelly's procedures. The differences in the approach might stimulate thought about the development of further methods, more closely related to the theoretical requirements of personal construct theory, or the development of other theoretical assumptions appropriate to such essentially empirical measures.

Traits in isolation and combination: another approach to the study of trait implication is presented by Bruner, Shapiro and Tagiuri (1958). Bruner's theoretical position is in many ways similar to that espoused by Kelly, though less fully developed. In this discussion, Bruner and his associates describe a model which deals in specific and concrete form with his interest in the general question of how *partial* information gets coded and organized, to make possible the prediction of further information (cf. Bruner, 1957; Bruner and Tagiuri, 1954, and Cronbach, 1955).

In forming impressions of a person, Bruner notes, we usually start with partial information which, though far from complete, generates a host of inferences about the person, inferences which are made with various degrees of certainty. "One 'knows' more about a person," Bruner and his co-authors suggest, "than what seems to be immediately connoted by the acts one has witnessed or the information one has gained about him. To 'know' is not used here in the sense of 'know' correctly." The interest of these writers is in what they describe as "lay conceptions of personality." Similarities with some of Kelly's and Hinkle's arguments can perhaps best be illustrated by direct quotations. "What we infer about others is based upon a set of expectations or a 'coding system' about the nature of persons, derived in part from experience with behavior . . . It is characteristic of trait words like *honest, brave, vulgar* or *clever* that they do more than denote specific acts of a person; that, indeed, they summarize or 'package' certain consistencies of behavior . . . When we know a person possesses certain traits, we infer the presence or absence of certain other traits. If a person is *considerate* he is very likely to be *reliable*, but he may or may not be *clever*."

"The meaning of a trait can be defined by the positive and negative inferences that can be made, with varying degrees of certainty, to other traits. Each inference adds a new facet to its 'meaning' . . . If we say of a person that he is *intelligent* and this predisposes a listener to infer that he is also *witty*, then *wittiness* is part of the meaning of *intelligence*. But the meaning of a trait depends in part upon its trait context, i.e., upon the traits with which it is coupled."

Bruner and his colleagues are here concerned to examine the implicative meanings of various traits considered singly, and to note how traits combined in groupings may possibly change their meanings. Previous work done by Asch (1946), Haire and Grunes (1950), Wishner (1960) and others had directed attention to some of the ways in which traits combined in different groupings could yield rather different meanings. Bruner's concern is to establish something of the degree of predictability of inference from certain traits to others; knowing the implications of certain single traits in relation to a set of other traits, he hopes to assess the rules which allow predictions from knowledge of inferences from single traits to inferences from the same traits when the single traits are combined in various ways.

The basic methodology is similar to that used by Hays in his implication model and by Hinkle in his Implication Grid. Each subject is given a list of traits, and at the top of the list are the introductory words: "People who are *considerate . . .*" The subject is asked whether such people –

> very often are
> tend to be
> may or may not be
> tend not to be
> seldom are –

aggressive, active, etc.

In the example given by Bruner *et al*, each subject was required to make choices of this kind for 59 traits; but clearly, in further work, characteristics could be added or deleted by the experimenter. In the list used, common words were selected to represent various aspects or dimensions of personality, and both ends of each dimension were used separately. In the worked example, all inferences rated in any category other than the middle one (may or may not be) were classed as *definite* inferences (in either the positive or negative directions), though again it would be possible, and perhaps sometimes useful, to make greater use of the differences in degrees of probability of inferences implied by scalar ratings.

The traits used were *considerate, independent, intelligent* and *inconsiderate*. These were presented singly, in combinations of twos and in groupings of three (always excluding the simultaneous presence of considerate *and* inconsiderate). A large group of subjects was used in the example given, and each subject was tested on only *one* of the inference rating tasks. This was done to ensure the independence of inferences from one arrangement to another.

As stated above, the main purpose of this investigation was to explore the principles that related the inferences drawn from single traits to the inferences made from combinations of the same traits. It must be borne in mind that the results obtained refer to the specific group procedure used, and no evidence was obtained to imply that anything like the same conclusions would be derived from the single case.

The conclusions were as follows

(i) When the direction of inferences made from two or three single traits is the same, the inference from their combination is almost always in the same direction, and agreement among subjects about direction is greater for grouped traits than for component traits presented singly.

(ii) When, within groupings of two or three traits, single traits yield inferences of unlike sign, the *sign* of the inference from their combination is apparently governed by the component on which there is more general agreement. When there is "conflicting" information, the resulting inference does not show the same relative increase in agreement observed in the first instance.

(iii) For combinations of three traits, where the single inferences differ in sign, the inference from the combination tends to be in the direction of the dominant sign.

These principles, based on sign of inference and degree of agreement between subjects, apparently accounted for the sign in 97% of the inferences made from trait combinations. It seemed also that a greater number of definite inferences are made from trait combinations of two or three than from the traits given singly, regardless of whether the component single inferences were of like or unlike sign.

Perhaps the most interesting implication of this work relates to the observations made on cases of opposite sign or of conflicting pairs of traits. Such an instance was in relation to the inferences from *intelligent* and *inconsiderate* to the trait *modest*. The first tended to be positive and the second negative. When the two were combined, the inference to modest showed a *gain* in the certainty of the inference, along with a slight reduction in the agreement among subjects about the direction of the inference. The generality of this finding, or its applicability to the individual subject is obscure; but it strengthens the concept of a personal *system*, as opposed to the concept of a simple, additive collection of "responses."

Bruner and his colleagues point out one limitation of the procedure they describe, namely, that only a very limited sample of traits can be examined at any time, if adequate balance and controls in the design of the study are to be maintained. While this difficulty is certainly real, it is one shared by other conceptual measures. Exhaustive groupings of single traits may not always be necessary in practice, though employed in the present academic example. If, within an individual or group, the implications of some particular traits or concepts singly and in combinations were to be examined, there might be no necessity to explore all possible groupings, but only those of primary interest.

One useful point raised by this study is that, in conceptual analyses, single dimensions, as commonly used in grid format, may introduce unnecessary artificiality. Kelly was certainly aware of the importance of avoiding the limitations imposed by too concrete a use of his methods but the tendency to use single-word descriptions of constructs is still common in grid work. The differential implications of construct groupings (expressed in phrases) as contrasted with their single word constituent constructs, within individual systems, remain an uncharted area, but one which will increase in importance as stress is placed on the more "real life" behaviour likely to come under study in the future.

In the example provided by Bruner *et al.*, trait names were used singly and in combination. As the procedure stands, it involves the difficulty noted earlier, namely, that variations in meaning (implication or inference pattern) for the same word are not accommodated or controlled. Changes in the meanings attributed to words could well be made by subjects within a single study, and the degree of confusion resulting from such an occurrence could make any interpretations of general principles derived from the results somewhat questionable.

This work, like most studies in the area of measurement and analysis of conceptual structure, has intentionally been limited to the examination of one grammatical class – adjectives. Such a limitation is not essential, but in practice it has become the norm. Certain modifications of Bruner's methodology might allow investigation of some aspects of variations in meaning of trait names, and at the same time might help to extend the range and type of constructions involved. People use the same words to summarize different situations, events and characteristics, and sometimes the same words are used by a person to imply different things within different contexts. For example, one person may distinguish between generosity (of spirit), generosity (with money) and generosity (with sexual favours). Differences in the implicational patterns surrounding *generous* might then appear if the modifiers – "of spirit," "with money" and "with sexual favours" were introduced, instead of, or in addition to, further trait modifiers. Again, instead of studying differences in inferential patterns of concepts singly or in groups, where the concepts in the groups are all "descriptive adjective" modifiers, contexts, or groupings of ideas, juxtaposing trait characteristics with constructions involving time, place, opportunity, intention etc. might lead to some understanding of the range of alternative inferential patterns available to a person in these terms.

ASSOCIATION OF IDEAS

In the studies discussed, concern has been shown with problems of investigating links between concepts – the links under scrutiny having been of the similarity or implicational kind. The study of conceptual links has been popular, in one form or another, in the associationist tradition for a very long time. In the verbal sphere, the free association test situation has had perhaps the greatest application and influence. In such a task, few constraints are placed on the kind of conceptual link which may emerge, and certainly the usual formats do not apparently prejudice the outcomes in favour of associations of either the similarity or the implicational type.

Deese (1965), in a recent book on the structure of associations in language and thought, presents a useful historical analysis of associationist theories, highlighting some of their inadequacies, and arguing enthusiastically for the use of a free association test method, as the most general and least biasing framework within which to study the conceptual links underlying language and thought.

The general point of view held by Deese and argued in this book is that "the most important property of associations is their structure – their patterns of intercorrelations." He indicates, however, that nearly all previous writing on associations has stressed temporal order – expressed in the law of contiguity – rather than structure. If this dominant trend in association theory is taken seriously and literally, Deese suggests, we shall find ourselves facing a theory which describes almost no orderly arrangement among successive events. Such a theory tends to emphasize external control, and in so doing appeals to the experimentalist, who is in a position to modify external conditions more readily than internal ones. "In association theory, then, almost all of the organization or structure of mental events is determined by the organization of input conditions. The major organization so imposed is the result of frequency of various contingencies in perception."

He argues that almost all the older theories ignored one aspect of associative contingencies which seems of particular importance – namely, their *multiplicity:* "a given element C is not only contingent upon A but also upon B. There is little attention in older work to the concept of *distribution* of contingencies among a relatively small number of basic elements."

Another limitation and persistent problem in association theories has been the notion of *similarity*. Deese argues that the idea of similarity is essentially structural, and that it is a property of the perceiver. "Objects can only be similar or dissimilar to one another in perception (or thought) . . . . Things are similar which appear to be similar." Compare this with Kelly's more general contention that each person "erects a structure within the framework of which the substance (events, things) takes shape or assumes meaning. The substance which he construes does not produce the structure; the person does." In tracing departures from the rigid mechanics of associationism, Deese considers the work of the Wurzburg school, Gestalt psychology and the particular merit of Bartlett (1932), who comes "closest to describing the organization of relations among associations though he never mentions the term 'association' and deals with none of the traditional problems of associationism." Bartlett, he contends, provides nearly the first suggestion that associations are not simple straightforward echoes of previous experience, but may be organized in terms of some kind of simplified structures or schemata. These make it possible that obtained associations may never have occurred together in the experience of the person who gives them, but may be the outcome of schemata which serve the function of bringing together structurally related elements from diverse experiences.

Deese sees this principle operating in the context of a free association test, in the following way.

Having obtained distributions of associations for a population to specific stimulus words, the next problem is to find some means of assessing the relationship between any pair of linguistic forms. Deese suggests that "If the associative meaning of any stimulus is given by the distribution of responses to that stimulus, then *two stimuli may be said to have the same associative meaning when the distributions are identical, and they may be said to share meaning to the extent that these distributions agree*."

Distributions are accepted as agreeing when they possess examples of the same words. The occurrence in each distribution of common elements is the measure of the relationship between two stimuli, in associative terms.

The basic free association task, used by Deese, requires each person in a group to provide only one association to each stimulus word. This avoids at least some of the problems introduced by using series of responses to any particular stimulus, where each subsequent association may in part be constrained by the preceding associations, rather than only by the *original* stimulus, Thus, he is concerned to elicit group distributions of responses to a stimulus, where each response is provided by a different person.

In designing his equation to estimate commonality in distributions of associative meaning, Deese argues that it is possible to take the conditional frequency of occurrence between pairs of stimuli as the measure of the commonality in distributions of responses to these stimuli. A response is considered to have a conditional frequency of occurrence if it appears in both distributions. Thus, the joint frequency of occurrence of any word is always the smaller frequency of the pair (i.e. if the association *fly* is given to the stimulus word *insect* 9 times, and *fly* is given as an association to *moth* 10 times, the joint frequency of occurrence is 9). The commonality in a distribution of associations is, then, the sum of the conditional frequencies of occurrence divided by the geometric mean of the Ns of the two distributions. If, however, the two distributions are equal in size – the same number of associations having been obtained to each stimulus – the denominator is standard for any distribution.

In defining his idea of associative meaning, and in presenting a method of comparing different distributions of associations, Deese notes the similarities between his approach and others discussed by Marshall and Cofer (1963), Bousfield (1961) and Garskof and Houston (1963), the latter specifically referring to the problems encountered in dealing with the study of verbal relatedness in the individual case.

Deese concludes by suggesting two new laws of association, stated in the following form

"(1) Elements are associatively related when they may be *contrasted* in some unique and unambiguous way, and (2) elements are associatively related when they may be *grouped* because they can be described by two or more characteristics in common." Thus, in his conclusion, he fails to envisage the possibility which is centrally embodied in construct theory – that constructs are bipolar and essentially group *and* contrast simultaneously, and that it is precisely this simultaneous signifying of "same" and "different" which provides a differential network of implications.

A prime interest of Deese's work resides in its self-conscious attempt to break away from the "contiguity learning" type of principle. He acknowledges, and seeks to elaborate, ideas about man as a system builder, and can therefore be aligned with a broad construct theory approach. However, his work contrasts with such an approach in four major respects.

Firstly, (with due apology) his experimental focus is on groups, and on the gathering of normative data. In this, he follows the practice which equates a nomothetic approach with the totting of averages, rather than seeing it as the elaboration of a unitary language within which individual processes can be meaningfully described and understood.

Secondly, he sees virtue in the fact that free association, as an experimental tool, can be regarded as context-free. This can be viewed as the quality which does most to deprive it of value. Thinking is never context-free; men always think to some purpose, however vaguely that purpose is defined. It is this relationship, between construing and predictive contexts, on which construct theory focuses. To dispense with it experimentally does not reveal basic man; it reveals man as he never was on land or sea, but only as he is in the laboratory of the free associationist.

Thirdly, a great deal of effort is put into integrating grammatical concepts into the psychological explanation of language which is being propounded. This examination of noun *versus* adjective implications, and so forth, is part of the growing tradition in psycholinguistics which counts, say, noun/verb ratios, apparently because we can identify nouns and verbs and we can thereby count them. Grammar is a system for analyzing language, as is literary criticism and phonetic analysis – but we do not have to incorporate concepts from these undertakings into a psychological analysis of language, unless a useful end is thereby served.

Finally, in the empiricist tradition, Deese has built a micro-theory in conjunction with a favoured method (free association), rather than having elaborated methods out of a comprehensive theoretical framework. In so doing, he has burdened his theory with the assumptions of his method, and while pointing towards a promising road, he has moved only a short distance.

AN EXPERIMENTAL COMPARISON OF METHODS

The methods discussed in this chapter have received relatively little experimental attention. The Semantic Differential (Osgood *et al.*, 1957), however, has a large experimental literature; and its relationship to grid method will be discussed in detail later. One study compares the Semantic Differential, as a technique of conceptual analysis, with Hays' Implication model (Todd and Rappoport, 1964); and this merits attention.

Todd and Rappoport were concerned to study (a) the degrees of similarity in trait relationships emerging from the two different approaches (b) the degree of agreement in dimensional structure derived by the statistical procedures relevant to the two methods, and (c) the psychological validity of the trait relationships and conceptual dimensions resulting from both models.

They chose to compare the methods of Hays and Osgood because, while both provide estimates of subjective relationships between traits and of the dimensional structure implied, they do so in very different ways. Hays' method involves the estimation of "distances" between traits, derived from judgments of the likelihood of associations between them, while Osgood's is a factorial method, involving the analysis of clusters of correlations resulting from ratings.

Using a modification of Kelly's Role Construct Repertory Test (RCRT), Todd and Rappoport obtained from all subjects the constructs or trait names they used to describe themselves and others. The elements used for the elicitation of these constructs were people known to the subjects, each appropriate to one of 25 commonly occurring role titles used by a student population. Each subject used two sets of 12 triads, and in each instance was required to indicate the characteristic according to which of the two people constituting the triad were alike and different from the third. For each characteristic, subjects also supplied its opposite. For each subject, synonymous construct labels were eliminated.

Probability judgments required by Hays' implication model were then obtained, using the trait names elicited from each subject.

The factor analysis resulting from the Osgood method was based on *two* sets of ratings by each subject. In both instances, the bipolar trait names derived from the RCRT were used as seven-point rating scales. In one case, the 25 people chosen by the subject as appropriate to the role titles in the RCRT were each rated on the bipolar scales (and described as Person-objects). In the other case, hypothetical or *concept* persons, each being described by only one of the trait names used as scales (e.g. "intelligent person") were each rated on the scales. Fourteen students acted as subjects.

Statistical analysis of the Hays implication data provided a matrix of implicative distances between traits, and a set of dimensions on which the traits were "loaded." The process was completed for each subject, and in each case the number of dimensions obtained was arbitrarily limited to five. For the Osgood method, two factor analyses were done for each subject – one, using the ratings of the 25 real people, and the other, the ratings for the "concept people."

The similarity in implicative relationships between traits, resulting from the two procedures, was examined. The authors point out that the implicative distances between traits obtained by Hays' model are interpreted as the degree to which one trait implies another. They suggest that a similar interpretation can be made of the correlations between traits resulting from Osgoodian factor analytic procedures. They thus compared, for each subject, the correlation coefficient between the implicative distances yielded by the Hays model, and the equivalent correlations between traits derived from the two factor analyses. A similar comparison between the trait correlations for the two factor analytic procedures was also made.

The resulting *mean* correlations were as follows:

Implication Model/Factor analysis for real persons, 0·73:
Implication Model/Factor analysis for concept persons, 0·79:
Factor analysis for real persons/Factor analysis for concept persons, 0·83.

Todd and Rappoport conclude; "there is a high agreement among the three procedures with respect to the *degree* of implication indicated between traits. Nevertheless, there are statistically significant differences among procedures with regard to the extent of their agreement. The direction of these differences indicates that correspondence is greatest when the methods are the same, but the stimulus objects differ; correspondence is less when the methods differ but the stimulus objects are the same; and correspondence is least when both the methods and the stimulus objects differ."

They next compared the dimensional *structure* derived from each procedure. The comparison here involved arbitrary solutions to a number of problems arising from the facts that, for the Hays procedure, (a) no criteria had previously been erected to limit the number of dimensions extracted (b) no criteria were available to determine the relative importance of the dimensions obtained, and (c) no convention existed for deciding what constituted a "significant" loading on the Hays model dimensions. In addition, the authors had available no generally accepted method for the quantitative comparison of dimensions by the two procedures. They therefore attempted what they describe as "an overlapping content" comparison, in which two factors or dimensions were considered as having essentially the same content if two thirds of the elements loaded on them, meeting certain specified criteria, were identical.

From this comparison, they concluded that there was little agreement between the two methods concerning the dimensions of cognitive structure yielded. Only 3 subjects showed any considerable agreement between dimensions from the implication and factorial models. Indeed, 6 of the 14 subjects showed little agreement even in the comparison of dimensions derived from the two factor analytic procedures. Furthermore, for 9 of the 14 subjects, fewer factors were obtained when the "concept person objects" were rated than when the "real person objects" were rated.

Todd and Rappoport describe further studies aimed at evaluating the psychological significance of the implicational relations and the conceptual dimensions provided by the two statistical models.

Firstly, concerning implications, they report two studies designed to test variations of the hypothesis – "If according to the models, Trait 'x' implies Trait 'y,' then given the information that a person-object has Trait 'x,' the subject should infer that he also has Trait 'y.'"

In the first experiment, the subject was told that a hypothetical person showed one of the characteristics (stimulus trait) given by the subject in his RCRT. He then selected from his RCRT list three other traits he would attribute to the hypothetical person (response traits). This procedure was repeated five times with each subject, a different stimulus trait being used in each case.

The second experiment aimed to discover from what response traits the subject would infer particular stimulus traits. Each subject was here asked to imagine that he had to decide whether a hypothetical person possessed a specified trait (stimulus trait). He was then asked to indicate the three other traits on the list which would assist him most in making such a decision. Again, five presentations involving different stimulus traits were used.

In both studies there appeared to be some relationship between the response traits predicted by the models and those actually chosen by the subjects; and the authors suggest that "implication," as measured by the models, appears to have psychological significance.

Their final concern was to compare the dimensions extracted by means of the two models with groupings of traits arrived at by more direct means – to see whether either statistical procedure provided dimensions similar to those intuitively produced by the subject.

In this experiment, the traits produced by each subject in the RCRT administration were written separately on cards. The subject then took his set of cards, and was required to place them into groups indicating traits which he considered belonged together. Subjects were told that they could re-sort the cards as often as they wished, and that the same trait could be included in more than one group.

These groupings were compared with the dimensions and factors resulting from the two models, by the overlapping content measure used earlier. In general, there was little agreement between the groupings and the factors, or dimensions. In the Hays model, the overlapping content constituted 25% of the total, while the comparable figures for the concept-person and the real-person factor analyses were 38% and 40% respectively. Differences between subjects were striking, however, with a few subjects showing quite marked overlap between the direct groupings and one of the other results.

This study has been quoted in some detail not only because of its intrinsic interest, but also because it highlights some persistent problems in the whole area of conceptual analysis.

It is of interest that two different approaches to the study of implications between traits should provide similar patterns of implicative relations, but that when further statistical analyses were effected, the dimensions or factors involved in each were not comparable. The further the transformation of the data from their original form, the less comparability appears between methods, and the less agreement there is between the results from statistical models and those from direct sorting behaviour.

It is perhaps the most important limitation of the various methods outlined here that none is based on a theory elaborate enough to make much sense of discrepancies in results when they emerge.

Todd and Rappoport indicate that other methods are available for extracting dimensions from the type of data presented by them. However, it seems very doubtful if the retreat into more "refined" and complex mathematics will solve the more basic psychological problems of adequately conceptualizing the processes involved, for both the experimenter and subject, in the test situations used.

INTERPERSONAL PERCEPTION

Two studies, Laing, Phillipson and Lee (1966) and Drewery and Rae (1968), though not concerned with conceptual *structure*, are of interest because they show a concern with role relationships and role construing, which represent a basic point of emphasis in both construct theory and method.

Laing and his colleagues present the Interpersonal Perception Method, by which the members of a dyad (e.g. husband and wife) are separately faced with a series of statements in groups of four and asked to rate each statement on a four-point scale, from very true to very untrue. For example, in relation to "understanding," each partner first rates the statements "She understands me: I understand her: She understands herself: I understand myself." The statements are then rated by each partner as he *predicts* the other will rate him; and finally each partner rates them as he thinks the other has *predicted* for him. This is the complicated but essential game of "if he thinks that I think that he thinks." Analysis is in terms of possible congruencies, disjunctions, and so forth, of the interacting perceptions of the pair. The rationale of the test echoes Kelly's definition of role (sociality corollary) which stresses that "to the extent that one person *construes the construction processes of another* he may play a role in a social process involving the other person."

Drewery and Rae faced their dyads (husbands and wives) with a similar task, but used the Edwards Personal Preference Scale as the source of the statements to be judged. Each partner completes the scale three times, first answering in terms of "myself as I am," then in terms of "my spouse as I see him or her" and finally in terms of "myself as I think my spouse sees me." Analysis, in this study, was primarily in terms of a comparison of the profiles, as yielded by the Edwards Scale, intra- and inter- the two subjects. Thus, if the three viewpoints are 1, 2, and 3, and husband and wife are A and B, then raw score correlations and congruence scores can be obtained between $A_1 \times B_1$, $A_1 \times B_2$, $B_1 \times B_2$, and so on. Drewery and Rae have here fundamentally altered the status of a standard test (the Edwards Scale) from the absolute measuring rod of the experimenter, to a portable construct system, through which the subjects can view themselves in relation to each other.

Both these approaches differ from some aspects of grid method in that they supply constructs but do not elicit them, they do not examine the interrelationships of the constructs within the individual subject's system (in contrast to Bender's 1967 "interpersonal" grid study) and they create a special psychology for "interpersonal" construing not linked to a general theory of construing. Yet both reveal a concern with the subject's elaborated role construing which is akin to that evident in grid method and construct theory, while providing variations in method.

CONCLUSIONS

Most of the reported work on conceptual structure (except that by Zajonc and some by Deese) has been "self-centred" in the sense that few, if any, attempts have yet been made to *use* the methods in experimental or clinical investigations. Furthermore, the one comparison discussed between two of the methods involved only an internal comparison, since the relative *usefulness* of the Hays and Osgood methods in guiding predictions or controlling conceptual change was not assessed. One of the dangers of developing theories and methods concerned with conceptual structure in an abstract, academic and context-free fashion is that some idea of "conceptual structure" may develop, and hold as general and as detrimental a sway as, say, the concept of "intelligence." Unless theories and methods are developed to take account of constructs *in action* – incorporating functional strategies and processes of change – they are likely to show the usual natural history (of enthusiastic expansion followed by unpublicized decay) of work in other areas of psychological investigation.

All the methods described assume that analysis of aspects of cognitive structure is possible and of central importance. However, in no instances have the assumptions underlying the methods used been explicitly stated; nor have the techniques been articulately evolved from the theoretical ideas associated with them. The theories outlined, more or less explicitly by the different writers, have generally been very limited in scope and definition, and the main emphasis has been on the advantages of finding generalized methods of examining groups of people, rather than on finding ways of incorporating aspects of individual uniqueness into a study of group similarities. The rationale of many of the methods of analysis discussed is of the *ad hoc* empirical variety, or is dictated by the statistical techniques adopted.

Perhaps the most marked contrast between the approaches discussed and that of Kelly lies in their automatic acceptance of segmentalism in psychology – the chapter-heading theory of man, which has erected separate psychologies to deal with "emotions," "memory," "sensory perception" and, of course, "cognition." This segmentation shows itself in two ways in the studies discussed.

Firstly, (a minor feature with major implications), it shows itself in the degree to which these writers fail to cross-refer to each other – Deese, for example, makes no reference to Kelly, Zajonc, Bruner or Hays. This is presumably because they are thinking in terms of the specific chapter headings under which they work. Deese is working on "associations," Bruner on "conceptualization," Hays on "person perception," and so forth. Concepts have been transmuted into "topics" or "fields" or "areas," and thereby reified to a point at which cross-reference thinking is grossly hindered.

Secondly, these studies, and many of a similar kind, seem to imply that thinking about people is a special process requiring its own psychology, because, in unspecified ways, it differs fundamentally from thinking about things. Hence, the study of "person perception," the concern with "traits" and the special terms erected to deal with the "interpersonal" field. Construct theory explicitly argues for construing as a fundamental process, and for construct systems as changing strategies for dealing with the person's world – not purely his interpersonal world.

CHAPTER 5

Repertory Grid and Semantic Differential

IN ATTEMPTING to construe the repertory grid, psychologists have often sorted it as an element along with the Semantic Differential, (Osgood, Suci and Tannenbaum, 1957[1] and Osgood, 1962) construing both as measures of meaning. Indeed, many regard the repertory grid and Semantic Differential as kissing cousins in the area of psychological measurement, and a similarity-difference analysis of the two seems relevant here as a way of defining the grid in relation to more familiar ideas and practices. Initially, the research basis and procedures of the Semantic Differential will be described, and these will then be reviewed in terms of the assumptions underlying them as contrasted with the assumptions underlying the grid.

OSGOODIAN MEANING

Before reporting the experimental substructure for his method of measuring meaning, Osgood briefly expounds his theory of meaning, which is cast within a learning theory framework. He argues (p. 7) that "words represent things because they produce in human organisms some replica of the actual behavior towards these things, as a mediation process." In more formal terms, this is rephrased as follows: "a pattern of stimulation which is not the significate is a sign of that significate if it evokes in the organism a mediating process, this process (a) being some fractional part of the total behavior elicited by the significate and (b) producing responses which would not occur without the previous contiguity of non-significate and significate patterns of stimulation." This seems to make the traditional and intriguing arrow between S and R a compound of fragments of R and fractions of S, to be termed a "mediating process." The word "significate" is used in the traditional sense to refer to, say, the word "hammer," as opposed to the object hammer. Acknowledging that the word is not the object, Osgood argues that the word is a stimulus which "in a given situation regularly and reliably produces a predictable pattern of behavior," presumably a pattern of behaviour relating to the pattern produced by the object itself.

Osgood then re-defines his concept of meaning in a form obviously designed to allow for the factor analytic procedures which he intends to use in construct-

[1] Page numbered quotations are from this work.

ing his measuring instrument. Briefly, he argues that "meaning is a multi-dimensional space and that a particular word will be represented by a point in this multi-dimensional space."

Osgood and his co-workers carried out a number of experiments which were to be the basis of the Semantic Differential, and since all were of similar form, one generalized example is given. A large number of subjects were provided with booklets containing, say, 50 descriptive seven-point scales, each end of each scale being defined. These scales were randomly chosen from a thesaurus and included such items as *rough-smooth, good-bad, large-small, beautiful-ugly, yellow-blue, hard-soft, sweet-sour, strong-weak, clean-dirty* and so forth. On each of these seven-point scales, subjects were asked to rate a number of concepts such as *lady, boulder, sin, father, lake, symphony, Russian, feather, me* and so forth. Assuming, say, 50 scales, 20 concepts and 100 subjects, such a study would generate a $50 \times 20 \times 100$ cube of data, with each scale position being assigned a number one to seven arbitrarily from left to right, and each cell in this cube containing a number representing the judgment of a particular concept on a particular scale by a particular subject. The data were summed over both subjects and concepts to produce a 50 by 50 intercorrelational matrix of every scale with every other scale. Such matrices were then factor analyzed and the resulting factors labelled on the usual, somewhat speculative basis of subjectively perceived similarities in terms of scales highly loaded on particular factors.

A series of such studies tended repeatedly to yield what was called an *evaluative* factor, which usually accounted for about 35% of the total variance in the matrix, and which was best defined by the scale *good-bad*. Other scales which loaded on this factor (with their loadings shown in brackets) were *wise-foolish* (0·57), *beautiful-ugly* (0·52), *cruel-kind* (0·52), *successful-unsuccessful* (0·51), *true-false* (0·50) and so forth. A second factor which frequently emerged and usually accounted for about $7\frac{1}{2}$% of the total variance was labelled *potency:* this was usually best defined by the *potent-impotent* scale, and carried high loadings for scales such as *hard-soft* (0·97), *masculine-feminine* (0·47), *strong-weak* (0·40). A third factor which also emerged fairly regularly was labelled *activity*, and this was usually best defined by the *active-passive* scale, with loadings from *excitable-calm* (0·26) and *fast-slow* (0·26). This factor also accounted for about $7\frac{1}{2}$% of the total variance. Other factors varied considerably from study to study and usually accounted for so little of the variance as to be of doubtful explanatory value.

The three most frequently occurring dimensions were made the basis of the final measuring instrument and assumed to be the basic dimensions of a semantic space in terms of which an individual's concepts of particular entities, such as *mother, me, Communist*, could be plotted. In any individual case the usual procedure is to select a number of scales which previous studies have shown to define these major nomothetic dimensions. Concepts are then selected which have particular relevance to the individual subject or group study in hand. Subjects are asked to rate each concept on each seven-point scale. The scoring can then be either in terms of simply who rated what concept where on what particular scale, or, if one wants to compare the meanings of two words or to compare two people for the way they rate a particular word, a D (difference) score is used. The precise score used is designated D_{il}, and it is the total linear distance between the concepts in the Semantic space defined by the three dimensions. The formula for D_{il} is

$$D_{il} = \sqrt{\sum_j d_{il}^2}$$

where D_{il} is the linear distance between the points in the semantic space representing concepts i and l and d_{il} is the algebraic difference between the co-ordinates of i and l on the same dimension or factor, j.

For example, for the ratings of two concepts X and Y by a single subject on three scales a, b, and c (which may be assumed to define the three major dimensions) the worked-out formula is shown below.

```
        1    2    3    4    5    6    7
        X                   Y
   a ——:——:——:——:——:——:——
                  X         Y
   b ——:——:——:——:——:——:——
                       X    Y
   c ——:——:——:——:——:——:——
```

$$D_{il} = \sqrt{(1-5)^2 + (3-5)^2 + (4-5)^2}$$
$$= \sqrt{16 + 4 + 1}$$
$$= \sqrt{21}$$
$$= 4{\cdot}65$$

The difference score may be compared, in the absence of other information, with the expected zero, if the words have completely the same meaning, and the expected 10·4, if the words have completely different meanings from each other.

Osgood and Luria (1954) provided a dramatic example of the use of the Semantic Differential when they described its application to a case of multiple personality, in which the three personalities of the patient were respectively known as Eve White, Eve Black and Jane. Successive Semantic Differentials showed changes in the patient's semantic space, as depicted by the test, depending upon which personality was in control at the time. An example of a group study utilizing the Semantic Differential is available in Tannenbaum (1956) where the instrument was used to study the differential effects of television and stage presentation of drama on a sample audience.

In summary, the Semantic Differential is an instrument which utilizes seven-point, bipolar rating scales, and the main difference between it and other rating scale procedures is that the rating scales themselves are based on an extensive series of factor analytic studies. The instrument therefore offers the opportunity for cross comparison of the meanings of two different words for one subject, or the meanings of the same words for a number of subjects, by enabling the experimenter to sum ratings in terms of three allegedly major dimensions of meaning.

It seems probable that the perceived similarity of grid and Semantic Differential arises from the fact that both are techniques rather than standard-form static tests, and both are concerned with the interweave of concepts (elements) and scales (constructs).

THEORY AND PRACTICE

In evaluating the Semantic Differential and comparing it with the repertory grid, we are faced, first of all, with one apparent similarity – both appear to be methods of measurement related to articulated theories. In fact, it will be argued that this is a dimension of difference between the two measures in that, on closer examination, the Semantic Differential seems not to be clearly related to the theory with which it is formally linked.

Osgood seems aware of this. In trying to link the two together, he admits that he must make what he calls "a rather tenuous assumption, but a necessary one," and goes on to say (p. 27) "Let us assume that there is some finite number of representational mediation reactions available to the organism and let us further assume that the number of these alternative reactions (excitatory or inhibitory) corresponds to the number of dimensions or factors in the semantic space. Direction of a point in the semantic space will then correspond to what reactions are elicited by the sign, and distance from the origin will correspond to the *intensity* of the reactions." Such an argument seems to contain more analogy than inference. There seems to be nothing in Osgood's S–R account of how meaning is acquired which would make an inhibitory response to, say, "soft" produce the concept "hard." The paralleling of the notion of excitatory and inhibitory reactions with the Semantic idea of bipolar opposites seems an arbitrary act. On a learning theory basis one would expect the organisms to wind up with softness *versus* non-softness, and Osgood's recognition of the usefulness of the idea of bipolarity may derive more from his common sense and the dictates of test practice, than from his theory (see Carroll, 1959).

While recognizing the importance of bipolarity as an aspect of meaning, Osgood noted neither how widely the idea can be applied nor how specific it must be in its application to the individual. Thus his concepts are not bipolar, though his scales are, and he seems to regard the two notions as qualitatively different, while construct theory argues that the distinction between "elements" and "constructs" is an empirical one, indicating merely the level of superordinacy at which two *constructs* are being considered. Construct theory accepts that each individual erects his own *personal* contrasts (in terms of both verbal labels and operating discriminations) and that the practice of supplying universal pairs of opposites may do violence to the individual's construing.

Osgood concludes his theory and precedes his practical discourse by commenting on the gap between the two. He says (p. 30)

"It is true that many of the practical uses of the semantic differential, indeed its own empirical validity, depend little, if at all, on such a tie-in with learning theory–On the other hand, if we are to use the semantic differential as an hypothesis–testing instrument, and if the hypotheses regarding meanings and changes in meaning are to be drawn from learning-theory analyses, some such rationale as has been developed here is highly desirable. Further, from the writers' point of view, it is an awkward and somewhat embarrassing state of affairs to entertain simultaneously a theoretical conception of the nature of meaning and a procedure for measuring it which have no relation to one another. Whether this attempt at resolving this state of affairs has reduced awkwardness is another matter."

Indeed, if we look further at Osgood's theoretical substructure, we can see that not only does this instrument not specifically relate to it; at one point it specifically contradicts it. Osgood repeatedly stressed that he viewed meaning as a multi-dimensional space, but his instrument, as finally organized, treats meaning as essentially a three-dimensional space, with three axes labelled *evaluative*, *potency* and *activity*. It is not difficult so see why Osgood departed from his theoretical concept of a multi-dimensional space when constructing his test. He was working with the usual assumptions about test construction, and these include the idea that content dimensions of a generalized kind are almost inescapable in psychological measurement. This is the kind of assumption which is carried to its extreme in trait psychology, but is also present in most attempts to create psychological measures. Thus, although his theory led him to believe that meaning should be conceived of as multi-dimensional, he accepted that it would have to be measured in terms of a limited number of publicly specified dimensions. Furthermore, Osgood says (p. 9) "the meanings which different individuals have for the same signs will vary to the extent that their behavior towards the things signified have varied," – thus recognizing that meaning is also *personal*, as well as multi-dimensional. Yet when the measure is finally constructed, the individual's personal meanings are only recognized *within* publicly designated dimensions.

Again, while the whole factor-analytic procedure underlying the construction of the Semantic Differential is an example of the psychologist's searching for superordinate constructs in terms of which he may subsume the constructs of his subjects, and while this is an implicit recognition of the hierarchical nature of construing, nothing in the measure allows for the possibility that subjects, also, may have a hierarchical system of concepts, so that meaning cannot be adequately measured in a pre-determined framework.

A central argument of construct theory, that personal construct systems are hierarchically structured, is embodied in the organization corollary: each person characteristically evolves, for his convenience in anticipating events, a construction system embracing ordinal relationships between constructs. The accessibility of the grid to forms of cluster analysis and the more recent development of the implication grid (Hinkle, 1965) reflect, albeit crudely, this aspect of the theory in its methodology. The explanation proposed by Osgood leaves unexamined the question of whether semantic space is flat or hierarchical, but Osgood's own factor analytic strategies assume superordinate dimensions which can subsume the subordinate contributions of his subjects. At instrumental level, however, the subject tested by the Semantic Differential cannot reveal hierarchical structure, try as he might; the test permits no ready examination of the way a single subject links and organizes concept and concept, scale and scale or concept and scale.

In short, the Semantic Differential can be seen as a logical conclusion of orthodox test construction procedures, and it embodies no more than the rationale implicit in current ideas on the structure of rating scales and inference from factor analytic method. It does not relate specifically to any systematic theory and in some major respects it contradicts the outline theory which Osgood proposed as its basis.

By contrast, repertory grid technique is, for better or worse, logically related to personal construct theory. For example, the theory argues that psychological space is multi-dimensional, and the repertory grid accepts this, in that all constructs are compared with all other constructs, and they are not matched against any universal axes.

Grid usage thus recognizes the multi-dimensionality of psychological space, as proposed in construct theory, yet leaves the experimenter free to attempt any parsimonious method of subsuming the subject's dimensions, such as might be achieved by subjecting *the matrix of the individual subject* to a form of cluster analysis.

Kelly uses the term "element" to describe a *relationship* between constructs (an element is a construct within the range of convenience of a superordinate construct). This is reflected in the interchangeability of "elements" and "constructs" in grid administration; and concepts such as "range of convenience" are not only theoretical tenets but are basic to grid construction. Throughout, many correspondences between theory and grid method can be argued.

FACTOR ANALYTIC MEANING

There is one major statistical objection to the basis of the Semantic Differential which has an interesting theoretical moral to it. This objection was raised by Gulliksen (1958) and is well illustrated in a study by Dalziel (1960). The latter replicated Osgood's factor analytic procedures on 100 subjects, using 50 scales and 20 concepts. As a precautionary measure, to test for homogeneity, he first worked out the intercorrelations between scales for each concept separately. It was obvious that there was a massive scale-concept interaction which rendered illegitimate any pooling of scale correlations across concepts, and any subsequent calculations that might be performed on pooled data. Whether two particular scales correlated positively or negatively or not at all, was to a significant degree a function of the particular concepts which were being rated on the scales. Osgood, in a personal communication quoted in the same work, confirmed that this concept-scale interaction had been found in his own factor analytic studies, but failed to provide any argument for the analyses which he had made. Thus there are serious grounds for believing that the findings of orthogonality between major factors, which Osgood used as the basis for his instrument, are invalid, since they are based on a matrix of inter-correlations which in themselves probably do not meaningfully reflect the true state of affairs but are a pooling of error.

There are two contentions of personal construct theory which would have forewarned against the kind of procedure which Osgood undertook. The first is the central notion of range of convenience. Throughout his work Osgood ignored the idea that constructs might have a limited range of convenience, and the effects of this will be discussed in more detail later. For the moment, we can use it to explain in part the existence of concept-scale interaction. Suppose we have two scales *tender-hard hearted* and *warm-cold*, and a large number of the subjects are rating the concept *Mother* on these scales. It is quite probable that the scales will correlate positively in terms of this concept, since a large number of subjects may tend to rate *Mother* as both *tender* and *warm*, with perhaps a few exceptional subjects of unfortunate experience and cynical outlook rating *Mother* at the *hard-hearted* and *cold* end of the continua, contributing thus to the finding of a positive correlation between the two scales. Suppose later in the test we have the concept *freshly baked bread* to be rated on these two scales. It is quite probable that the majority of subjects will rate it as clearly at the *warm* end of the *warm-cold* continuum, but they may be baffled by the question whether *freshly baked bread* is *tender-hearted* or *hard-hearted*, and if they are unwilling to be whimsical about it, may simply rate it in the meaningless centre of the continuum (point 4 of the seven-point scale). We then have data pointing towards a zero correlation between the two scales. The existence of elements, within and without the ranges of convenience of the scales used, is a guarantee of varying intercorrelations dependent upon the particular concept-scale interaction.

This general argument can be re-stated in terms of the concept of *context*, by the argument that the relationships of constructs must be seen and assessed within a specific context, and that it is essential to maintain the distinction between the symbol of a construct (verbal labels etc.) and the construct as used in a given context. Hinkle (1965), elaborates this idea as follows.

"Construct definition should include a statement of the subordinate and superordinate implications of the construct. The problem here is how much can these implications change from context to context before the identity of the construct is lost? Essentially, a construct is a specific basis for differential anticipations or responses. Since a given construct symbol may represent a variety of specific bases (constructs), it is important that a construct and its symbol not be equated. For example, what a person considers to be "honest" in the context of criminals may be vastly different from "honest" in the context of intimate friends. Since the subordinate and superordinate implications of "honest-dishonest" could be expected to differ widely between these two contexts, in what sense could we say that the same construct is being used in each situation?"

One example of the way in which the Semantic Differential has fallen foul of this kind of distinction is Osgood's own finding that the scale *deep-shallow* loads on the *evaluative* dimension in terms of the concept *sonar* but not in terms of other concepts. In general, Osgood constructs his method as if each word had a single unitary meaning and does not allow for the possibility of explaining the different meanings which may underlie a single word. Osgood does recognize, but is not apparently willing to shoulder the burden which the scale-concept interaction problem places on the Semantic Differential. "In the last analysis it may prove necessary to construct separate meaning instruments for each class of concepts being judged, but for both theoretical and practical reasons we hope this will not be the case." (Osgood *et al.*, 1957, p. 188).

RANGE OF CONVENIENCE

Both in the factor analytic studies which were the basis for the Semantic Differential and in the form given to the test itself, the theoretical argument by

Kelly that "a construct is convenient for the anticipation of a finite range of events only" is ignored.

This sort of objection has been made on general grounds by Brown (1958) in a review paper significantly entitled "Is a boulder sweet or sour?." Brown also deals with Osgood's defence of the practice of ignoring "applicability of scale" arguments, on the grounds that what he is measuring is connotative meaning. Brown argues (p. 114)

"The authors say that the meaning measured by the differential is 'connotative', but, in terms of any standard semantic analysis, the differential must be considered a mixture and a mixture that changes with the problem at hand. Consider, for example, the concept called *boulder*. The *denotation* of this concept is the population of objects which may be so designated. According to some usage the *connotation* of the concept would be a listing of the attributes that define the class called *boulder*. Such scales as *large-small* and *hard-soft* might be considered connotative in this sense. There is, however, another way of using the term *connotation*. It is sometimes said to indicate any non-defining accidental associate of the concept; anything 'suggested' by the concept. There are many kinds of these. *Boulder*, for example, would probably be scaled as more *loud* than *soft*. This might be because (a) when boulders fall they make more noise than do pebbles; (b) among animal species the larger adult specimens are generally able to make more noise than the smaller immature specimens and this rule is extended to stones; (c) *soft* means yielding as well as not-loud and boulders are not yielding; etc. In some cases differential research even involves something very like denotation. When *things* are scaled rather than words, the thing (a Rorschach blot or a sonar signal) may belong to a class denoted by one or another term in the scales. A blot may be more *dark* than *bright*; a signal may be more *loud* than *soft*. The reason why the meaning measured by the differential seems to be best designated *connotative* can only be because *connotation* is a very ambiguous term."

The loose use of the term *connotation* criticized by Brown is also interesting in that it indicates that Osgood's theory of meaning needs to be supplemented with terms taken from non-psychological forms of analysis. In construct theory terms the denotation-connotation distinction can be handled in terms of the element-construct distinction, or, if the wider "accidental association" (apperceptive mass) meaning of the term connotation is required, then it is fairly covered by the loose-tight distinction made in construct theory about both constructs and construct sub-systems.

Apart from its contribution to the problem of scale-concept interaction, which has previously been mentioned, the problem of range of convenience might well have other consequences in Semantic Differential measurement. For example, ignoring the idea of range of convenience may have led to a kind of devaluing of meanings for all individuals, so that a whimsical reaction is indistinguishable from, and given equal weight with, a stable and well elaborated semantic relationship. One of the present authors has for years, in papers and lectures, used the attempt to designate false teeth as either *religious* or *atheist* as an example of possible difficulties over range of convenience. One outcome of this has been the ultimate conviction on his part that false teeth are clearly *atheist*. However, this element allotment has shown little tendency to elaborate, and few predictions within his construing system are based on it. It is what is called in lay terms, whimsicality or humour, or, in terms of psychological testing, obliging the experimenter, or in personal construct theory terms, an example of the permeability of the construct *religious-atheist* within one particular person's construct system. However, if this ever occurs in completing a Semantic Differential (and equivalents may often occur for many people) then all things will be considered equal, and it will contribute as much as anything else towards the total picture of the person's semantic space.

If the person taking the Semantic Differential is unable to "stretch" his construing and simply reacts by allotting to the mid-point 4 (which indicates "no meaning on this scale") any concept which he finds irrelevant, difficulties may still arise. Thus, if two subjects are faced with allotting the same concept to three scales embodying the three major dimensions, the first may find the concept unscalable on two of them and record 4 on these scales, and at the extreme end of the third and record 1 on this scale. The second subject may, on the first two scales, find the concept very meaningful and record 7 and 7, and meaningless on the third scale and record 4. This will give a difference score of 5·19. A second pair of subjects may record respectively 6–6–6 and 3–3–3, also achieving a difference score of 5·19. Thus we have an apparently identical degree of difference in meaning for the two concepts for both pairs of subjects; yet one pair cannot see the concept on the same scales at all, and in the second case both subjects are agreed as to the relevance of the scales but consistently differ about where the concepts should be rated. Obviously these are very different kinds of "difference."

This, then, is a major difference between grids and the Semantic Differential. Personal construct theory lays great stress on the idea that constructs and construct sub-systems have limited ranges of convenience, and specifically argues that in this respect traditional logic is not a fair reflection of human psychology.

In traditional logic everything is either A or not-A, whereas in construct theory elements may be subsumed under the emergent pole of a construct or under its implicit pole or be outside the *range of convenience* of the construct. True, Kelly does not see constructs as having fixed and inflexible ranges of convenience; a construct has a focus of convenience (those elements which it was originally designed to subsume and discriminate between) and a range of convenience, (all those elements to which the construct can be later applied) but an examination of any particular construct system at any point in time will rapidly reveal finite ranges of convenience for the constructs and construct sub-systems which compose it.

Osgood comes some way towards recognizing the idea of range of convenience in making his seven-point scale bipolar; and again he seems aware of the problems in his use of the concept of connotative meaning. Yet neither his specific theory of meaning nor his test procedures take account of the concept of finite ranges of convenience.

ORTHOGONAL DIMENSIONS – ORTHOGONAL FOR WHOM?

The central characteristic of the Semantic Differential is its utilization, on the basis of factor analytic research, of three major, allegedly orthogonal dimensions which, since they are thought to be independent of each other, are designed to give maximum dispersion of concepts in the semantic space so ordered, and provide an optimal description of the meaning of concepts thus plotted.

There are general grounds for criticizing such a procedure. For example, although the *evaluative* dimension occurs repeatedly and accounts usually for around 35% of the total variance, the two other dimensions are of very different calibre, in that they account between them for only about 15% of the variance, and have a curious habit of merging (used on political concepts they appear together as *dynamism*), or inverting themselves in terms of loaded subscales in some of the studies. Furthermore, Gulliksen (1958) has criticized the subgrouping of scales as loaded on the major dimensions, since it is quite possible that the relationships between these subscales are curvilinear, and such relationships are misconceived if they are treated as parallel. Again, there is the more fundamental criticism, previously cited, that the whole process of pooling for factor analytic purposes is illegitimate in view of scale-concept interaction. The same objection would apply to the cluster analysis of grids in which the contexts of the elements vary, and thereby differing relationships between the same constructs may be compounded.

There are also theoretical grounds for doubting the usefulness of the whole "orthogonal dimension" approach. This approach does not derive from Osgood's theory of meaning, but seems rather to result from his use of factor analytic method.

Kelly's individuality corollary states simply that "Persons differ from each other in their construction of events." This is tantamount to a statement that persons differ from each other in the relationships between their constructs. Thus, from a construct theory viewpoint, we would not expect to find three major dimensions which were truly orthogonal for all, or even a majority, of mankind. In what sense has Osgood found that his three dimensions are orthogonal for people in general? The answer is that he has found this only on a pooling basis which effectively conceals individual variance. Thus, it is likely that if the individual Semantic Differential protocols of

Osgood's studies were examined, it could be shown that for a large number of individual subjects, two, or all three of the major dimensions were in fact correlated either positively or negatively. In other cases (as illustrated by Fransella, 1965) the individual's factor picture might bear no relation to Osgood's normative model. In the factor analysis of a pooled matrix, individual differences tend to cancel themselves out. The final statement that specific dimensions are orthogonal may be true in some general arithmetic sense, while being both statistically and psychologically misleading in a large number of particular cases.

In the grid, no prior assumption about orthogonal dimensions is made. In any particular grid, all possible pairs of constructs can be correlated for a given individual, and no assumptions about independence of constructs need be made; the data about each particular case being actually available. Even a relatively small amount of experience in the administering and scoring of grids will convince the psychologist concerned that broad generalizations of the "three orthogonal dimensions" type are almost invariably an oversimplification in terms of the detailed matrices provided for each individual by grid technique. In this respect, then, a further difference between grid and Semantic Differential is that, where the latter makes an assumption, the grid asks a question and attempts an answer.

A further difficulty which arises out of this idea of three basic orthogonal dimensions, is that in itself it discourages the practice of eliciting constructs. Although nothing in grid technique prevents the experimenter from supplying constructs to his subjects, if he feels that this is both necessary and valid for his particular experimental purposes, the whole structure of the grid readily enables him to elicit constructs from his subject. This property of the grid is not only a tenet of construct theory, but has been shown to be empirically important in studies by Landfield and Nawas (1964), Isaacson and Landfield (1965) and Caine and Smail (1967) who revealed some of the distortions which result from making the subject a dummy to the psychologist's ventriloquist.

The pooling procedure of factor analysis and the basing of a test on such a procedure rest on the assumption that future subjects will be legitimate members of the population on which the original factor analyses were carried out. This is a traditional but still valid criticism of all factor analytic procedures (see Block, 1955), and although the replication of factor analytic pictures on further populations somewhat narrows down the problem, it does not dispense with it. All factor analytic pictures are portraits of the population from which they were derived, but only hypotheses in relation to future individuals and populations. In the case of the Semantic Differential we have to assume not only that new subjects will adhere to the rule of three orthogonal dimensions, but also that the subscales used to define these dimensions will adequately express some aspect of the outlook of each new subject.

In short, the Semantic Differential *assumes* generality of meaning in the words used to label scales and concepts – a strange assumption for a *measure* of meaning.

COMPARISONS

Little direct experimental comparison of grid and Semantic Differential exists in the literature. Perhaps this is because, although they are often said to be similar, in practice the kind of assumptions they make and the kind of data they produce very nearly defy comparison.

Following the work of Bieri (1955), there are a number of studies which, utilizing grid technique, have hinged on the idea that people may be compared in terms of whether they use a large number of relatively independent dimensions through which to view their world (cognitive complexity) or a small number of highly clustered dimensions (cognitive simplicity). Jaspars (1963) was interested in the question of whether the designation of subjects as cognitively complex or simple in test terms would vary, depending on whether constructs were elicited from, or supped to the subject. He used the Semantic Differential as a form of supplied construct test, and estimated cognitive complexity in terms of the amount of variance accounted for by the first (*evaluative*) factor. In parallel, he used an early form of the Role Construct Repertory Test, and analyzed the results for factorial complexity. His results showed that the two measures agreed fairly well, except that the correlation between them fell fpr subjects who were more neurotic, more intelligent or more introverted than average. Jaspers concluded that it makes less difference to the normal person than to the neurotic whether or not he has to express himself in provided dimensions. He went on to suggest that neurotics have a more unusual cognitive structure than normals, but that this could not be assessed by the Semantic Differential because with this instrument, neurotics are "forced into normality." He concluded that, in this respect, the Rep test was more sensitive to individual difference.

Fransella (1965) used a number of forms of both repertory grid and Semantic Differential in studying stutterers, including a special form of the Semantic Differential devised for such patients by Smith (1962). Fransella illustrates a number of difficulties with both techniques; but it is particularly interesting that when she analyzed the Semantic Differential down to the level of factoring results for the individual subject, she found it difficult to locate the traditional three independent dimensions. This last procedure is interesting in that it shows the wheel coming full circle. It is possible to factor analyze the Semantic Differential of an individual, thereby in effect converting it into a grid.

Indeed, Slater's Principal Component Analysis for grids (1965) allows for entries in the form of seven-point scales and therefore readily accepts Semantic Differential material. However, when this is done it seems that the whole of the procedure on which the Semantic Differential is based has been implicitly rejected, in that a form of cluster analysis on an idiographic basis (essentially the form of the grid) has been accepted.

This latter point suggests a definition for the grid in relation to the Semantic Differential. A grid may be seen as carrying out on each individual subject something like the procedure which Osgood applied to large populations in his attempt to derive normative axes of meaning. Grid results can either be analyzed individually or pooled. The Semantic Differential should not be regarded as a rather simple, quick equivalent of grid method. Grid method can be cast in such a form as to give all the information that might be derived from the Semantic Differential, plus additional information which is not obtainable from the normal use of the Semantic Differential method.

In grid terms, the Semantic Differential is concerned with the placement of certain specific elements in relation to a number of constructs. Grid method also allows the examination of the elements in the construct space, but, in addition, allows examination of the relationships between constructs in the element space.

CONCLUSIONS

The history of the Semantic Differential can be viewed as a story with a moral. It is a story which begins on a note of high endeavour, in that its area of attack – "meaning" – is one central to the study of man. Many psychologists, particularly learning theorists, have tended to buy an apparently high degree of scientific precision at the cost of limiting themselves to the most fragmentary and unrewarding aspects of human behaviour. In making his goal the study of meaning, Osgood turned his back on the kind of psychology which relegates much that is interesting about human beings, and much that differentiates them from non-human species, to "higher processes" which are to be studied at some unspecified date, when so-called "fundamental processes" have been fully analyzed. This perpetual dodging of issues, justified by a kind of naïve reductionism (see Jessor, 1958) has given us a literature replete with muscle-twitch psychology. If the Semantic Differential work of Osgood had done nothing more than to draw the attention of psychologists to the area of meaning, it would have been well worth while.

The outcome of the story illustrates what is probably the best that can be done with an area as complex and as fundamental as meaning, using an orthodox test construction approach of a largely a-theoretical kind. Basically, the Semantic Differential is a sophisticated form of rating scale procedure, with the underlying factor analytic rationale which is common for such procedures. Its extensive use could possibly add considerably to our knowledge of specific empirical relationships in a number of applied contexts, but would add no more to our theoretical understanding of the nature of meaning than, say, the vast history of intelligence tests has added to our understanding of thinking. In the case of both the Semantic Differential and the intelligence test, developments have been marked by a common sense rationale and statistical sophistication in the development of instruments; however expedient such ventures are in relation to specific experiments, they contribute little to the cause of explanatory science.

Far from being related instruments or approaches, the repertory grid and the Semantic Differential are perhaps better viewed as contrasting outcomes of different types of psychological approach.

CHAPTER 6

A Definition of Grid Method

THE FORMAL properties of grids have been illustrated and discussed, so it is possible to take a perspective view of grid method, to attempt to summarize its defining characteristics and to consider the ways in which it contrasts with earlier methods of psychological measurement.

A grid may be defined as any form of sorting task which allows for the assessment of relationships between constructs and which yields these primary data in matrix form.

The possible variations in grid method are such that no definition more detailed than this can be inclusive. The nature of the elements sorted cannot be prescribed (e.g. as "people") since this is entirely dependent on the subsystem of construing under investigation. The presence of elements, as such, cannot be prescribed, since in Hinkle's Implication Grid, for example, the subject explicitly constructs the matrix by directly indexing the implications which relate constructs, without reference to specific elements. Different types of grid yield many scores (e.g. the mal-distribution score) other than "relationships between constructs" but these latter represent the only invariable and general data provided by all grids. The definition cannot specify constructs as "verbal," since grids can be administered which require the subject to make no explicit verbal formulation of the basis of his sorts (cf. Scott, 1962 and 1963), and it is at least theoretically possible to imagine dichotomous behaviours being analyzed in grid form, where neither experimenter nor subject had, at that point, ventured a verbal label as the basis of discrimination. The definition cannot prescribe that the constructs shall be "the subject's," since constructs may be supplied and only be the subject's insofar as he is prepared to try and use them.

The three prescriptive characteristics included in this definition are legitimate in the following sense. All grids are sorting tests, in that they involve the subject in acts of serial and systematic categorization: either categorization of elements in terms of constructs, or constructs in relation to each other, expressed in terms of their mutual implications, or the relative allotment of constructs on a third construct (e.g. the construct *preferred self—not preferred self*) as in the Resistance to Change grid. All grids involve the exploration of construct relationships, in that they assume that the subject will find it meaningful to make the kind of bipolar discrimination implied by the term construct, and it is precisely the bipolarity of the discrimination that enables constructs to be related to one another by the experimenter. The experimenter is here using himself as a model, in that he expects the subject to have related, and thereby predictive, dimensions, just as experimenters erect dimensions and hypothesize relationships between them. "Concepts", as the term is traditionally used, cannot have relationships, other than can be specified by commonalities of class inclusion or class exclusion of elements, since they specifically lack the contrast pole which makes the construct a dimension and therefore relatable to other dimensions. All grids yield, primarily, a matrix of cells with rows representing constructs, and columns representing elements or representing other constructs. It is this matrix to which the term "grid" refers.

The basic components of a grid are constructs and elements. A construct can be described as a bipolar abstraction which a person uses to summarize, give meaning to and anticipate events. Elements are the things or events which are abstracted by a construct. In construct theory terms, any construct can be an element within the range of convenience of a more superordinate construct. Thus, for a given individual, the construct *kind-unkind* may be subsumed by (be an element within the range of convenience of) the superordinate construct *good-bad*. In this sense, construct systems are hierarchical. It is assumed that reality cannot be directly apprehended but only construed; and the named units of any person's reality (a particular person, or tree, or time) are, for that person, the intersection points of a number of constructs which are in turn subsumed by constructs more superordinate within the system. In grid practice, elements can be of two kinds. In an Implication Grid, for example, there are no formal unitary elements to be sorted (such as people known personally to the subject). Instead the subject is asked to take construct X, state whether he can perceive it as an element within the range of convenience of construct Y and specify its superordinate relationships, and then to consider Y, decide whether it can be considered an element within the range of convenience of construct X and again specify the lines of implication.

Alternatively, elements given a unitary character and for which a common construction can be assumed (e.g. these are "people," or "political parties," or "paintings," or "chairs") can be allotted, by the subject, to one pole or another of his constructs. Thus, grids assume, in Kelly's terms, that a person "erects a structure within the framework of which the substance (events, things) takes shape or assumes meaning. The substance which he construes does not produce the structure; the person does."

A person, in construing anything, does not merely attempt to decide what it is. He attempts to decide what it is, in contrast with what it is not, though it seems to be in the nature of our conventional use of language often to leave the contrast pole implicit. In summarizing the defining characteristics of grid method, an attempt will be made explicitly to contrast it with other methods of psychological measurement, and the constructs, in terms of which the grid will be described, have been specifically chosen because they polarize the grid in relation to traditional techniques.

A THEORY-RELATED METHOD

Grid method, in its design, is a detailed application of some of the basic tenets of personal construct theory.

Other psychological measures are frequently used in relation to specific theories. The Taylor Manifest Anxiety Scale (MAS) has frequently been used as an index of drive in relation to the Hull-Spence theory; and the Thematic Apperception Test and Rorschach have a broad kinship, in language and assumption, with psychoanalytic theories. In no instance, however, is the relationship of the measure to the basic aspects of a theory so consistently close as it is in the case of grid method and construct theory. Thus, although the MAS is used widely as a measure of drive, its construction, form and content do not relate logically to that theoretical concept (see Jessor and Hammond, 1957 and Mair, 1964). It was constructed in relation to psychiatric categories, it took its form from current notions of questionnaire design and its content was prescribed by loose, commonsense and more-or-less socially accepted ideas about the correlates of anxiety. In constructing projective tests, the basic assumption was that subjects, faced with ambiguous stimuli, would project their wishes, hopes, problems into the interpretations that they gave. The basic mechanism, thought to be involved, was that of projection. This concept is certainly important in Freudian theory but is clearly not *the* basic concept of that theory. Furthermore, the actual concept of projection used in relation to projective tests differs in a number of important respects (for example, it does not necessarily carry the implication of defending the subject from guilt) from that which is elaborated in Freudian theory. In the case of many other tests, the idea of theory-to-test inference seems to have been at least half-reversed. It can be argued, for example, that the logic of intelligence test construction has dominated theories of intelligence, rather than the reverse.

Every aspect of grid method (e.g. the assumption of bipolarity of constructs, the assumption of finite ranges of convenience for constructs, statistical methods of analysis which assume that constructs are hierarchical, the assumptions underlying elicitation of constructs, the focus on construct relationships rather than element allotment, and so forth) is close kin to an equivalent assumption in construct theory; and tests of the assumptions of grid method can be translated into tests of some of the assumptions of construct theory.

If we disallow the current belief of many psychologists that wheresoever two or three concepts are gathered together they are entitled to be called a theory, and if we apply the term theory only to comprehensive and elaborate frameworks, then we must come to the conclusion that most psychological tests are notion-generated, rather than theory-generated. In considering the advantage of theory derivation for a test method, we might note that constructs within Kelly's theory can be viewed as theoretical constructs, in the sense implied by Cronbach and Meehl (1955), and various methods of construct validation would thus seem important. Jessor and Hammond (1957) point out that an important derivative of the idea of construct validation is that the psychological theoretical model has implications for psychometric as well as for experimental procedures. They point out that "there is no fundamental reason why theories should make unequivocal demands on the experiment and permit the test to satisfy psychometric requirements only." Russell (1961) also commented on the suggestion that items in a test should be derived from the concept being measured. He considered that such a method would be advantageous in the event of negative findings. One might then be able more accurately to place blame on the theory, rather than on the test; and this procedure would encourage more stringent tests of the theory. It may be that grid method will facilitate clearer tests of construct theory than has previously been possible with other methods of measurement, in relation to other theories.

The fact that grid technique is so closely related to construct theory presents an interesting problem for users of the grid who approach it without a construct theory orientation. A personal construct theorist, using repertory grid technique, sees himself as measuring aspects of personal construct systems, as elaborately defined within the theory. A psychologist using the technique purely in an empirical manner, or within another framework, is faced with the problem of deciding what he is measuring. He may decide he is measuring some aspect of "meaning," or "concept formation," or "attitude," and so forth. He must ask himself why he felt it necessary to follow construct theory-dictated assumptions in his construction of the grid, while feeling free to ignore them in his interpretation of the data generated by it. An infinite number of contradictions can be foreseen. For example, a psychologist might be tempted to use the grid as a method of ascertaining the hierarchical gradient of situations required for behaviour therapy with a particular patient (Fransella, 1965). He would thus assume that his patient was capable of meaningfully abstracting situations, and potentially capable of reconstruing them. If orthodox, he would then move on to a form of behaviour therapy which implicitly assumes that the patient is the mechanical outcome of his reinforcement history, which merely needs a few laboratory-manufactured additions.

There seems little doubt that, in the empiricist tradition of much psychology, repertory grid methods will be frequently divorced from their origins in personal construct theory; but whatever short-term advantages may accrue to particular psychological ventures, it is contended that grid methods can be most meaningfully used in relation to the theory which defines them.

Grid method allows for the assessment of aspects of *both* the content *and* the structure of an individual's construct system. Here, the term content refers to the things which interest or concern any particular person; whilst structure implies the type of organization he has erected to deal with these things. A simple analogy could be found in industry. Six factories may be concerned with the production of different goods e.g. matches, tinned peas, aircraft engines etc. – their content is different. The organization of their production methods, communication between departments, hierarchical arrangements of departments, and so forth, can to some extent be examined, apart from this content, and various aspects of similarity or difference in organization – i.e. structure – can be specified. So also with grid method. It is possible, in analyzing data yielded by a single grid on a single individual, not only to make statements about which particular elements he has allotted to which poles of which constructs, or which constructs relate to which, but, at a higher level of abstraction, to make general statements about the structural qualities of the sample of his construct system. For example, it may be deduced that it is closely knit correlationally, or relatively diffuse and unstructured in correlational terms. The format of the grid allows for a detailed mathematical analysis of the structure of the resulting matrix.

Psychologists have often been concerned with both content and structure; but test methods generally seem *content*-oriented – their scoring methods directly reflect what the subject says or does in particular contexts. Statements about structure have been loose inferences made from an examination or simple count of the content of responses. Thus, for example, various projective tests might be used to examine ideas related to notions of "ego structure." Here, the definition of ego structure may remain vague, and the "evidence" relevant to the concept will almost certainly be derived from a speculative interpretation of the meaningfulness of the things the person has said in response to the test items. Alternatively, "structural" statements about a given individual are made on the basis of plotting his particular score in terms of group-analyzed data. This is the sort of procedure manifest in personality and cognitive test "profile" methods. But, here again, the structural statements are a second-order inference (albeit a mechanically made one) dependent, for their value, upon the tenuous assumption of some massive homogeneity in the standardizing population.

With grid method, it is possible to examine *what* constructs any individual uses in any particular context (e.g. interpersonal relations, paintings, politics, etc.), and also to abstract further and quantify something of the organization of these constructs. Within grid method, statements about structure are neither dependent on interpretations of content, nor derived from any summary of group responses. They are directly derived, mathematical summaries of the grid data themselves. They are entirely "objective," in the sense that different scorers will arrive at the same mathematical expression of the data, though, in the present state of our knowledge, the statements that psychologists will be tempted to make on the basis of particular structural scores may differ. Nevertheless, statements about aspects of structure and content can be made for an individual or group whose constructs are examined in terms of grid method.

Be it noted, however, that preoccupations with "structure" and "content" are not mutually exclusive. Both are complementary *viewpoints* in terms of which construct systems may be analyzed. Grid strategies are not inherently concerned with either content or structure. Thus, the procedure of laddering can be construed as a method of eliciting constructs, as a means of noting linkages between specific constructs (content analysis) or as a basis for examining the structural "height" (the number of constructs between top and bottom) and the organization of the system (structural analysis).

ABSENCE OF PRECONCEIVED DIMENSIONS

Historically, psychologists seem to have developed their ideas about psychological measurement by accepting, as their model, measurement in the physical sciences – the concept of the calibrated rod. A number of scales in areas such as intelligence testing, personality assessment, memory and sensory acuity have been set up on the basis of conceptualizing and naming a broad dimension, formalizing it in terms of a series of problems or questions and precoding the subject's responses in such a way that they will, in total, yield a scale position on the preconceived dimension. Such responses have been assessed in terms of their relationship to a key which was derived normatively (as in personality questionnaires), or in terms of correct responses as determined by traditional logic (as in intelligence tests), or in terms of the intuitive norms and the personal philosophy of the psychologist (as is certain projective tests). Various forms of cluster analysis (factor analysis, principal component analysis, Q-sort) were introduced at an early stage, but were used largely on group data, either to derive further, more parsimonious standard scales or to check hypotheses about expected commonalities of response within the subject population. With the introduction of grid method, tradition was breached; instead of seeking to place the subject on the preconceived dimensions of the psychologist (*intelligent-dull*, *introvert-extravert*, *good memory-poor memory*, *high threshold-low threshold*) we are primarily involved in attempting to discover what dimensions each person uses to make sense of his own world, and only then, and on that foundation, do we attempt to subsume these dimensions under further constructs of our own.

Unlike previous types of measurement, the grid does not necessarily impose any *content* dimensions on the subject. Each subject can be encouraged to express the constructs which he uses to make sense of areas of his life. Once this freedom has been allowed to the subject, the experimenter is at liberty to view the subject's responses in terms of particular content or structural dimensions; and he may either evolve these for himself, or use those proposed in personal construct theory – that is, dimensions such as *tight-loose*, *superordinate-subordinate*, *permeable-impermeable*, *core-peripheral*. This practice of allowing freedom for the subject to express his own content dimensions and subsequently allowing the psychologist to view these in terms of given structural dimensions, makes it likely that grid methods will provide data and allow generalizations about behaviour which are more "culture-free" than those yielded by most psychological measures. They will be culture-free, in the sense that structural summaries of grid data are mathematical in nature; and mathematics is the nearest approach to a culture-free language. They will also be culture-free and subculture-free, in that the subject will have been allowed to work in terms of his own preferred language, thus throwing the problem of translation onto the experimenter rather than, as is the case with many current tests, forcing the subject to talk in an alien tongue for the convenience of the psychologist.

ABSENCE OF ASSUMED MEANINGS

The grid is a method for investigating *personal* constructs. Many constructs are symbolized by verbal labels – a word or a group of words. All words in general use in any language have commonly agreed dictionary meanings; but individuals may often use similar words to describe different experiences or ideas, or different words to describe similar experiences or ideas. Almost all psychological measures dependent on words have relied heavily on the assumption that different people will understand broadly the same thing where a standard set of words is used (e.g. in questionnaires) and will mean the same thing when they reply in some standard form. Grid method does not assume that the subject means what the experimenter means by particular verbal labels involved in the test – on the contrary, the method is designed to help ascertain what the subject means by particular verbal labels. With grid method, it is possible to attempt an assessment of the particular and personal definitions which a subject attaches to the words he uses, by examining the element selections made on the basis of his constructs, and by quantifying the interrelationships between these constructs. It is then possible to compare these personal "meanings" for words either with their public meaning (the construct interrelationships implied by dictionary definitions, or normative relationships yielded by grid administration to groups) or with the experimenter's meanings (either by having the experimenter complete a similar grid, or by having him predict the construct relationships which would reflect his particular explanatory stance). Kelly distinguishes between commonality and individuality in construct meaning; and while other types of psychological measures depend primarily on commonality of meaning, grid method can readily allow exploration of either commonality or individuality in construct usage.

THE MEASUREMENT OF SYSTEMS

Personal construct theory stresses that an individual uses constructs, not as isolated descriptive categories which can be picked out and examined separately, but as changing categorizations of events which are systematically interrelated with each other and ordered into various hierarchical sub-systems within a total system.

Other sorting tests seem to have either partially or totally ignored this idea. For example, Epstein (1953), in devising a test to measure "over-inclusion," required his subjects to state which of a series of concepts was "absolutely essential" to a named initial concept (e.g. LOVE: hate, feeling, kisses, marriage, sex). Such a test explicitly acknowledges that concepts are interrelated (it is difficult to see what use they would be if they were not); but does not allow free exploration of *how* they are related for a particular individual. On the contrary, it rests on a public distinction between "right" and "wrong" relationships, and then sets out to see if the subject agrees with society, as conceived by Epstein. This immediately makes the purely individual aspects of a person's construing (however viable they may be in terms of his own experience) "wrong," and liable to get him diagnosed as schizophrenic. Equally, if we accept the complexity of the *personal construct system* as described by Kelly (a system with many hierarchical sub-systems unified into a total system through a multiplicity of lines of implication) then a test such as Epstein's would clearly be an inadequate way of sampling it.

Grid method permits an examination of the relationships between different construct dimensions, and allows the possibility of studying aspects of the systematic and hierarchical arrangement of constructs in use by any particular person. In this way, the grid differs markedly from other measures, and seems to make possible the experimental examination of many different aspects of the psychological functioning of the subject which are excluded by the fragmentary approach typical of unitary concept measures.

GRIDS AS EXPERIMENTS

In applying a conventional psychological test, we are using as assumptions, the hypotheses of an experiment which has already been carried out, in that the test has been validated in a specific context for a particular purpose. In contradistinction to this, every grid is an experiment in itself. The construction of the grid, in terms of choice of elements, choice of constructs and selection of scoring procedures, represents a complete experimental design. The need to avoid *post hoc* licence in the interpretation of results means that specific hypotheses are better proposed before the grid is administered. Since the grid allows internal tests of significance, no prior validation specific to the problem in hand is necessary, even though the basic assumptions underlying the method have to be met. It must again be stressed that the relation of grid method to a specific psychological theory means that each grid application is, to the extent that the underlying assumptions of the theory are met, an experimental test of certain tenets of that theory.

ARTICULATION OF SAMPLING ASSUMPTIONS

Since the grid is a flexible method or framework rather than a static test with specified content, each occasion for its use explicitly demands that sampling requirements be met.

It is true that test constructors traditionally lay great stress on sampling considerations; but since most tests, once constructed, are static, the limitations of the original sampling are often forgotten or ignored. Thus, for example, a well known and relatively well standardized test like the Wechsler Adult Intelligence Scale is widely used on populations which differ in important respects from those on which the norms are based (e.g. English populations normal and abnormal: test standardized only on normal Americans); and scores on different parts of this test are sometimes used to guide decisions about vocational problems, when no adequate validational evidence for their appropriateness exists. Similarly, the limitations of *item* sampling are likely to be ignored. Users of the Rorschach may make statements about varied aspects of a person's real-life functioning in many areas, on the basis of having sampled his responses to ink blots. Implications are drawn from an individual's responses to these very particular items to aspects of behaviour related to very different circumstances. Such generalizations need not be invalid, but are certainly likely to be so, since the relevance of the items sampled for the test, to the life areas in which predictions are being made, may not be specifically checked.

Users of grid methods are faced on each occasion with an explicit sampling problem, in that they must select elements, constructs, methods of administration and methods of analysis appropriate to the context in which they are attempting to make predictions. This certainly does not relieve them of sampling problems, nor does it guarantee that they will adequately solve them; but it does mean that they have explicitly to face them time and again, and they are less likely to ignore the dangers of sampling error by resting content with a pseudo, once-for-all solution of the problem.

THE INDIVIDUAL AS A POPULATION OF DATA

The fact that the grid produces data for each individual subject in the form of a matrix, means that each individual grid can be subjected to statistical tests of significance of the kind normally reserved for group data. This makes the "population" surveyed (the population of interrelated responses within the single subject) a paradigm of the conventional experimental population. Hypotheses can be erected and tested for a single subject, in a manner not possible with conventional normative tests; and a range of conventional population statistics (including forms of cluster analysis) is potentially available for use in analyzing individual grids. The individual can be studied, not merely in the sense of taking subjects one at a time, nor in the sense of making the content of test items relate to a particular individual, but also in the sense of developing a complete experimental design for a single subject. In this sense, the grid meets the requirements for single-case study design suggested by du Mas (1955).

"DIFFERENCE" AND "SIMILARITY" IN PEOPLE

In all test situations, the psychologist is concerned with the examination and interpretation of responses to stimuli. In most tests, the assumption is made that if two people respond similarly to the same items, they can be considered similar people *both* in this respect *and* in other important respects. If they respond differently to the same items, they can be considered as different *both* in these *and* in other important respects. The total of responses to the specific stimuli determines statements about similarities and differences between subjects.

In terms of grid method, people who respond similarly to the same "stimuli," or elements, will be considered similar in that respect, i.e. in relation to their element allotment and construct relationships in that particular area. They will not necessarily be considered alike in other areas of construing, as yet unexplored. If two people respond differently to a set of elements in terms of a number of constructs, they need not necessarily be considered as different people as regards their *construct system* for dealing with these elements. In construct theory terms, similarity between persons is seen in terms of similarity of the constructions they have placed upon experience, not in terms of similarity of the experience they have undergone. This conception is embodied in grid measurement, in that it is possible for two people to allot the same elements quite differently to the poles of the same constructs; yet when the grid is analyzed they may be shown to be operating very similar construct systems. That this is not only mathematically but psychologically possible is demonstrated by Bannister (1962). Relative to grid methods, most psychological tests can be said to be "stimulus-bound." Whether this is considered to be a point of strength or weakness will depend on the theoretical standpoint of the individual psychologist; but it is clearly a point of difference between grid method and conventional psychological techniques.

CENTRALITY OF CHANGE

For grid method, as for all other psychological tests, any aspect of the subject's view of his past can only be assessed from the standpoint of the present. What a person is now will probably affect his statements about what he was in the past. Interpretations of a subject's past are not usually made from results of psychological tests: allegedly less rigorous methods, such as case-history record interpretation, are used for this purpose. Psychological tests are generally used to assess some aspect of the subject's present state, so that an assessment can be later made of changes which have taken place (e.g. following treatment), or to facilitate predictions about future behaviour. While it may often be possible to derive predictions about possible changes in future behaviour from responses to various "projective" tests, such possibilities seldom derive from observations of responses to "objective" personality measures. The emphasis on the "reliability" of such measures (see later discussion) seems to force the psychologist into a trait-psychology posture, from which he can only predict that the subject will behave in the future as he has behaved in the past, and argue that although some aspects of his situation may be changed (e.g. so as to make the effects of the same behaviour less catastrophic), the person himself cannot change or be changed.

Grid method, because of its close relationship to personal construct theory, seems, at least potentially, to offer a framework within which a more systematic approach can be made to the problem of detecting areas within which a person's behaviour may change, and the general nature of such changes can be defined. Kelly argues that people erect constructs to simplify and make sense of their world. These constructs he conceives of as bipolar abstractions which apply to a limited range of events. That is to say, a construct is not defined by either of its poles, but by the inclusiveness and exclusiveness of *both* poles *and* the *contrast* between the two poles. Knowledge of a person's polar position on any of his important constructs defines something of his present self-conception *and* his notion of the alternative to this conception. Kelly suggests that the simplest and perhaps the most probable immediate change in construing, under stress conditions involving personal invalidation, is a change from one end of relevant and important construct dimensions to the other. Thus, a person who uses the construct dimension *introvert-extravert* as the central one in organizing his life, and sees himself at the *introvert* pole, may be expected, if he perceives massive invalidation of this role construction, to swing to the opposite extreme and view himself as *extravert* – with all that follows, in terms of related conceptual changes within his construct system, and with resulting behavioural changes, in terms of his newly envisaged relationship between himself and his interpersonal environment.

Of course, Kelly does not imply that the only construct change a person may make when facing disconfirmation of some of his predictions is that of polar change. Many other types of change, some of which have been mentioned earlier, are possible. Yet the most immediate and likely changes under stress may well involve sharp movements to contrasting constructions, and consequent behavioural changes.

American construct theory psychologists, like American clinical psychologists generally (and unlike their British counterparts), are frequently involved in psychotherapy, and this in turn may have given them a greater readiness to envisage change as a possibility. Faced repeatedly with the explicit demands of patients who ask to be helped to change, one is less likely to go chasing after those great immutable stabilities which trait psychologists try to embody in their tests. Behaviour therapists in this context often have an interesting compromise position. They seek to obtain a contractual agreement with the patient (with clauses couched in the learning theory language of discrete habits) which will specify and limit the changes which are legally allowable in the course of behaviour therapy. In return for his co-operation, the contract promises the patient change of a limited kind, and promises the psychologist freedom from the confusions which face a therapist when the patient insists on changing in a multiplicity of ways, including changing his notion of what is really wrong with him.

Few experimental studies of change in construct theory terms have yet appeared; but it seems likely that grid method – particularly if its associations with construct theory are explored rather than ignored – will repeatedly focus the attention of the investigating psychologist on the central importance of change, and offer him at least the possibility of predicting and monitoring its direction. The recent development of Implication and Resistance to Change Grids (Hinkle 1965) explicitly encourages both experimenter and subject to consider the implications of change within the subject's construct system.

THE ROLE OF THE EXPERIMENTER

The acceptance and use of grid methods and some of their associated theoretical considerations imply, and may induce, marked changes in the role of the experimenter in psychological investigations. In perspective, it may not be completely fanciful to suggest that the experimental use of construct theory methods and ideas may help the psychologist to a clearer conception of his own scientific role, and of some of its essential differences from that of the physical scientist whom he has copied for so long.

Construct theory insists on the importance of *personal* constructs and *personal* construct systems. Understanding of another person must take account of the particular dimensions which he has constructed, and of the structural arrangement of such dimensions which he uses to organize his life. If the experimenter is concerned to study some aspect of the content and structure of another person's view of the world, then he must, at least temporarily, recognize that the other person is the informed expert in the situation, and not constantly insist on the dominant role for himself. Furthermore, having taken the unusual step of eliciting the constructs, or at least the verbal labels which identify some of the constructs, the experimenter may find himself in the difficult and embarrassing position of having to make some sense out of the diverse data he has collected. He may have to convert the information he has collected from his various subjects to some common and personally meaningful base, or frame of reference. This is one of the problems which Osgood's use of standard scales manages to avoid. It is important to note, however, that the imposition of verbal uniformity merely avoids the real problem; it does not solve it. In trying to make sense of his subject's responses, the psychologist may well be faced with the necessity of examining his own personal or personal/professional construct dimensions in the grid and construct theory framework proposed for his subject.

Current grid methods, or elaborations of them, may offer the beginnings of an adequate structure, within which measurable translations between individual construct systems may be effected. This type of "translation" has been used tentatively by the second author, in both an experimental and a clinical context.

In an experimental situation (Mair, 1966), the dimensions used to make sense of, and discriminate between different types of paintings were elicited from a group of people; and an attempt was made to explore the degree to which these subjects could take in limited information about each other's preferences, and use it to make accurate predictions about the kind of pictures the others would like best. The relationships between their own system and their success as predictors could thereby be investigated. In this experimental procedure, each subject is enacting both the role of the predicted and the role of the predictor.

In a clinical investigation, a translation was attempted between the personal construct dimensions of a married couple seeking help for problems arising from marital disharmony. Again, the same elements were used by both as the basis for eliciting constructs, (i.e. people known well by, and important to them both). Here, it was important and possible to get an assessment of the similarity of each partner's view of his or herself and the other, in terms of both their own and the other's important construct dimensions.

Construct theory and its associated methods of measurement force the experimenter to take more than usual note of the point of view, and meaning system of his subject; and in doing this he is likely to be less prone arbitrarily to impose his own construction on the experimental events. He is likely to find himself in a position much more familiar to the clinician than to the experimentalist – the position of having to make sense of various aspects of his subject's construction system through a greater understanding of his own, and through a careful interpretation and translation of one to the other.

One of the psychologist's major concerns as a scientist is prediction; construct theory's central postulate is that *man* is essentially concerned with the anticipation of events; the construct theorist, as a psychologist, is likely to be concerned directly with exploring, perhaps by means of various grid techniques, the constructs used by his subject, and the *predictive* systems implied by the person's organization of these constructs. The experimenter will find himself using his own personal, or personal/professional predictive system to organize and predict aspects of the predictive system and predictive processes of his subject. His conclusions, from any such study, must not only account for some aspects of his subject's behaviour, as most experimenters at present try to do, but should also relate to and encompass the nature of his own predictions about the subject, and the processes whereby he made and elaborated these predictions. He will be using a single language within which to subsume his own and his subject's processes. This distinctive aspect of construct theory, namely, its reflexivity (cf. Oliver and Landfield, 1963 and Bannister, 1966) may not obviously be implied by the formal characteristics of grid method, but will almost certainly be involved if grid methods are used in relation to the parent theory. This would put the experimenter in a markedly novel role in relation to the things he does in his experiments. No longer could they be regarded as wholly external to himself – he would have to see himself as operating within the same type of predictive context as he assumes his subject does. Introspection might again enter, as an important and recognized aspect of even the most rigorous experimental study.

OBJECTIVE OR PROJECTIVE

When a person is confronted by a novel element, he will initially attempt to construe it in terms of dimensions previously applied to elements having a formal similarity (in terms of his ongoing construct system) to the new event confronting him. Since construct theory attempts to take psychologists and their doings, as well as people and their behaviour, within its range of convenience, this statement should be true of psychologists facing grid method for the first time. One of the traditional constructs used by psychologists to describe psychological tests is *objective-projective*; and an initial attempt may be made, by psychologists, to categorize grid methods as fitting one or other pole of this construct.

Kelly made a number of statements which underline the difficulty of construing grid method along this dimension.

He stresses some of the ambiguities of the distinction itself, when he points out (p. 207) "It is not so much the tests which are 'objective' or 'projective' as it is the way in which clinicians use them. It is possible to examine a client's performance on an 'intelligence' test not so much from the standpoint of its accuracy, as from the standpoint of the client's interpretation of the test. Yet intelligence tests are carefully designed as 'objective' tests and the construct of *intelligence* is definitely a clinician-imposed yardstick."

He anticipates some constructions which would underline similarities between grid and projective methods (p. 213): "the Rorschach Test and later the Thematic Apperception Test have done much to bring into the clinical setting a new and interdisciplinary appreciation of the measurability of personalized constructs. The notion of projective testing, which in a sense is not testing at all, is built basically upon the idea that the client's own constructs are to be *revealed* rather than his efficiency in using the examiner's constructs *tested*."

Again, he sees at least one sense in which grid method as an extension of construct theory could be objective, in that he points out, as quoted earlier, that "the psychology of personal constructs invites each psychologist to examine his client's performance as a projection of the client's outlook. This does not mean that the clinician cannot also be objective. Indeed, we see this approach to the client as being more *objective* than that of the old-fashioned psychometrician. It is more objective, not because it is more legalistic – a feature which is often confounded with objectivity – but because it is more object-oriented. It recognizes that it is the client who is the primary object of the psychologist's investigation and not the test. Thus, we would argue that the psychology of personal constructs *is more objective because it is more projective*." (p. 207)

If we argue that mechanical scoring systems, which give absolute interjudge agreement, are the essence of "objective" tests, then clearly the grid is objective, in that it is amenable to many such quantification procedures. If we argue that a focus on the subject's structuring of his environment in personal terms is the essence of "projective" tests, then clearly the grid is projective. If we argue that predetermined dimensions and a supporting substructure of normative data are essential to objective tests, then clearly the grid is not always "objective." If we argue that ambiguous stimuli and unrestricted speculative freedom for the experimenter are the hallmark of "projective" tests, then clearly the grid is not always "projective."

The answer may well be that this traditional dichotomizing of psychological methods of measurement cannot adequately subsume grid method, and its failure to subsume it may be an indication of limitations which must be overcome in our concept of what psychological measurement is or can be.

ASSESSMENTS OF GRID METHOD

Grid methods represent a break with orthodox traditions in psychological measurement. This implies that psychologists may find them initially difficult to construe, and may well arrive at distorted pictures, in an attempt to place them in conventional pigeonholes. An indication of one possible misconception has just been given, in the discussion of the objective-projective dichotomy. In order to test out this prediction, and as a brief essay in the psychology of psychologists, the assessment of grid method given by six authors of standard psychological textbooks is briefly considered.

Vernon (1964), following a brief description of the Role Construct Repertory Test, makes the following comments.

"Note that this procedure is wholly intra-individual. Its aim is to allow the subject to display his own constructs, not to force them onto dimensions provided by the tester, or by other people in general, nor to facilitate comparisons with the constructs of other Subjects. Kelly appears to use the results much like those of TAT as a source of therapeutic hypotheses and gives scarcely any indication of how the factors can be interpreted. Presumably they represent the ways in which the Subject groups qualities: e.g. if intelligent then trustworthy and likeable etc. – something which might be found out equally well by correlating his ratings of acquaintances on a standard list of traits.

Since a major object of the technique is to provide the clinician with a framework for viewing his client in terms of the client's own 'vocabulary' it offers little scope for predicting how the client will measure up against vocational or other external criteria. It could, presumably, be used purely idiographically – to guide the psychologist's understanding of the person; but its value would then depend wholly on the psychologist's skill. Kelly seems to claim that Rep test results are *more* communicable to other clinicians than are the findings of other diagnostic techniques. This may be true of the raw data: the test is easily administered either to an individual or a group and easily 'processed.' But there are even fewer rules for interpreting and communicating the implications of such data or relating them to the case-study and other material than with Rorschach or TAT. It is interesting that the only evidence of the values of the method, apart from clinical usefulness, that Kelly quotes is that Rep test results can be matched successfully with diagnoses based (a) on TAT or (b) on observing the Subjects in brief role-playing sessions.

A further limitation of the Rep test is that its constructs refer solely to people; and even if the people listed include most of the key figures in the individual's adjustment, it ignores many other important attitudes – likes and dislikes for different kinds of work, for leisure pursuits, for types of people rather than particular acquaintances, etc. Perhaps these could be covered by additional sortings; but all the objects included in any one sort have to be alike or unlike in some respect.

A strong point in favour both of the Semantic Differential and Rep Test which cannot be claimed for Q-sorting, is that they may reveal concepts of which the person is barely aware or which normally operate at the emotional rather than the verbally formulated level; i.e. they penetrate to our third level of Self. For example, he may be construing his wife in much the same way as his mother, and the test helps him to realize such connections. In this respect one might reasonably claim that the Rep test involves less subjective interpretation by the clinician than does TAT.

In many ways the Rep test resembles the Word Association or Sentence Completion tests. All three yield samples of the person's concepts and linkages which often give the clinician valuable leads. But though the responses can be classified or quantified in various ways, the resulting *scores* convey very little useful information to the diagnostician. Sentence Completion has indeed worked better than the other two, since it is comparatively easy to score for personality conflict or neuroticism vs. stability; whereas there is no evidence so far that the Rep test can be interpreted other than idiographically."

There would seem to be two important constructs in terms of which this commentary on grid method was written. Firstly, it was viewed as a test rather than a method. Kelly, in his original discussion of the mathematics of psychological space, repeatedly stressed the general assumptions and ideas from which grid instruments of various kinds could be derived, and repeatedly affirmed their flexibility. He then went on to illustrate and use these assumptions by giving details of the first form of grid, the Role Construct Repertory Test. It is significant that Vernon selects the Role Construct Repertory Test as *the* test, and confines his discussion to a consideration of this one particular form. This may well be because, in psychology, we are so used to the idea of tests, and have so poorly elaborated our notion of methods and approaches, that automatically we view any new venture as merely one more addition to the endless catalogue of unitary psychological tests. Having thus concretized grid method by viewing one form as *the* test, Vernon then calls into play one of the great traditional dichotomies of psychological thinking – *idiographic versus nomothetic* – using the term idiographic, presumably, in the sense of characterizing an account of particular or individual cases or events and contrasting it with the term nomothetic, as characterizing procedures and methods designed to discover general laws. The combination of the view of the grid as a single test, and the view that idiographic-versus-nomethetic is a universally valid way of categorizing tests, results in statements such as that grid procedure "is wholly intra-individual," or "there is no evidence so far that the Rep Test can be interpreted other than idiographically." This assertion is made in spite of the fact that, almost immediately following the publication of construct theory and details of the Role Construct Repertory Test, this specific form of grid was used to set up the clearly nomothetic dimensions of cognitive complexity-simplicity (Bieri and Blacker, 1956). Later (Bannister, 1960) a standard form of grid was devised, complete with normative groups, validating criteria and standard scoring methods. Quite apart from the actual and frequent use of grid forms within a nomothetic universe of discourse, even a cursory examination of grid method and format reveals that it can be used to generate group or individual data, depending upon the inclination of the psychologist. Attempts to categorize it as one or the other suggest that the nomothetic-idiographic construct itself is too rigidly and superordinately embedded within the construct system of the psychologist.

In construct theory terms, problems conventionally discussed by construing along the nomothetic-idiographic dimension are dealt with in terms of the permeability or impermeability of constructs, and the level of abstraction in terms of which a problem is specified. Thus, however standard the tests a psychologist uses, however vast and generalized the dimensions underlying his tests and however large the normative populations with which he is going to compare his subjects, he will make some "idiographic" decisions. He will initially decide that his generalized test is relevant to the problems of his individual subject, and, given the test results, he will try to make predictions about behaviours which will evolve in the individual context within which his subject lives. It is clear that, for communication purposes alone, the psychologist had best talk a language which has a wider reference than one person; but it is also clear that he will never meet a perfectly representative person manufactured to fit the dimensions of his tests. There seems little point, then, in using nomothetic *versus* idiographic as a way of distinguishing between tests, or as a way of distinguishing between "scientist" and "non-scientist" approaches. The psychologist (whether he is concerned with groups or individuals) might more profitably specify whether he is using subordinate or superordinate constructions, acknowledging the prime importance of the *linkages* between the two. The danger to beware is a failure to articulate such linkages – a failure which is all the more likely to occur if the psychologist takes up permanent intellectual residence in the "nomothetic" or the "idiographic" camp. A psychologist who cannot go beyond the concrete details of his subject's life is neither more nor less useless than a psychologist who cannot apply his major scientific dimensions to a given individual's life situation.

The other interesting aspect of this commentary is the way in which the view taken of the grid method leads the author to speculate on certain possibilities, without apparently being aware that he has been explicitly invited to explore them. Thus, he notes as a limitation of the Rep test, that its constructs refer solely to people, then instances other areas which could be explored by grid methods (e.g. leisure pursuits, different kinds of work, and so on) and concludes "perhaps these could be covered by additional sortings; but all the objects included in any one sort have to be alike or unlike in some respect." The range of convenience rule, which is here referred to, in no way prevents the psychologist from constructing new grids other than those in which people are the elements, just as Kelly's reluctance to prescribe specific dimensions for the grid (in the manner which the author applauds in the Sentence Completion Test) in no way prevents the psychologist from undertaking such a venture.

Three other writers of standard textbooks briefly summarize the Role Construct Repertory Test (again they seem to assume that this is *the* test, rather than an exemplification of a method), but do not attempt to subsume it under general dimensions. They concretistically compare it with what they seem to assume is its closest relative in the test field, the Semantic Differential. Thus, Anastasi (1961) says, of the Rep test, "this test has common features with a number of other personality tests, notably the Semantic Differential and the various sorting tests used to study concept formation. In the Rep Test, however, the objects to be sorted are persons who are important in the subject's life. And unlike the Semantic Differential, the Rep Test requires the subject himself to designate the scales, dimensions or constructs in terms of which he characterizes these persons." Cronbach (1961) similarly comments "the Role Concept Repertory (Rep) Test of G. A. Kelly (1955) is much like Osgood's procedure save that the subject himself now picks the scales on which he will respond." Semeonoff (1966) (illustrating the genetics of textbooks) echoes previous writers in saying "the main differences from the Semantic Differential are that the technique allows the subject to define his own scales and that the ratings are applied to persons."

The question of the relationship between grid method and the Semantic Differential approach has been discussed earlier, but it is interesting to note that these authors assert a general similarity between the two techniques, specifying as the major differences only that the elements used are people known personally to the subject, and that the subject selects his own dimensions along which to construe. None comment on what would seem to be an obvious and primary difference – namely, that the Semantic Differential defines the conceptual structure of the subject in terms of three prescribed nomothetic dimensions derived from pooled data, while the grid allows for a cluster analysis of each subject's individual responses, and thereby generates a mathematical picture of the unique psychological space of the subject, rather than defining it in terms of an approximation to some generalized, cultural, psychological space.

The varying degree to which psychologists commenting on grid method are constrained by the concept of the standard-form test is illustrated in the contrasting summaries of Costello (1966) and Oppenheim (1966). Costello, like the authors previously quoted, implies that the grid has one kind of material (people), and omits reference to its various forms and functions. In contrast, Oppenheim stresses that the repertory grid "is not a single test but a highly flexible technique which can be evolved afresh for each new investigation." However, the tendency of psychologists to assume that flexibility must imply subjectivity in scoring, is evident in Oppenheim's misleading suggestion that scoring is by "inspection," rather than by count.

Just as the psychotherapist might pray that his patient will begin to explore the possibilities of his life situation, instead of rigidly categorizing them, it is to be hoped that psychologists will, at least initially, view grid method in terms of the philosophy and the theory from which it derives, by regarding it as an open-ended approach. It is not formal, though it can be given many forms: it is not mechanical, though it can have many mechanisms built into it. It is not arbitrary or whimsical, in that its assumptions are explicit; but it may help to make our psychological exploration of man both more systematic and more adventurous. While attempting to define what grid method is, we should not thereby seek to limit what grid method might yet be.

CHAPTER 7

Reliability

SUCH HAS been the influence of trait theory in personality psychology that the concept of "reliability" has long since acquired value connotations. As in cognitive tests, high reliability in personality measures is considered one of the most important indices of a "good" test.

Grid methods and the theory underlying them stand in sharp contrast to this tradition. Since this is a procedure relating to a theory which affirms that "man is a form of motion," it is necessary to challenge the orthodox notion of high reliability as an invariably desirable characteristic of tests. In this context, Kelly once defined reliability as "that characteristic of a test which makes it insensitive to change." This shift of emphasis does not mean that we have to become the happy victims of so-called error variance. We can perhaps substitute, for simple general reliability, the idea (Mair 1964a and 1964b) that within the broader context of assessing the validity of grid scores, we are essentially concerned with *predictable* stability and *predictable* change.

A similar idea is evident in McQuitty's (1957) argument that "a more fundamental test of constructs is their value for prediction. The truth of this statement is realized by recalling that if two tests are of equal validity but of unequal reliability (stability) the less reliable one offers the greater hope for increased validity; this is especially true if the more reliable test is near its saturation point with respect to stability and the less reliable one is considerably below a corresponding degree of stability."

Another aspect of grid method is relevant to this concern with the *predictable* stability rather than the *general* stability of scores. As stated previously, the grid is not a test, but a variable technique: it can be cast into many different forms, involving any number of different types of constructs and elements, and many kinds of scores can be derived. Since there is no such thing as *the* grid, there can be no such thing as *the* reliability of *the* grid.

Any consideration of a specific reliability coefficient, quoted for a particular instance of the application of grid method, must take into account, firstly, the particular measure extracted from data supplied by the grid, secondly, the type of experimental situation within which repeat grid data were obtained and, thirdly, the general parameters which affect reliability coefficients in any grid context. What follows is an attempt to describe the possibilities and variations under each of these three headings, to outline the kind of expectations about them which are derived from construct theory and to indicate the type of empirical data which is available in relation to each aspect.

This treatment of the problem is not exhaustive, but data relating to a range of grid scores will be considered. However, no work on any aspects of reliability in relation to Implication or Resistance to Change Grids is yet available. A further review discussion is available in Bonarius (1965).

RELIABILITY OF DIFFERENT MEASURES

CONSISTENCY OF ELICITED CONSTRUCTS

Some early Repertory test studies in the United States focused on the problem of whether the constructs elicited by the triad method were *representative*, in the sense of being central and enduring features of the subject's construing, and thereby likely to appear again when he considers new sets of elements. In the earliest reported consistency study of the Repertory test (Hunt, 1951), groups of normal subjects and psychiatric patients supplied elements (people known personally to them) to fit a list of 41 role titles. In the first testing session each subject was faced with 40 triads, made up of combinations of 20 of his elements, and he was asked to supply a construct in response to the question "tell me some important way in which two of these are alike and thereby different from the third?" One week later, each subject repeated this task with the other 20 elements. Equivalence between constructs given in the first and second sessions was decided by asking the patient if he saw a similarity between the two constructs, if he could apply the two constructs to the same figures and, finally, if he thought that a person who was described in terms of the emergent pole of one construct would almost always be described in terms of the emergent pole of a second construct, and *vice versa*. In terms of this measure of equivalence, subjects reproduced (on average and with very little variability) about 70% of their constructs. Again, in terms of the same measure of equivalence, it was found that very few new constructs were produced after between 20 and 30 triadic sorts, and virtually no novel constructs were generated after 40 sorts. It must be noted that in this kind of study the elements were being used only to generate constructs; they were not being sorted in order that their allotment might quantify the relationships *between* constructs. The experimenter was asking the question: if we elicit constructs at two sessions a week apart, will there be any kind of detectable similarity between the two samples of constructs elicited?

Fjeld and Landfield (1961), using 80 normal subjects, applied a more elaborate version of Hunt's criteria for equivalence between constructs, under varying conditions of Rep test administration. They concluded that (i) given the same elements, the subjects, after a two-week interval, produce very similar constructs (Pearson r = 0·79); (ii) when allowed to take the test entirely afresh and considering new elements, subjects equally reproduce their earlier constructs (Pearson r = 0·80).

This type of experiment illustrates the interlocking of the usual concepts of validity and reliability when applied to grid methods, in that they can be looked on as experimental explications of the dichotomy corollary, which states that "a person's construction system is composed of a finite number of dichotomous constructs." These studies suggest that the grid tests are "reliable," in the sense that where constructs about people are concerned (and, one would tend to assume, where other types of construct are concerned), normal sampling procedures apply. Grids are delving into a limited repertoire of constructs which the subject has available, and there is no fear of being confronted with the everlasting pages of an infinite personal dictionary.

ELEMENT CONSISTENCY

Again, in terms of *elements*, experimenters have asked whether an elicited sample can be considered representative, in the sense that most of it will recur on re-test.

Pedersen (1958) required his subjects to supply figures to fit role titles, and found an average of 77% agreement between these figures and figures supplied by his subjects to fit the same list of role titles a week later. That this was not purely a reflection of the restricting effect of role titles is indicated by the previously quoted study of Fjeld and Landfield (1961) which showed that, when subjects were given a blank form of the original test, they provided, on average, 72% of the figures they had given for the original role title list.

In turn, the degree of representativeness of the elements may affect construct reliability. Mitsos (1958) showed that, over a three-month period, 9 out of 10 subjects repeated a significant number of their constructs when using the role title list, originally recommended by Kelly, to select their elements. Only 2 out of 9 equivalent subjects gave a significant number of construct repeats, when their elements were simply a sample of "nineteen friends" without further specification (group difference p < 0·02). The current practice of abandoning role title restrictions may, in itself, have lowered reliability findings.

Granted that subjects have a fairly stable number of significant others, whom they are prepared to provide for grid purposes, the question can be raised of whether or not particular elements are allotted to the same poles of each construct, or to the same position in rank orders on constructs, from one testing session to another.

That this question has not been experimentally asked reflects the central difference between ordinary rating scales and yes/no questionnaires, on the one hand, and grids, on the other. Grids are primarily measures of *internal proportions*, and they focus attention on relationships between constructs. Changes in element allocation do not necessarily produce any change in the manifest relationships between constructs. Thus, if a subject completed two grids with the same elements and constructs, on two different occasions, he could, on the second occasion, (assuming some massive change of mind as to who were friends and who were foes), completely reverse the polar position of all his elements on all his constructs. Yet this would leave the construct relationships, as expressed by matching scores, completely unchanged. It is true that questionnaires can share this property, to the extent that, given a questionnaire which yields a score on one dimension (e.g. *anxious—not anxious*) the subject could change a number of his actual responses without changing his score, provided that the changes cancelled each other out. In this sense, a one-dimensional questionnaire is rather like a single line from a grid, in which the questions are elements and the subject is allotting them to the poles of a construct, whose nature and label is known to the experimenter but kept secret from the subject.

Grids, by their nature, tend to relegate element allotment to a content status, to focus attention on the structure of the network of constructs (assumed to underlie the subject's view of the elements of his world) and to accord primacy to the investigation of this view. Nevertheless, it can be surmised that for particular purposes it might be useful to know how stable was the element allotment for a given subject or subjects. For example, in trying to evaluate, for clinical purposes, a particular re-allotment of a significant person by a patient, it would be possible to take into account the general element stability, or lack of it, which the patient normally showed in his interpersonal evaluations. Such measurement of element stability involves no more technical difficulties in grids than it does in any conventional rating scale analysis.

MATRIX PATTERN MEASUREMENTS

The data provided by a grid are in the form of a matrix (of correlations or matching scores), which is assumed to represent the pattern of relationships between the constructs used in the grid, and to be an index of the network of implications between the obtained sample of constructs for the individual subject. This matrix of relationships (or any specified part of it) can itself be the object of "reliability" assessment. Thus, for any given subject, a test-retest coefficient can be calculated, by rank ordering each of the matrices, which his grid performance has yielded on two separate occasions, from the highest positive relationship through zero to the highest negative relationship, and then calculating the Spearman rho between these two rank orders. Such a rho is, in one sense, an index of factorial similarity between the two matrices, and represents an estimate of the degree to which the pattern of the construct inter-relationships of the subject has remained stable across the time interval. Again, in terms of such a derived measure, no general estimate of reliability can be given, because, as will be shown, it will be grossly influenced by factors such as the elements and constructs used, individual and group differences, methods of administration, and so forth. However, as a kind of statistical platitude, it can be said that using elements such as people known personally to the subject, with supplied constructs of a conventional type and with either a rank order or split-half matching administration, normal subjects, doing repeat grids, on either the same or different elements, tend to yield co-efficients of reliability which fall largely within the range 0·6 to 0·8.

CLUSTER ANALYSIS SCORES

The question of assessing reliability becomes even more complicated when the basic raw matrix of construct relationships is subjected to some form of cluster analysis (e.g. principal component analysis, factor analysis, anchor analysis). Factor pictures are always difficult to compare, since no agreed rationale is available which would reveal the relative amounts of "sameness" and "difference" between, say, two factors, where one was loaded on five constructs, and the other, on the same five plus two additional, as compared with one loaded on five constructs, and the other loaded on four plus one which was different – to say nothing of the question of the order in which factors are generated, (e.g. the third factor yielded by matrix I, looks suspiciously like the fourth factor of matrix II, except that it has an air of some kind of curious combination of factors five and six). The Gordian knot can be cut in a variety of ways; but the attempt to assess the reliability of clusters from a series of grids will remain relatively arbitrary until the psychological meaning of the clusters yielded by a single grid can be better assessed.

TOTAL STRUCTURE SCORES

In investigations specifically concerned with schizophrenic thought disorder (Bannister, 1960, 1962 and Bannister and Fransella, 1966), much use was made of a score labelled "Intensity." This represented an attempt to assess the total amount of structure manifest within the matrix of construct relationships of a single subject, by calculating the arithmetic total of all the relationships. This kind of measure was meant to reflect the gross difference between a grid which manifested a massive interrelationship of constructs around one central dimension, and a grid where each construct seemed to be a law unto itself – the kind of grid which one would imagine would be yielded by some random coin-tossing or ballot-drawing procedure.

The reliability of this type of global measure of structure is likely to be low since it is a patently compound measure. For example, a middle-range Intensity score could reflect a matrix with one large cluster plus a number of residual independent constructs, or two moderate clusters, or one cluster of middle-value correlations. For the 30 normals in Bannister (1962), the reliability (immediate retest, same constructs, new elements, split-half scoring) of the Intensity score was 0·352, which, though significant, (p < 0·05) is low. It is worth noting that, for 23 out of the 30 subjects, the Intensity score increased from first to second grid (a common finding), which suggests a process operating during testing which tightens construing. The nature of the process is obscure; but it is unlikely to operate equally for each individual, and thus reliability is inevitably reduced. For the quoted experiment, Intensity was an acceptable measure, since the question at issue was the simple one of whether structure, broadly speaking, was present or absent; but the importation of such measures into investigations raising more subtle issues would be a dubious strategy.

CONSISTENCY OF CONSISTENCY MEASURES

Because grids can readily provide a reliability coefficient for a single individual, the consistency of grid performance in the single subject has already become an individual difference measure in its own right (Bannister, 1960 and 1962 and Bannister and Fransella, 1966, 1967). The implications of such a measure will be discussed in more detail in other contexts, particularly in relation to varying validational feedback experiments; but there is so far no specific evidence as to what consistency might be expected between reliability coefficients themselves, when tests are repeated over time on either the same or equivalent forms of the grid. On a speculative basis, it might be that such serial test-retest coefficients could operationalize some aspects of Kelly's particular way of defining "emotion." There is no concept of drive or emotion or affect in construct theory, equivalent to the type of concept which exists in what Kelly calls hydraulic theories – theories which postulate some specific energizing system contrasted with "cognition." Construct theory does not involve separate notions of drive and direction. However, Kelly does use some of the terms originally used to denote "emotions" (guilt, hostility, anxiety, threat and aggression) to refer to construct systems which are in a state of transition, or, more specifically, to refer to the awareness on the part of the individual that his construct system is undergoing, or is on the verge of change. There might be a marked lowering of serial retest coefficients in individuals who are overtly undergoing a constructional change process e.g. patients in psychotherapy or people in stress situations.

MEASURE OF LOPSIDEDNESS

In Kelly's form of the grid, subjects were allowed to allot their elements to either pole of each construct freely, so that the obvious was made operationally manifest – people do not invariably divide their environmental elements half-and-half. They often "see" many more *kind* people than *cruel* ones, or many more *philistines* than *aesthetes*. Kelly gave this phenomenon the term lopsidedness; the first author later substituted for this the rather more pompous title of "mal-distribution." Unfortunately, the fact that people's construing habits, in this respect, represent an awkward statistical problem for the computation of relationship scores (cf. Bannister, 1959) led to a tendency to force the subject to split his elements equally, and this in turn may have distracted attention from an aspect of construing which is fascinating in its own right. It can be argued that a construct is (like a chi-square) maximally useful the nearer it approximates to dividing up the world half-and-half, and presumably becomes totally useless when all elements occupy one pole. The construct then discriminates nothing from anything else. If all men are *bad*, then there is little point in thinking of men as *good* or *bad*, since no differential predictions are generated to test and no differential implications are available to explore.

Any talk of lopsidedness as a measure implies that the relative allotment of elements to the two poles of a construct for any given individual is more or less stable, in the sense that we would expect the proportions in each pole to be roughly the same when an individual uses the same construct on two random samples of elements. There is some evidence that the measure is relatively "reliable" in this sense. Bannister (1959), reported a study in which each of a small group of normals provided the names of 38 people known personally. These were randomly sorted into two groups of 19, and, for each group of 19 elements, the subject was asked to allot them freely to one pole or the other of 22 constructs which had been elicited from him. For each subject, for each of the 22 constructs, a count was taken of how many had been allotted to the emergent pole of the construct for both the first and second sets of 19 elements; and the two sets of figures were then correlated. This measure was termed "consistency of reference," and was designed to find out how well the subject maintained the proportions of elements allotted to each pole of a construct, on two samples of people known personally to him, on his own elicited constructs. The mean correlation for a group of five normal subjects was 0·70. In a later experiment (Bannister, 1962), a further attempt was made to examine the consistency of distribution of elements between poles, this time across two forms of the test – one, in which the elements were people known personally to the subject and the second, in which the elements were photographs of people unknown to the subject; these were judged in terms of the same constructs, as for a "personality from faces" test. Thirty normal subjects were supplied with only three construct labels (*fair-minded*, *hard-working* and *timid*), and asked, for each construct, to say whether each of 40 people, known personally, belonged in the stated pole of the construct or not. The subjects made similar allotments for 40 photographs of people unknown to them. The measure of mal-distribution, in this case, was the discrepancy between the subjects' allocation of elements to the two poles and a 20 : 20 split. Whereas many structural measures had poor reliability, as from people-sorting to photo-sorting, this measure (although only three constructs were used) had a reliability of 0·76.

The tentative indications of these two studies that mal-distribution, as a measure, is reasonably reliable, raise the question of the conditions in which it might become "unreliable." What are the general psychological implications of shifts in the proportions of the environment which an individual sees as being subsumed under the two poles of his various constructs? When a man, who has previously seen his fellows as being either *good* or *bad*, says that he now realizes that all men are "really" *good*, what does he mean? Is he creating a new superordinate construct of *good*, for which he has not yet found a contrast pole? Is he, for practical purposes, dismissing the construct and rendering it useless within his system? Is he notifying us of some major transition in his system? So much of construct theory hinges on the notion of the bipolarity of constructs, that the reliability or unreliability, in different individuals, or under different conditions, or between different constructs, of the distribution of elements between the poles must be a matter of major interest.

INSIGHT MEASURES

Many grid measures are oblique. What is measured is not what the subject imagines is being measured. The majority of subjects focus on the allotment of elements, and seem unaware that it is the relationship between judgmental categories which is the usual focus of the experiment. This being so, it is possible to compare the relationships between constructs as quantified in a grid by a particular subject, and the relationships between his constructs which the same subject declares to exist in reply to direct questioning. We need not regard the relationship between the two as a measure of the grid's "validity". If the subject could draw an exact diagram of how he related his constructs, there would be little point in putting him to the trouble of completing a grid.

While not using a concept of "the unconscious," construct theory argues that many aspects of our construct systems are unverbalized. One of the purposes of psychotherapy is to enable a person to articulate his construct system to a greater degree, and thereby subject it to more crucial and clear-cut tests, so that its validity, as a monitoring device for life experiences, can be assessed, by both patient and psychotherapist. The discrepancy between the person's report (on face inspection) of his construct relationships and the statistical relationships which manifest themselves when he uses his constructs in a grid format, could be looked on as some sort of index of how well acquainted he is with the network of implications which constitute his construct system.

In two studies (Bannister, 1960 and 1962), the discrepancy was used in this way, and, as a measure, was given the label "Insight." The meaning attached to the term Insight here was wider than the meaning it is sometimes given in psychiatric parlance, where it indicates the degree to which the patient is prepared to agree with the psychiatrist that he is "ill". In both studies, normal subjects and psychiatric patients completed grids on a series of supplied constructs, and were then asked, for each construct, to indicate which of the other constructs they thought was nearest to being "the same," and which was "the most opposite." The actual deviation scores between the constructs selected by the subject as being "same" and "opposite," in relation to each construct in turn, were noted and added (unless the signs were in the opposite direction, i.e. the subject claimed, as "opposite," two constructs which actually had a positive relationship). Each total was transformed to a proportion of the total of matching scores for each subject. In the 1962 experiment, where Insight scores were calculated in this proportional manner, they were largely successful in discriminating normals (high scores) from most psychiatric groups: but little information is available about the reliability of this type of score. For the 30 normals used in the second experiment, the correlation between Insight, as measured on people-sorting, and Insight as measured on photograph-sorting (equivalent form), was 0·53.

Again, if man is considered a process, the interest lies not in making any definitive statement about the reliability of the measure of Insight as such, but in discovering what is implied about individuals whose Insight scores rise or fall over time, as compared with those whose Insight scores remain stable. Equally, with reference to subsystem differences, which are discussed later, interest might focus on the characteristics of subjects who showed a high degree of Insight when explaining their construct network in relation to one kind of element, but much less Insight in relation to some other subsystem.

SOCIAL AGREEMENT MEASURES

The relationships between constructs, as quantified in the grid, can be compared with the subject's verbal declaration of the relationships which he imagines apply. Similarly, the relationships between constructs, as quantified in the grid of a particular subject, can be compared with the grid relationships for the same constructs (or more accurately, for the same verbal labels) of a normative group assumed to reflect, however crudely, normative social usage.

The commonality and sociality corollaries of construct theory seek to re-define concepts such as "groups" and "similarity" between people. They specify a way of conceptualizing interpersonal relationships and the kind of problem covered in other psychological languages by the term "communica-tion". Given that a construct system is a complex process, any sampling in grid terms is likely to distort our estimates of possible degrees of similarity or difference between people. Nevertheless, even in its present embryonic state, the grid offers at least one useful operational definition. In Bannister (1960 and 1962), supplied construct grids were given to groups of normal subjects, and a mean relationship for each pair of constructs derived; the resulting matrix was assumed to be a kind of crude normative dictionary of the relationships between the constructs under examination. The average relationships matrix from Bannister (1962) is shown in Fig. 9.

Each individual's matrix of correlations was compared, cell by cell, with this normative matrix, and the discrepancy termed a measure of "social deviation" – high discrepancies indicating that (at least as sampled) the

Fig. 9. Normative Matrix

	Mean	Good	Unusual	Narrow Minded	Sincere	Selfish	Unreli-able	Kind
Likeable	−10	+9	−2	−7	+8	−7	−5	+8
Mean		−9	+3	+8	−8	+10	+4	−8
Good			−4	−6	+10	−8	−6	+8
Unusual				+2	−3	+3	+2	−3
Narrow Minded					−7	+7	+4	−7
Sincere						−9	−7	+9
Selfish							+5	−9
Unreliable								−7

The average relationships (Bannister, 1962) between nine constructs for 30 normals shown in this figure are in terms of deviation scores which, for the grid used (40 elements) could range from +20 to −20. Since the constructs were supplied to the subjects and the elements were photographs, the individual matrices could only crudely represent a sample of each subject's construct system. Averaged to compound individual differences they represent a very simplified normative "dictionary" indeed. It is interesting to note, however, that the observed relationships between the constructs represent what "common sense" would predict. The exception, for some, might be in the rather unfavourable "definition" given to the construct *unusual*. The general effect of sampling individual systems and then compound-ing them into an averaged mass is inevitably to highlight a *good–bad* dimension, as in this example.

subject's construct system was highly idiosyncratic, low discrepancies indicating that it approached the norm. A later, reversed title for this measure was "social agreement." Although, in terms of predicting normal versus psychiatric group differences, the measure appeared valid (if we accept that one would expect less commonality in a psychiatric population), little is known about the reliability of this kind of measure.

In the second experiment, the normative matrix, calculated from grids in which the elements were people, was compared with the matrix of average correlations derived from photograph-sorting grids. The correlation between the two was 0·981. This very high equivalent-form correlation suggests that estimates of mean *population* patterning in construct relationships may have a high degree of reliability, though estimates of individual construct relationship patterns may have far less.

EXPERIMENTAL CONTEXTS FOR THE ESTIMATION OF RELIABILITY

In order to show the difficulties of talking about reliability of grid technique, a summary has been given of the kinds of measures which have been derived from grid data. The summary was neither exhaustive of possible measures, nor complete for variants of quoted measures. For any given measure, the experimental context within which its reliability can be assessed may vary in at least three major ways.

Firstly, reliability can be calculated simply over time. The main value of test-retest coefficients, with varying time intervals, would seem to lie in their use as a baseline, against which to calculate the effects of intervening experimental manipulations, which reduce or raise the size of reliability coefficients.

Secondly, reliability can be calculated across equivalent forms. Equivalent form construction is a relatively easy undertaking with grids. The same sets of constructs can be repeatedly applied to new sets of elements; it is also reasonable to regard different sets of constructs as equivalent, in the sense that they are a "fair sample" of a system. Repeat measures of structural, though not content, stability can thus be made.

Thirdly, the stability of various aspects of construing can be estimated, when the validational fortunes of predictions based on the constructs under study are experimentally varied. Construct theory argues that construct systems are subject to continuous change, though such change is not random. The experience corollary states that "a person's construction system varies as he successively construes the replications of events". Since any construction is intrinsically a prediction, the construing person can experience three basic kinds of outcome. His construction can be validated, in that he experiences the events as meaningfully subsumed by his construction, and the outcome is seen as being in line with his polar allotment. He can be invalidated, in that, while the elements can meaningfully be viewed in terms of his construing, their subsequent behaviour implies (to the person) that they would be more appropriately construed in terms of the *opposite* poles of the constructs used. The unfolding situation turns out to be (in the person's view) outside the range of convenience of the constructs used. In Kelly's terms, "the constructions one places upon events are working hypotheses which are about to be put to the test of experience. As one's anticipations or hypotheses are successively revised in the light of the unfolding sequence of events, a construction system undergoes a progressive evolution." (p. 72)

The notion of "validation" is quite different from the idea of "reinforcement," as the latter term is commonly used. Reinforcement carries the implication of meeting the person's needs, of satisfying him in some way, of gratification. Validation does not involve a concept of specific need or drive, but refers solely to the verification of a prediction, even though what was predicted was something "unpleasant."

What then may happen when a person's predictions in a particular area have gone wrong – when he interprets the outcome as invalidation? Kelly suggests a number of possibilities. The person may change only his specific prediction, e.g. allot the element to the contrast pole of the same construct; he may turn to another construct in his system, and base his next prediction on that instead; he may revise the dimensional structure of his constructs, or tighten or loosen related aspects of his system. Any of these changes could be reflected in changes in reliability coefficients, as calculated on measures which reflect relevant aspects of the system.

Poch (1952) and Newman (1956) both dealt with the first type of change (the re-allotment of elements from one pole to the other of a construct), and studied its relationship to varying validational fortunes. Since they predicted change, they did not set out directly to assess the "reliability" of the measures which they hoped would reflect change. Nevertheless, if a reliability estimate had been made, they would have found lowered score stability, in that they repeated their measures following specific experimental manipulation (in this case invalidation).

Does repeated validation result in a tightening of construct relationships in the area involved? Does repeated invalidation lead to a general loosening of construct relationships? Bannister (1963 and 1965) reported four experiments which indicated that the answer to both questions is yes. A re-calculation of these data provides some information more directly relevant to the problem of reliability, by showing the effect of repeated validation or invalidation on the stability of overall construct pattern interrelationships. Two particular weaknesses in the experimental design should be noted. Firstly, no attempt was made to elicit the subjects' views of the total experimental situation, and the extent to which they credited the experimentally supplied validation and invalidation is not known. Secondly, the varying validational evidence supplied was of a somewhat indirect type. Subjects were asked to make character judgments about photographs of people unknown to them; they were then told that they were doing well, or doing badly, or nothing was said. Thus, they did not explicitly formulate any *specific* expectations, in terms of the constructs (personality traits) they were asked to use. Validation and invalidation, in these studies, were reflected in a rather global procedure of being made generally right, or being made generally wrong. In one of the four experiments, 18 normal subjects were tested, on 20 separate occasions, over a period of 10 days. On each occasion, they were faced with 10 photographs of people unknown to them, and asked to rank order these on six constructs (*mean, good, sincere, selfish, intelligent*, and *kind*). For each subject, on each occasion, a matrix of 15 Spearman rhos (between all possible pairs of constructs) was derived. It must be stressed that, on each occasion, the subjects were faced with a *new* set of 10 photographs, and that what is being examined in the reliability analysis is, in effect, equivalent form reliability over time, with the test having 20 equivalent forms. The 18 subjects were equally divided. One group (the invalidated group) was told, after each testing, that they had been performing very badly, and were mistaking the photographs, as witnessed by detailed biographies which the experimenter claimed to possess, and which were illustrated from time to time. A second group (the validated group) were always told that they were doing very well. The third group (no information group) were told that results could not be scored until the whole series was complete; these subjects, therefore, worked without experimentally supplied validation or invalidation. The key term here is *experimentally* supplied validation or invalidation, since the "no information" subjects could have been reacting to their own estimate of task difficulty, or to other aspects of the situation, in such a way as to provide, for themselves, validation or invalidation.

For each individual, the 15 Spearman rhos, representing the relationships between constructs for a single occasion of testing, were rank ordered from highest positive, through zero, to highest negative. These rankings, for each occasion, were serially compared for each individual subject, so as to provide a construct pattern reliability estimate from each trial to the succeeding one. Thus, for each subject, 19 reliability coefficients were available, showing each successive tendency to stabilize or change a given pattern of construct relationships. The 19 coefficients for each individual were averaged (by z transformation), and are shown individually in Table I, along with the grand mean for each group.

The amount of individual variation (individual variance in general will be discussed later) can readily be seen, and many individual comparisons would certainly be statistically significant. However, of major interest here is the group variation in "reliability" – groups being defined in terms of varying validational experience. A comparison of the coefficients of 0·560 and 0·585, for the validational and no information groups respectively, with the coefficient of 0·740, for the validation group, shows that the latter differs significantly

TABLE I

Mean reliabilities of pattern of construct relationships for 18 subjects over 20 trials (from Bannister, 1965)

	Validated group	Invalidated group	No informa-tion group
	0·180	0·180	0·040
	0·664	0·220	0·270
	0·800	0·380	0·580
	0·800	0·730	0·730
	0·835	0·745	0·780
	0·865	0·805	0·780
Grand Mean	0·740	0·560	0·585

from the former ($p < 0.001$). It must be remembered that what is being measured as changing is not the specific judgments of the subjects (which cannot be compared because they never ranked the same set of photographs twice), but the relationships between their judgmental categories.

Within the limits of this series of experiments, it can be argued that varying validational fortunes will affect "reliability," and, more specifically, that validation seems likely to lead to a stabilizing construct pattern, and thereby higher matrix pattern reliability. This type of experiment illustrates what is meant by saying that the focus should be on predictable stability, as contrasted with predictable change, rather than on "test reliability," as traditionally conceived.

GENERAL FACTORS AFFECTING RELIABILITY

Bearing in mind the multiplicity of measures which can be derived from grids, and the varying experimental conditions under which the consistency of grid measures can be assessed, consideration can be given to the broad parameters within which the reliability of grid measures may change. For no set of parameters or professional situations can a cookbook of reliabilities be compiled – even assuming that such a document were desired – but experimental evidence exists which indicates some of the factors affecting grid measure reliability.

SUBSYSTEM VARIANCE

The range corollary states that "a construct is convenient for the anticipation of a finite range of events only." Construct theory extends this to argue that not only does any given construct have a limited range of convenience (a limited number of elements among which it can discriminate), but also construct systems as a whole can be seen as composed of a number of subsystems, each with different ranges of convenience. Thus, structural differences between subsystems seem inevitable, and consequently, reliability differences seem likely to exist between grids (or other types of measure) designed to investigate different subsystems.

Consider constructs which deal with people and interpersonal relationships, as contrasted with constructs which deal with physical objects. Separate grids were constructed[1] to measure stability within the two construct subsystems. Ten subjects were asked to rank order 10 photographs of people on the constructs, *sincere, kind, friendly, mean, selfish* and *energetic*. They were asked to repeat the task immediately, on a different set of 10 photographs; and six weeks later, they used the same constructs on the original set of photographs. Each grid was analyzed to provide a matrix of construct relationships, and the consistency of this matrix was calculated over time, across elements and across elements and time; correlations were averaged for the group. Such measures are approximate indices of the degree of factorial similarity between grid matrices. The mean reliability of matrix pattern across elements was 0·72, across time it was 0·86 and across elements and time it was 0·73.

The same group of subjects were given a similar series of tests, in which the elements they were asked to sort were two sets of 15 names of common physical objects (anchor, toy balloon, cricket bat, building brick, carrot, etc.) and they rank ordered these in terms of the constructs *large-small, smooth-rough, heavy-light, fragile-tough, curved-straight, long-short*. The mean stability of matrix pattern for this task was: across elements 0·92, across time (again six weeks) 0·93 and across elements and time 0·93. In terms of this experiment, it can be tentatively argued that people (as assessed in terms of the stability of their conceptual structure in two subsystems) are more confident as physicists than they are as psychologists – they have more stable systems through which to view objects than those through which to view people.

The reason for comparing a 10-element "people-construing" grid with a 15-element "object-construing" grid was that, in an experiment to be discussed later, it was found that increasing the number of elements in people-element rank order grids appeared to reduce the reliability coefficient sharply.

---

[1] This, and other studies described, for which no specific references are given, are background research by the authors specifically undertaken for this volume.

It must be stressed that the *elements* do not, in themselves, determine the subsystem, or the operating characteristics of the subsystem. A grid with people as elements could be completed, by a subject, in terms of constructs such as *light-heavy, large-small*; and the high reliabilities noted in the "object-sorting" grid might well appear. The contrast is between "physical" constructs and "psychological" constructs, and not between the elements, as such.

In construct theory terms, these results might be taken to indicate that the subjects had fared better, in their lives, as construers of objects, than as construers of people. A more elaborate form of this experiment is reported in Bannister and Salmon (1966), where group differences (normals *versus* thought-disordered schizophrenics) were shown to relate to subsystem differences. The results again indicated that varying degrees of stability of construct relationships are to be expected, depending upon which subsystem is under examination.

With the exception of the two studies quoted, and work by Hall (1966), to be discussed later, the vast majority of grid work has focused on interpersonal construing. In future, grids involving varying types of elements may be frequently evolved; and it will be more than ever necessary to remember that, at best, a grid can only be a more or less inadequate sampling of a single subsystem. No single grid, however extensive, can sample the whole construct system of an individual.

CONSTRUCT VARIANCE

The idea of change as an intrinsic feature of construct systems directly implies that particular constructs will show differential degrees of stability over time. Superordinate constructs may be more stable than subordinate, core role, more stable than peripheral and tight, more stable than loose constructs. The difficulty here lies, in part, in identifying different types of construct (cf. Mair, 1964b).

The confusion between theoretical and operational definitions is exemplified by the fact that Bannister (1960 and 1962) opted for degree of overall closeness of relationships within constructs, as a way of discriminating between tight and loose, and then went on (Bannister, 1965a) to imply that this was a way of discriminating between superordinate and subordinate constructs; while Levy (1956) had used an almost identical operation to distinguish between constellatory and propositional constructs. Hinkle (1965) has perhaps come nearer than anyone else to penetrating this confusion by showing, in his Implication Grid study, that a threefold definition of superordinancy yielded significant intercorrelations. He showed that constructs which have the most implications for an individual are those on which he is least prone to contemplate changing his preferred polar position, and are also the constructs which he offers as justification for his preferred pole position on other constructs in a "laddering" interview.

Whatever the most appropriate interpretation of close construct matchings, a re-analysis of data from Bannister (1962) throws some light on the relative stability of particular constructs across two grids, involving two arrays of elements. The grids involved the construct *good-bad*, which accounted for more of the variance within the matrix of interrelationships than any other construct, and the construct *usual-unusual*, which accounted for least variance. Thirty normal subjects completed two grids in which they rated, on a one-zero scale, two different sets of 20 photographs on 10 constructs (split-half matching format). The stability of the construct *good-bad*, in relation to all other constructs, across elements, and the equivalent stability of *usual-unusual* were calculated. The mean stability for the construct *good-bad* was 0·80, and for *usual-unusual* it was 0·50 (difference p $<$0·05).

It should be noted that this finding did not replicate when Mair and Boyd (1967) used a different set of elements, constructs and subjects, but examined a similar aspect of differential construct stability over a period of two weeks. No stability difference between two groups of constructs, selected on the basis of high and low Intensity scores, was found. The difference between high and low Intensity constructs may be, in part, an artefact. Constructs which account for little of the variance in grid matrices are likely to be those with many near-zero relationship scores; and this restriction of variance, plus the tendency of low correlations to wobble randomly around zero, may, of itself, reduce the reliability coefficient.

Nevertheless, however difficult it is to specify the characteristics of constructs which lead to differential reliability, it would seem wise to assume that, for any given individual, some constructs may be stable and others unstable in their network location. Certainly, any examination of repeat grids, from an individual, tends to reveal that the source of a low reliability coefficient lies largely in radical matrix position changes for one or two, out of a large number of constructs.

INDIVIDUAL VARIANCE

It is a prime tenet of construct theory that *individuals* differ in their construction of events (individuality corollary).

When two grids are administered, either with varying elements or with a time interval, it is possible to obtain a measure of construct relationship pattern stability *for each individual subject*. This in turn allows for consideration, not merely of "the reliability of the test," but also of "the reliability of the individuals taking the test." An examination of data for individuals, from a large number of studies, shows individual reliability coefficients ranging from negative correlations to correlations near unity. Mair and Boyd (1967) report a study which assessed the pattern of construct relationships of the constructs *like me*, *like my father* and *like my mother*, matched with 15 other constructs, over a two-week interval. Test-retest stability correlations for different individuals, ranged from −0·61 through zero to 0·90. Furthermore, the differences between individuals varied with different constructs e.g. for one subject, the stability correlation for *like father* matchings was 0·77, and for *like mother* matchings it was −0·61; while another subject provided correlations of −0·25 and 0·74 for these constructs. Here is a compounding of individual differences with the specific construct differences discussed in the previous section.

The practice of pooling individual reliability coefficients to give a group coefficient tends to hide the enormous amount of individual variance which almost every grid experiment seems to make manifest. The size of such individual differences in reliability suggests that they might be viewed as matters of psychological interest in relation to the subjects, rather than purely as indices of test merit in relation to official standards. Whatever experiments may derive from an interest in individual differences, it seems clear that group reliability coefficients are less meaningful in relation to grid measurements than in relation to almost any other type of psychological assessment. Fortunately, the grid, by providing individually calculated estimates of reliability, and estimates for each individual construct, frees the psychologist from the limitations of group data.

GROUP VARIANCE

The sociality corollary argues that "to the extent that one person construes the construction processes of another, he may play a role in a social process involving the other person." Reference has already been made to a group which signally fails to play an adequate role in social processes, thought-disordered schizophrenics. In a series of studies (Bannister, 1960 and 1962; Bannister and Fransella, 1966; replicated by Bridges, 1965 and Foulds and McPherson, 1966), the immediate test-retest reliability of construct relation-ships, for different groups, using either people or photographs as elements, was calculated. The reliability correlations for normals, in the three primary studies, were 0·60, 0·72 and 0·80; and for thought-disordered schizophrenics, they were 0·33, 0·35 and 0·18. These differences, in what would conventionally be termed "the reliability of the test," have been used as part of a diagnostic measure of schizophrenic thought disorder (Bannister and Fransella, 1967). This is possible, since a reliability coefficient can be calculated for each subject separately, within the format of grids.

Although other populations might not differ in such an extreme fashion for the measures quoted, they may differ as markedly on other grid measures (existing and potential); and it seems clear that reliability coefficients obtained for a specific score for a specific population should not be rashly generalized. These studies represent a clear example of the use of the notion of reliability as a measure of the subject's psychological processes, rather than as an estimate of the error variance of the test.

Bannister has suggested that the relatively low Intensity and Consistency scores of thought-disordered schizophrenics, as compared with normals and other psychiatric groups, may be the result of a history of early and/or repeated invalidations of predictions about people. Insofar as repeated invalidation leads to a loosening of linkages between constructs, it might cushion the individual against yet further invalidation, but also make it impossible for him to make clear-cut or stable predictions about interpersonal events.

Thus, differences in the validational history of individuals may account for group differences in aspects of their construct systems, just as it was earlier suggested that differences of the same kind might account for changes in structural characteristics *within* individuals (intra-subject subsystem differences).

It may be that simple test-retest assessments with grids will prove less useful than serial reassessments at different points in time – longitudinal rather than cross-sectional approaches may be more appropriate to grid method.

ADMINISTRATIVE VARIANCE

Many types of administration have been used for grids, and, because of ignorance, the variations have had to be justified by arguments of expediency. It seems reasonable to expect that format will affect grid results generally; and there is some evidence that it affects reliability assessments.

In one study, 13 subjects completed a grid with six supplied constructs and 15 elements (photographs of people). Each subject completed a second, equivalent-form grid, with a new set of photographs, immediately after the first, and a third grid, using one of the original sets of elements, six weeks later. The mean reliability coefficients for the pattern of construct relationships were: across elements 0·54, over time 0·56 and over time and elements 0·30. Later, a similar group of subjects completed a similar type of grid (rank order format) the primary difference being that only 10 elements (photographs of people) were supplied, instead of 15. The resulting mean matrix reliability coefficients were: across elements 0·72, over time 0·86 and over time and elements 0·73. It seems likely that the differences in stability estimates, which these two sets of grids yielded, were largely due to the inability of many subjects to use interpersonal constructs in the finely graded scalar fashion required by what was, in effect, a 15-step scale. It should be noted, however, that no absolute number of elements can be quoted as ideal, since, in the object-sorting grids referred to earlier, high reliability coefficients were obtained with 15 elements. The general rule would seem to be that the number of elements used should reflect the subject's discriminating capacity, if a rank order method of sorting (with no allowance for ties) is used.

In a further study (Mair and Boyd, 1967), one aspect of the relative reliability of the rank order method *versus* the split-half method was explored. Twenty subjects completed a 16-construct split-half grid and a rank order grid, using the same elements and constructs for each, repeating both after a 14-day interval. The stability of each of three whole-figure constructs (*like self*, *like father* and *like mother*), as related to the other 15 constructs, was examined. The mean reliability coefficients, for the split-half grid, for *like self*, *like father*, *like mother* were: 0·59, 0·52 and 0·43 respectively; and for the rank order grid they were: 0·57, 0·57 and 0·72. It seems likely that some of the variation in reliability coefficients was due to the combined effect of varying the constructs under examination and varying the administrative method.

Even on the basis of such slender evidence, it would seem wise to assume that reliability will be, in part, a function of grid form and type of administration.

CONCLUSIONS

Although information on specific reliabilities for different types of grid in particular contexts is scarce, the illustrative studies cited should serve to outline the dimensions of the problem, and to stress the pointlessness of trying to make any single generalized statement about "the reliability of the grid." In terms of the (by no means exhaustive) list of grid measures given, the types of experimental situation in which reliabilities can be calculated and the general parameters affecting reliability, it would be possible to take one subject, administer three or four elaborate grids at three or four sessions, in the presence or absence of intervening experimental manipulation, and then calculate, for that subject, over 100 reliability coefficients. Even the scattered and unsystematic studies quoted in this section have resulted in experimentally observed reliabilities ranging from significant negative correlations, through zero, up to coefficients well above 0·90. To ask the question "how reliable is the grid?" is akin to asking the question "how reliable is psychological measurement?" and it may take as long to answer.

One practical rule must be that if the reliability of a particular grid in a particular context needs to be known, for either theoretical or practical reasons, then it will have to be specifically assessed as part of the experimental venture. It is to be hoped that the day of the comprehensive cookbook of tables of grid reliabilities will never come. Such a volume might help perpetuate the tendency to regard high reliability as an experimental necessity, rather than encourage the view that "reliability" is, in itself, a target for experimental investigation.

The presentation of views on "validity" and "reliability" as two separate chapters in this work is designed simply to make the layout look familiar – it does not imply that the two concepts are regarded as separate, or that they are accepted as they are usually defined. In many contexts, reliability estimates will themselves be a test of the validity of particular grid measures; and it may often be the case that particular validities hinge on the finding of *low* reliability. This possibility was clearly recognized by Cronbach and Meehl (1955) in their discussion of construct validity. The grid may prove a method whereby this kind of possibility can be explored.

CHAPTER 8

Validity

KELLY ONCE defined validity as "the capacity of a test to tell us what we already know." This definition draws attention to the fact that there is a tendency to assess the validity of a novel measure in terms of its degree of association with dimensions whose natures we, supposedly, already understand. If the criterion dimensions are mysterious (e.g. diagnostic categories in psychiatry), they are embraced as *familiar* mysteries. Rephrased in construct theory terms, the meaningfulness of a new construction is assessed by examining its implicative relationships with constructs already defined by their position within a publicly acknowledged network of constructs.

Face, or content validity seem to be little more than the assertion that the test operations are obviously subordinate constructions, directly implied by the given superordinates – that these implications are of a kind so public, and universally agreed that there is no need to argue about them, e.g. speed in peg-shifting implies degree of manual dexterity.

The concept of predictive validity focuses attention on checking the assumed relationships between the subordinate constructions, (often termed "operational definitions") and superordinate constructions. For example, one of the implications of the construct *neurotic-normal* may be *breaks down under stress-does not break down under stress*; one of the subordinate constructs (elements) within the range of convenience of *stress-not stress* may be *conscripted into the army-civilian*; one of the constructs subordinate to *breaks down-does not break down*, within the context defined by the *army-civilian* construct, may be *given psychiatric discharge-completed service*. Returning to the superordinate *neurotic-normal*, another series of implications may have been derived which links subordinately into, say, a questionnaire test, in such a way that *high scorers-low scorers* are genealogical descendants of the original *neurotic-normal*. *Ergo*, if the test of neuroticism predicts which men among a newly arrived batch of conscripts will break down and be psychiatrically discharged, then, as far as this little network of implications is concerned, the test is "valid." It should be noted that this validity is purely in terms of this particular sub-network of constructs. It does not, however, confirm the whole series of interlinkages, nor does it bear on the problem of what further superordinations can be used to subsume this network. Thus, an assumption that the construct of *neuroticism*, as a whole, is a subordinate construction under, say, the *genetic* pole of the construct *genetic-learned* is neither supported nor denied by the subordinate implications tested in such an experiment. A new set of implications from the top of the hierarchical network would have to be derived and tested in terms of differential predictions.

On this last point, there is a danger that, if there is a sufficiently varied list of subordinate implications available, whose direct cross-associations are untested, then an argument about two contending superordinate implications of a construct can be kept going indefinitely, by always choosing different and unrelated subordinate implications against which to test them. Such a fate seems to have overtaken the argument hinging around the superordinate construction *behaviour therapy-psychoanalysis*, where the subordinate constructions directly defining *cured-not cured* seem destined never to meet.

LOGICAL VERSUS EMPIRICAL VALIDITY

The construct theory notion of validity does not hinge on separating logical from empirical validity – it implies that all validity is logical, in that failure to predict successfully implies some *non-sequitur* in the hierarchical lines of implication from which the prediction was derived. An exclusive concern with a special category of empirical validity fails to recognize that even the final experimental procedures are an intrinsic part of the same argument, and not a sudden breakthrough into an independent reality.

If it is decided that *pressing the lever quickly after the light-pressing the lever a long time after the light* is the "behaviour" which will ultimately be predicted by a particular construction of the subject and his total situation, then predictive failure signifies a break in implication somewhere along the line of argument. But even the most subordinate construction (the one about lever-pressing, which is subordinate to "reaction time") is a *construction* integral to the argument.

Logical validity, in construct theory terms, is meaningful because it has a contrast pole. It can be reasonably argued that some constructions cannot be valid because there are *differential* predictions running through intervening implications into the *same* ultimate prediction. What is the contrast pole of empirical validity? To say that an explanation is not empirically valid seems to mean that the location of the break in the line of implications is low down in the hierarchy of constructions – it is at the most subordinate level in the constructional hierarchy that trouble has arisen. But this does not take it right outside the realm of logical validity-invalidity; it merely becomes a question of whereabouts in the hierarchy of implications the difficulty lies. To give empirical validity a special status seems to imply that the most subordinate constructs are not constructs at all, but "reality," and this is not, in construct theory terms, acceptable. The theory argues that the reality which exists, and against which we measure our constructions, has still to be construed – it cannot be apprehended in some interpretation-free manner.

In thinking of psychology as "the science of behaviour," there seems to have been a tendency to assume that all are agreed as to what behaviour is, and that all there is to worry about is how to predict it. But is there agreement as to what constitutes behaviour? Consider the example of the behaviour *moving-remaining stationary*. This is a piece of construing (with possible alternative constructions such as *going to the cinema-staying at home* or *walking-sitting in a chair*). It may be that a subordinate construct of this kind has a high degree of commonality (high inter-judge agreement), in that its range of convenience is similar for most people, and that its immediate superordinate implications are similar for most people; but it is still a construction which may or may not be placed upon a particular element, and it is still a construction whose superordinate implications may not remain the same from one individual to another.

This is not simply an academic argument. It draws the psychologist's attention to a freedom which he possesses, but which he often does not use, and to a limitation which he labours under, but often tries to ignore.

The psychologist is free to ignore the customary subordinate constructions about behaviour which are commonly used within the profession, and to invent new ways of subordinately discriminating the behaviour, against which he can match his predictive wits. He may select subordinate constructions with a high degree of commonality, so that they can be replicated in experimental procedures; but, provided they are well indexed within his network of superordinate constructions, and can be expressed publicly, he need not worry if they give other psychologists trouble in linking them into their own superordinate constructions.

The limitation that cannot be avoided is that of being, in one sense, both defendant and jury. The construction systems of psychologists (like those of other people) provide their argument, their predictions, their measures and their standards for estimating the success or failure of their predictions. All that can be proved is that a construct system hangs together all along the line (from the superordinate selection of major abstractions, down to the subordinate selection of criteria), and that this may be publicly demonstrated. In the process, a language is created. Since science is a method, not a ritual, there is freedom to choose the target of predictions and the nature of theoretical assumptions; but, in terms of construct theory, constructs cannot be directly tested against an unconstrued reality. From this point of view, psychologists are in the same position as everyone else, in that validation or invalidation happen *in terms of* the construct system as a whole, for the construct system also selects and evaluates its validating criteria.

GENERAL VALIDITY

English and English (1958) state "there is no such thing as general validity. Nor is there absolute validity – we determine the *degree* of validity. And the validity index has no meaning apart from the particular operations by which it is determined."

These strictures apply to any consideration of the validity of grid technique in a highly specific way. Just as with reliability, to ask what is the validity of the grid is like asking what is the validity of the questionnaire. The question would be, what questionnaire, in what context, used for what purpose? The number and manner of grids is, for practical purposes, infinite. Perhaps all that can be done is to consider whether the basic rationale of grids makes sense, whether their application gives results which tally with the underlying assumptions and whether the use of grid methods to date justifies their continued elaboration.

What follows is not an exhaustive account of grid studies – only those which bear directly on questions of validity are discussed. Moreover, few studies have been completed which could be regarded as adequate explorations of even a single aspect of grid or construct theory validity. Mainly, isolated and unreplicated studies have been carried out, which serve only to illustrate the potential usefulness of grid method and construct theory ideas, rather than providing confirmation of their value. Studies will be discussed under three main headings: those concerned with information about construct system structure provided by grid method, those focusing on the direct meaning and content of construct relationships, and those which examine the relevance and usefulness of grid methods for the study of the single case.

GRID MEASURES OF STRUCTURE

If to ask about the validity of a measure raises the question "What is this measure associated with?" then it should be noted that a repertory grid *intrinsically* measures association.

A grid is a framework for measuring interrelationships between a subject's responses – the responses of a single subject are treated as a "population," and population statistics can be applied. The existence of statistically significant relationships in a subject's grid sorts indicates one kind of validity for the measure. If such demonstrably significant relationships did not appear within most grids for most subjects, then construct theory would collapse instantly. The theory rests on the notion that people construe in an organized way. Their categories are related, and these relationships are the sources of their expectations. If A, B, and C are seen as related, then C is expected (predicted, hypothesized) when something is construed as A or B.

This particular kind of validity has been demonstrated in thousands of grids. The measurement of internal relationships is a unique characteristic of grids; and the almost invariable appearance of statistically significant construct relationships in grid protocols is a fact of considerable theoretical importance.

Consider the protocol of a *single* subject on any psychological test other than the grid, e.g. an intelligence test, a Rorschach, a Semantic Differential, Anxiety questionnaire, and so forth. There is no way of proving that, in itself, such a protocol reflects meaningful behaviour (i.e. proof that it was not completed on a coin-tossing, or ballot-drawing, or any similar basis) which does not involve comparison of the single protocol with others (normative data), or with a set of specific predictions made for that subject on the basis of other evidence, or with some externally derived criterion of right or wrong. In this sense, all psychological tests, except the grid, are necessarily content-orient, and, in the broader sense of the term, culture-bound. Kelly pointed out that, if, from a subject's completed grid, the names of the elements along the top and the names of the constructs down the sides were removed, there would still remain information – information about the structure which had governed the sorting. This is true of grids, but not true of any other test, unless the test responses are analyzed for internal relationships, i.e. are analyzed in grid fashion.

SYSTEM SIMILARITY AND BEHAVIOURAL DIFFERENCE

It has been argued that the appearance of statistically significant internal relationships in grids gives validational support to the central tenet of construct theory – that people construe in an organized way – and this suggests in turn, that the grid is a useful means of objectifying this theoretical contention. Construct theory draws a distinction between people's broad structuring of their experience and their ordering of specific events. Thus, two people may agree that *good* people are *generous*, but they may not agree as to which specific people are either *good* or *generous*. This is formally stated in the commonality corollary, thus: "to the extent that one person employs a construction of experience which is psychologically similar to that employed by another, his psychological processes are similar to those of the other person." The behaviourist view is that people are similar when they do similar things; the construct theory view puts greater stress on similarity in terms of the significance which people attach to the things they do.

This raises the question; can grid method demonstrate the meaningfulness of the idea that people can respond differently to similar events, and still have similar construct *systems* for viewing such events? Does it make sense to talk of construct relationships as if they were independent of the elements construed; to talk of grid scores as separate from the absolute allotment of elements? Mathematically, it certainly does. The conclusion from grid analyses, that two subjects both have a high positive relationship between construct A and construct B, does not imply that they allotted their elements to the same poles of constructs A and B. The question remains – even if it is mathematically possible for subjects to give similar construct patternings which are derived from very different element allotments, is this psychologically possible?

Bannister (1962a) investigated this problem in a grid-based experiment. Twenty subjects were faced with 20 photographs of people unknown to them, and were asked to divide them equally as possessing or not possessing 10 qualities, such as *likeable, mean, good, narrow-minded*, and so forth. Each grid was then scanned to extract matching scores between the adjectives.

Three linked hypotheses were tested.

(i) Constructs within a single sub-system (in this case, constructs in the sub-system whose range of convenience is people) will be structurally related. Relationship was operationally defined as a statistical association in usage, i.e. a matching score. It was predicted that the table of matching scores as a whole would deviate significantly from chance expectancy. This is the general assertion that people will behave meaningfully and not randomly in grid sorting, and that the meaningfulness of the behaviour will be statistically demonstrable. The matching scores for every subject for every possible pair of constructs were subjected to a k sample chi-squared test, assuming a chance expectancy in each cell of 10, thus giving 419 degrees of freedom. Chi-square was 960·8 (p <0·001).

(ii) Within one culture, each individual tends to have construct relationship patterns which are similar to those of other individuals. Note, the phrase used here was "similar to" and not "identical with," and the assumptions being made are similar to those involved in Mair's (1966a) experiment. A Kendall coefficient of concordance was run between the rank ordered matching scores of the 20 subjects. The resulting W was 0·729 (p <0·001).

(iii) It is possible to have significant relationships between constructs for individual subjects, and similarity of patterning of construct relationships between subjects, without any consensus of agreement about the allotment of the elements construed. Each allotment by the 20 judges on the 10 adjectives of each photograph was examined, and it was noted whether it was allotted to the one pole of the construct rather than to the other. Chance expectation would be that each photograph would be alloted equally to each pole, i.e. would receive 10 allotments for each pole. A k sample chi-square test was made of the table of photo allotments, assuming a chance expectancy of 10 for each cell; the resulting chi-square was 139·4, with 139 degrees of freedom. This chi-square was not significant.

It was not the intention of this study to prove that there is never stereotypic agreement about photographed faces. In fact, a large number of photographs had to be sifted through in several trial experiments, in order to eliminate "stereotypes." There is a tendency, apparently, for subjects to agree that women and smilers are "goodies," and men and non-smilers are "baddies." However, what was at issue here was whether, *if* all inter-judge agreement about element allotment were eliminated, significant construct relationships in the individual grids, and similarity of construct patterning across subjects would also be eliminated. The results showed that neither was lost. This experiment was completed by a group of subjects who, in stimulus-response terms, would be considered quite different kinds of people. They responded differently to the same stimuli – they did not agree about which of the photographs were of people who were *kind* as opposed to *unkind*, or *selfish* rather than *unselfish*, and so forth. Yet these subjects were similar in the relationships they manifested between their constructs.

The experiment does suggest that grids can separate out the two aspects of the subject's performance, and differentiate between people's absolute agreement on stimuli and similarity between the personal theories underlying their approach to stimuli.

MEASURING CONFUSION

Analysis of most grids for most subjects demonstrates the presence of statistically significant relationships between constructs. This general finding would suggest that the *absence* of structure in a grid might indicate some unusual quality in the construct system of the subject. One approach to the problem of validating grid measures might be to focus on people whom society categorizes as grossly disordered in their thought and behaviour, to see if this is reflected in an absence of grid structure. Such a group, *prima facie*, is the psychiatric population known as thought-disordered schizophrenics, whose talk is clinically described as marked by irrelevance, vagueness, clang associations, word salads, neologisms and (in the experience of those who meet them) incomprehensibility. In terms of this validity argument, such a group might be expected to show little structure in their grid performance; and a number of studies (Bannister, 1960 and 1962; Bannister and Fransella, 1966; Bridges, 1965 and Al-Issa and Robertson, 1964) confirm this.

This argument can be extended to pose the question: can the grid distinguish between complexity and confusion, and, if so, does it indicate each appropriately?

Mathematically, any random sort, when subjected to cluster analysis, will manifest itself as a complex sort. Bieri (1955 and 1961) studied cognitive complexity in normals, using grid techniques. In these studies, he designated normals as cognitively complex if they tended to use their constructs orthogonally and not in tight clusters, and thereby produced grids with relatively low intercorrelations between constructs. It has been shown that when the construing of thought-disordered schizophrenics is measured by grids, uniformly low intercorrelations between constructs appear. How can it be shown that thought-disordered schizophrenics are not actually very complex construers, with a vast array of orthogonal constructs? The solution provided by Bannister involved giving each thought-disordered schizophrenic, in his groups, two grids using the same constructs but different sets of elements. The intercorrelations within each grid were then rank ordered, and the two sets of rank orders compared. The same procedure was carried out with normal subjects. It was found that, when they produced a pattern of low inter-correlations between constructs, the particular pattern (which constructs related to which, negatively or positively) was relatively stable, and was repeated from one grid to the next. Thought-disordered schizophrenics produced a pattern of low intercorrelations on the first grid, which was replaced by a *different* pattern of low intercorrelations on the second, i.e. the pattern was not merely weak, it was inconsistent over time and across elements. Thus, retest grid examination provides a means of differentially defining complexity and confusion.

The grid then appears to reflect the presence or absence of overall structure, and is valid in that it reveals structure in the vast majority of cases, where expected, and reveals absence of structure in the minority of cases, where absence would be predicted.

MEASURING SUBSYSTEM DIFFERENCES

Assessment of aspects of grid validity repeatedly involves assessment of aspects of construct theory validity. Individual constructs and construct subsystems have limited ranges of convenience (i.e. do not carry implications for all other constructs or subsystems within the construct system). Not all subsystems have the same general structural qualities. A statistician may have a remarkably elaborated and complex system for viewing numbers, but a very simple system for viewing people; a poet may have the reverse. Can the grid index differences in structure between subsystems? If it can, do differences appearing follow arguable expectations? Work on schizophrenic thought disorder can be cited, to give one answer to these questions. Psychogenetic theorists such as Bateson *et al.* (1956), Lidz (1964) and Laing and Esterson (1964), see distorted *interpersonal relationships*, dating back to early family experience, as a major part of the genesis of schizophrenia. It might then be anticipated that not all aspects of the thought-disordered schizophrenic's construing would be equally damaged – he may not be equally puzzled by all aspects of his environment. The concept of the schizophrenogenetic family would seem to predict that the maximum area of structural damage to construing would be in the subsystem for construing people, not in the subsystem for construing things.

This line of reasoning was implemented in an experiment reported by Bannister and Salmon (1966). Two types of grid were administered to thought-disordered schizophrenics and normals. In the one grid, subjects were asked to rank order photographs of people on people-relevant adjectives, such as *kind, mean* and *selfish*. In the other grid, they were asked to rank order the names of objects, such as *drawing pins, bowler hats, loaves of bread,* and *washing machines*, in terms of constructs whose range of convenience is objects, e.g. *long-short, curved-straight, heavy-light*. The degree of correlation between constructs inside each of the two types of grid was analyzed. There were three major findings. Firstly, all subjects showed higher and more stable (over time and across element) relationships between constructs subsuming things, than they did between constructs subsuming people. Secondly, it appeared that there was some degree of damage manifest in the thought-disordered schizophrenics' construing of objects, since the degree of conceptual structure manifested was significantly lower for them than for normals. Thirdly, at a highly significant level, it was apparent that there was a greater discrepancy between the thought-disordered schizophrenics' construing of people and their construing of objects, than existed for normals. The thought-disordered schizophrenics' construing of objects was only marginally less structured and stable than that of normals, but his use of people-relevant constructs was much less structured than that of normals.

It is interesting, in relation to this study, to note that Salmon, Bramley and Presly (1967a) were able to show the same characteristic for thought-disordered schizophrenics – i.e. that the area of maximum damage to construing was in the subsystem for construing people rather than things – using entirely different measurement procedures. They used a version of the Word-in-Context test (Cook *et al.*, 1963) in which the subject has to infer the definition of unknown words by an examination of various contexts in which they appear. The target words were divided into those with psychological (i.e. people) connotations, and those without such connotations. It was shown that relative to a control group, thought-disordered schizophrenics could make comparatively accurate inferences in determining the meaning of non-psychological words, but were poorer when the word in question had psychological connotations. This replication, using a different operational procedure, not only supports the experimental hypothesis, but also strengthens confidence in the sensitivity of the grid as a means of making these rather subtle discriminations.

Construct theory distinguishes between different kinds of constructs (or more accurately, different ways in which constructs can be used). For example, Kelly differentiates between propositional and constellatory constructs.

As indicated earlier, a constellatory construct is defined as one which fixes the other realm membership of its elements. It is the type of construct involved in stereotypic or typological thinking, the type of construct which argues that "if this is a ball, it must be round, made of rubber, bounce," and so forth. A propositional construct is defined as one which carries no implications regarding the other realm membership of its elements. This is construing of the "as if" type – "any roundish mass may be considered as if it were, *among other things*, a ball."

Can grid method be used to distinguish between constellatory and propositional constructs? If so, does the grid definition reflect theoretical expectancies about the use of these constructs in an experimental context?

Levy (1956), interpreting Kelly's differentiation, hypothesized that judgments made in terms of constellatory constructs would be more readily changed under conditions of high invalidation than would judgments made in terms of propositional constructs. Under conditions of moderate invalidation, it was predicted, there would be no tendency to change one type more than the other.

Levy first gave 55 subjects the original form of the Role Construct Repertory Test, with 22 constructs elicited from each individual subject, and 19 elements (which were people known personally to the subject) elicited in terms of defined roles. He subjected each individual's grid protocol to Kelly's form of non-parametric factor analysis, which aims to determine the major factors underlying the subject's grid sorts, and shows the loading of each construct on these factors. As his operational definition of constellatory and propositional, Levy argued that the five constructs out of the subject's 22 which loaded most heavily on the first major factor could be regarded as constellatory, since they would all be interlinked and form part of a network of closely related constructs. The five which had virtually no loading on any major factor, but which appeared individually as residual factors, were regarded as propositional constructs. He selected, in this way, five constellatory and five propositional constructs for each subject.

The subject was then presented with two photographs of people unknown to him and a list containing, in random order, his five constellatory and five propositional constructs, both emergent and implicit poles being indicated.

He was then asked to allot each of the photographs to one or other pole of each of his ten constructs. He was then presented with a series of predictions concerning possible behaviours of the people in the photographs (e.g. they will like going to parties) and was asked to pass judgment for each of the two people portrayed.

In the presence of the subject, the experimenter made a fake check on the subject's predictions for the people in the photographs, by apparently referring to biographical data about them. At this time, the *ratings* of the photographs by the subject on the 10 constructs were deliberately ignored, and he was told that they would be checked later. The subject was then given back both his prediction sheet and his construct rating sheet, and told that for one of the photographs he had done very poorly in making his predictions, and that for the other one he had been moderately accurate. He was then allowed to alter both his predictions *and* his ratings on the 10 constructs.

When the modified set of ratings on the 10 constructs was examined, it was found that, for the photograph for which they had been told they were doing *very poorly*, the subjects had tended to alter their construct ratings significantly more on their constellatory than on their propositional constructs ($p < 0.01$). For the photograph for which they were told that they had performed *moderately*, there was no tendency to alter more on constellatory than on propositional constructs.

Perhaps the most interesting aspect of this experiment was a *coda*. Levy presented the lists of 10 constructs from each subject to six trained psychologists, who were informed, in detail, about the difference between constellatory and propositional constructs. They were asked to divide, by inspection, the sets of constructs they had before them into propositional and constellatory. They failed entirely to reproduce the discriminations made in terms of the grid analysis. The judges' categorizing of the constructs did not successfully relate to the tendency of subjects to alter decisions more readily on some constructs than on others.

Thus, it appeared that it was difficult to judge whether a construct was constellatory or propositional, on the basis of an inspection of the verbal label, i.e. in terms of known dictionary definitions. The distinction appeared to be a matter of how the particular individual used that construct, and this might have to be determined by asking him to use it in an analyzable context, i.e. in a grid. This is a vital point, since many forms of psychological measurement can reasonably be accused of telling us the obvious, and it is rare that a psychologist checks to see if he has gained more than obvious information by his elaborate methods.

In summary, Levy's study demonstrated that grid method can provide a provisional operational definition for the constellatory/propositional distinction. This definition proved more useful, within the limits of his experiment, than the direct judgments of informed psychologists.

This discussion of the validity of grid measures of structure has omitted reference to Hinkle's (1965) investigations, quoted earlier, although these clearly constitute validational evidence for an alternative grid approach to measures of structure. It is clear that construct theory envisages many other aspects of construct system structure; and ways of indexing these in grid terms have yet to be developed.

GRID MEASURES OF CONTENT

Here, attention is directed to the grid's potential for reflecting meaningful aspects of the content of constructs, as contrasted with grid measures of the more formal mathematical properties of construct systems. Personal construct theory stresses the *personal* nature of constructs and the importance of under-standing the relationships between a person's constructs, that is, what he *means* by them. Is it important to know what an individual's personal con-structions are? Does the grid reflect meaningful relationships between constructs? Tentative answers to each of these questions are provided in the next two sections.

THE INFORMATION VALUE OF PERSONAL CONSTRUCTS

Bonarius (1965) reports a study by Payne (1956), who sought to assess the usefulness of the raw material of grids, namely, personal constructs. He was not concerned with measuring construct relationships, but sought only to assess whether knowing the verbal labels of another person's constructs was useful.

His hypothesis was that people would understand an individual better if they had access to the personal constructs *of* that individual than if they had access to constructs *about* the individual provided by others.

Payne's subjects were grouped in threes, and each member of each trio had to predict the answers of their partners to a questionnaire of a social nature, which they had previously filled out themselves. Each subject, for one of his partners, had access to the 15 personal constructs of that partner as elicited in preparation for a grid. As a contrasting source of information about the other partner, he had 15 constructs which peers had used in relation to him. "Understanding" in this case was measured by equating it with accuracy of prediction about the way in which the target subject would complete the social questionnaire.

The results supported the hypothesis, in that the subjects were better able to predict when they had a sample of the target subject's *own* constructs to examine before making their guesses, than when they were given an equivalent size sample of constructs which *other people* had used about the target subject (p<0·02). This experiment emphasized the value of knowing a person's constructs, even when this knowledge was limited to a set of verbal labels and prediction filtered through the construct systems of other lay judges.

Landfield and Nawas (1964) emphasized a similar point, when they studied the importance, for psychotherapeutic improvement, of the therapist's understanding of the *patient's* language system. Again the Role Construct Repertory Test, used by patient and therapist, provided the means whereby personal constructs were elicited.

Bonarius (1965) summarizes a number of studies which similarly relate to the individuality corollary, and which demonstrate the usefulness of the grid method of eliciting constructs.

THE MEANINGFULNESS OF GRID RELATIONSHIP SCORES

Both construct theory (individuality corollary) and common experience would predict that individuals will differ and be idiosyncratic in their pattern of construct relationships, and it would require monumental casework to prove that each individual's grid reflected some part of his particular network. However, a dictionary represents normative data on constructs; it is a kind of commonly agreed index of how constructs are publicly related. Dictionary definitions indicate the equivalent poles of highly related constructs, and often note contrast poles, ranges of convenience, and so forth. The fact that, to a greater or lesser degree, people can communicate suggests that they stay within striking distance of much of this publicly declared network of construct relationships, however much of their own idiosyncrasy they may add to it.

Mair (1966a) used this publicly documented network, and assessed the validity of the grid in terms of its ability to reflect it.

Using the "public" relationships between constructs (indicated by dictionary definition) as criteria, he sought to test three hypotheses:

(i) that the grid method allows reasonably accurate objectification of relations between constructs,

(ii) that known changes in construct relationships will be reflected in appropriate changes in grid scores,

(iii) that construct relations which are unaltered will be reflected in stable grid scores.

His subjects, on first testing, were presented with 20 photographs of people, and told that they were to try to judge the character of the people in terms of specified dimensions, (i.e. in terms of given adjectives) on the evidence of their facial appearance. Twelve supplied adjectives were used as constructs for the grid. One pair whose similar meaning would be generally recognized, (*anxious* and *easily upset*) and two general constructs (*like me* and *confident*) were presented. In addition, four pairs of synonyms were used: the first member of each pair was an easier and more commonly used term than the second (*diligent/sedulous, pompous/bombastic, menacing/minatory* and *petulant/ querulous*). This latter group of four adjective pairs was referred to throughout as the easy/difficult pairs.

Before completing the grid, all subjects were first asked to define all the adjectives, to determine in which instances the subjects knew the meaning of the first term in the four easy/difficult pairs, but did not know the meaning of the second. They were told to divide their photographs evenly (split-half grid method) as possessing or not possessing the 12 characteristics presented to them in random order. They were to guess a meaning for a construct if they did not know one. In the interval (approximately 11 days) between first and second testing, they were asked to look up the dictionary meaning of all the terms involved in the test. They then repeated the grid exactly as before.

As a test of the first hypothesis – that the grid method allows reasonably accurate objectification of the relationships between constructs – the following specific predictions were examined.

1. Within the easy/difficult pairs of synonyms on the first occasion, the grid relationships between pairs where the subject knows the meaning of the difficult word, will be significantly higher (more positive) than the grid scores between pairs where the difficult word is not known.

2. There will be a positive, and, in group terms, much higher than chance relationship between *anxious* and *easily upset*, giving an average matching score of 14+ (grid scores in this case would range from 0 to 20, with a chance relationship falling at 10) on the first occasion of testing.

3. Within the easy/difficult pairs, the average matching score between pairs where the meaning of the difficult word is not known, should be at chance level (i.e. 10) on the first occasion.

Each of these predictions was strongly supported.

As a test of the second hypothesis – that where experimental manipulation takes place, expected changes in construct relationships will be reflected appropriately in grid scores – the following specific predictions were examined.

1. Within easy/difficult pairs, between the first and second testing sessions, the grid scores for each subject, for each of the four pairs, should increase, or remain at the same level if originally high (equal to, or greater than 14).

2. Any variations in matching score between constructs from first to second testing sessions (other than in the easy/difficult pairs) should be distributed on a chance basis between increases, decreases and scores remaining at the same level.

3. Any variation in matching scores between constructs from first to

second sessions (other than for the easy/difficult pairs) should overall be smaller than matching score changes within the easy/difficult pairs.

Each of these predictions was strongly supported.

Finally, to see if grid scores remain constant in circumstances where stability would be expected, it was hypothesized that, within the easy/difficult pairs, the changes in matching scores between pairs where both words were known on the first occasion, and between pairs where one or both were unknown should be statistically significant. The known pairs should be more stable. This hypothesis was also supported.

In this experiment, a total of 61 predictions about expected grid scores, across subjects and across constructs, were specified, and all but four were fully confirmed.

The fact that public relationships and simply engineered changes are reflected in grid scores is no proof that private and very complex changes will be equally well reflected. There is some hope, however, for the latter possibility, in view of the support provided for the former. As noted earlier, the grid is sometimes regarded as merely an idiographic method designed for idiographic purposes. This is the sort of criticism that is sometimes, perhaps more justly, levelled at the Rorschach, which is often looked upon more as a method whereby the individual artist explores the unique immortal soul, than as a publicly available instrument for scientific use. Such a criticism of the grid does not seem valid, in view of the fact that, when using publicly available criteria of "right or wrong" relationships, the grid reflects them reasonably well.

The limited evidence available argues for the usefulness of eliciting *personal* constructs, and for the continued exploration of grid methods as measures of meaningful relationships between constructs.

GRID CONTENT AND BEHAVIOUR

The studies so far discussed have involved tests of hypotheses which relate directly to construct theory and grid method as such. This leaves open the question: is the information about construct relationships provided by grids useful for explaining and predicting behaviour that is not directly related to grid procedures?

Knowles and Purves (1965) carried out verbal conditioning studies in which subjects were asked to make sentences including a given verb, and beginning with any one of six personal pronouns. Whenever the subject began with either "I" or "we," the experimenter indicated approval. On a learning theory basis, it was expected (and often found) that this would reinforce the "I" and "we" responses, which would increase in frequency as trials proceeded. These authors decided to take into account each subject's view of himself and the experimenter, to see if this accounted for the considerable individual differences in verbal conditioning.

Prior to the experiment, subjects were given a form of repertory grid designed to assess their need for approval (i.e. the relationship between the construct *like me in character* and the construct *needs approval*) and their evaluation of the experimenter (i.e. the relationship between *like I'd like to be in character* and *like the experimenter*). One hypothesis was that subjects whose grid indicated that they needed approval (high positive relationship between the first two constructs) and that they thought the experimenter's approval worth having (high positive relationship between the second two constructs) would condition more readily than subjects who either did not need approval or cared nothing for the experimenter as a source of approval.

The results were analyzed in terms of a distinction between those who had shown themselves to be conditionable and those who had apparently been unaffected by the experimenter's reinforcement. It was found that subjects who were characterized, in grid terms, by needing approval and valuing the experimenter's opinion tended to be conditionable. Subjects who did not value the experimenter's opinion *or* did not appear to need approval conditioned less.

This effect was manifest mainly for male subjects in the experiment. As the authors recognized, since the experimenter administering the test was a young female, the grid should have examined linkages of constructs such as *needs approval* and *like the experimenter* with sex-relevant constructs.

This type of experiment might normally end with the statement that some subjects condition more readily than others. In this instance, an explanation (with some experimental support) of why some condition more readily than others can also be proposed – an explanation which does not involve tautological references to constitutional and genetic factors. It also brings the study into the interesting range of experiments which accept that any experiment is, in itself, a social situation, involving a social interaction between experimenter and subject. A further construct theory approach to the problem of experimenter-subject interaction is reported by McFall (1965).

Voting was taken as the focal behaviour in a study by Fransella and Bannister (1967). Seventy-four subjects completed a grid where the elements were 10 people known personally to them. The following 9 constructs were supplied: *sincere, likely to vote Conservative, proud of being British, like I'd like to be in character, likely to vote Labour, prejudiced, believe in equality, like me in character, likely to vote Liberal*. Subjects ranked their 10 elements in terms of each construct.

The testing took place in the two weeks before the British General Election of 1964. One week after the election, the subjects were asked how they voted, or would have voted, and what their second choice would have been, if there were no candidate standing for their preferred party.

Within each subject's grid, correlations for all possible pairs of constructs were calculated, and a series of predictions was tested concerning relationships between grid scores and voting behaviour for the group as a whole, and for Labour, Liberal and Tory supporters respectively.

The constructs covered three areas.

(i) Evaluative constructs, i.e. *sincere, prejudiced, like me in character, like I'd like to be in character*, covering the field of what may generally be referred to as personal and moral values.

(ii) Political constructs, i.e. *likely to vote Conservative, Labour* and *Liberal* respectively, which refer specifically to political behaviour.

(iii) "Brand image" constructs, i.e. *believe in equality* and *proud of being British*.

The primary hypothesis was that the pattern of intercorrelations between evaluative and political constructs would predict actual voting behaviour. Thus, if a subject had a correlation of $+0.75$ between *sincere* and *likely to vote Labour*, of $+0.13$ between *sincere* and *likely to vote Liberal* and of -0.20 between *sincere* and *likely to vote Conservative*, then the prediction would be that this person would vote Labour, with Liberal as his second choice. Chi-squares were calculated between the predicted and actual voting behaviour for all subjects, using, first, *sincere*, as the predictor; the result was in favour of the hypothesis ($p < 0.01$).

The same procedure was adopted for assessing the predictive capacity of the constructs *prejudiced, like I'd like to be in character*, and *like me in character*, except that, in the case of *prejudiced*, the highest negative relationship score with the political construct was counted as predictive of voting behaviour. All the evaluative/political construct relationships significantly predicted voting behaviour, the most highly significant predictor being the construct *like I'd like to be*.

The second prediction was that the construct *believe in equality* would tend to correlate positively with the construct *likely to vote Labour* for all subjects, regardless of their political allegiance; and that, similarly, the construct *proud of being British* would tend to correlate positively with *likely to vote Conservative* for all subjects. It was found that the construct *proud of being British* was significantly correlated with *likely to vote Conservative* for supporters of all parties, both collectively and individually. Similarly, the constructs *believe in equality* and *likely to vote Labour* were significantly correlated, though this tendency was much more marked among Labour supporters than among supporters of the other two parties.

The authors suggest a possible definition for the concept of "brand image" in construct theory terms, and a measurement of it in grid terms. A "brand image" might be defined as a construct whose applicability to a particular element (a political party or a soap powder) is generally accepted, there also being public agreement as to which pole of the construct the element occupies. However, the results of this study indicate that the position of the bipolar construct *within the rest of the construct system* may vary considerably where "brand image" constructs are concerned. Thus, while both Labour and Tory supporters were agreed that Conservatives are *proud of being British*, the Labour supporters see this as being *positively* and significantly related to *prejudiced*, while the Tories see it as being *negatively* though not significantly related to *prejudiced*.

A marginal finding hints at a way in which terms such as "interest," "enthusiasm" and "involvement," may be defined in construct theory and grid terms. A crude self-rating measure had been taken of each subject's degree of interest in politics. When two groups were selected, in terms of grid scores, as having either *very high* or *very low* correlations between personal and political constructs, then the former tended ($p<05$) to be those who expressed considerable interest in politics, and the latter, those who expressed relatively little interest. This suggests that a subject's degree of involvement in an area might be measured in terms of the strength of the links between constructs subsuming that area (chess, sex, politics, mechanics, and so forth) and more central constructs which govern the subject's construing of himself.

Although both these studies illustrate ways of predicting from grid content measures to diverse behaviours, in neither did the investigators check whether direct and more simple enquiry (of the type used by Levy to compare with his test procedure) would have provided equally effective predictive information. It can be argued, however, that the very abstract idea of construct inter-linkage provides a framework within which many ill-defined and disparate concepts can be given more coherent and related definitions. This was illustrated in relation to the notions of "brand image" and "interest."

THE SINGLE CASE

Personal construct theory is, by intent, a methodological, not a content theory. It provides a framework for studying how individuals pose and solve life problems, but it does not prescribe what people will have problems about or the particular solutions they will attempt. The theory provides constructs of a very high level of abstraction, such as permeability, superordination, tightening and loosening, which are not tied to the content of any particular life problem. They can be used by the clinician to subsume an individual's ongoing processes, but they need not turn his attention from the patient's construing of his life situation as the most meaningful and continuing focus. This contrasts with more content-oriented ways of viewing a person, such as those that insist that his problems constitute an "illness," or that all problems can be tied back to some universal source, such as "sex" or "agression," or that all approaches to life can be subsumed by some content-defined dimension, such as "introversion – extroversion." Construct theory is not simply an appropriate framework for the study of the single case; it assumes that the individual is the essential point of departure and the ultimate criterion of validation for social as well as individual psychological study.

Although the grid can be used normatively it reflects construct theory in that its basic form directs attention to the individuality of the person. Since the grid is a methodology and not a test, it can be used to structure diverse individual problems in terms of varying elements, constructs and forms of analysis.

There are few published studies of single cases where grid methods were used, and none of these make any primary use of construct theory. Those to be discussed violate a number of principles of grid construction, and are incomplete, in that they do not demonstrate the usefulness or validity of the data provided by the grid. They are cited to illustrate ways in which grids can be tailored to the single case, and to encourage the development of this line of work (e.g. Ryle, 1967).

THE CONCEPT OF ARSON

Fransella and Adams (1965) investigated a patient, admitted to a psychiatric hospital (via prison) after committing a number of acts of arson. Fire-raising has been variously construed – as a crime, as an illness, or as a distorted form of sexual activity. The purpose of the grid investigation was to discover how *the patient* construed his fire-raising activities.

Six grids were administered, over a period of a few weeks, with various elements (people known to the subject, names of emotions and photographs of people unknown to the subject) and with both supplied and elicited constructs.

The sex-substitute explanation seemed inadequate, in that sex-linked constructs repeatedly failed to relate to constructs about fire-raising. Nor did the subject's grids indicate that he regarded his fire-raising activities as either a crime or symptomatic of an illness.

The patient's grids implied a sharp distinction between his own fire-raising activities and arson. There were negative relationships between constructs such as *like me in character*, and *likely to commit arson*; and, while the grid indicated that he thought that arson was wicked, it also suggested that he felt himself to be a righteous man and not, morally and psychologically, an arsonist. It could be hypothesized that he viewed his fire-raising activities as a righteous punishment of wrongdoers. This might partly account for his poor response to treatment.

The fact that a number of grids were administered serially, over a period of weeks, enabled the psychologist to check the reliability and consistency of findings, and to test out explanations of patterns found in one grid by inferring from them predictions to be tested in the next.

THE MEANING OF AN ILLNESS

In relation to an agoraphobic woman, the question was "Does this woman regard her agoraphobia as a kind of 'measles' which has stricken her from outside, or does she regard it as an integral part of her personality and attitudes?". The patient completed rank order grids on photographs of people, using constructs such as *like me in character, like I would like to be in character, sincere, like my mother* and, representing the contrast pole of her major symptom, the construct *people who can go anywhere with confidence*. It became clear that the construct *people who can go anywhere with confidence* was orthogonal to all other constructs, and this might reasonably be interpreted as indicating that she did not regard her symptom as at all related to her characteristics as a person, or to her way of viewing her world.

Further grids were administered during the course of intensive psychotherapy and behavior therapy, and changes in the way in which she viewed herself, her psychiatrist and her major symptom were investigated. At one point, virtually all inter-correlations sank towards zero for 14 previously significantly related constructs; and she simultaneously began to complain of being vague, confused and indulging in excessive daydreaming. This might be viewed as indicating a loosening of her system for attaching meaning to her world, and as an opportunity for elaborating a new set of attitudes in the course of psychotherapy. However, the type of psychotherapy being used was non-directive, and no specific pressure for a given viewpoint was applied. Perhaps because of this, she gradually re-established her original conceptual framework. The overall picture was remarkable, in that, although the initial and final grids were almost identical, considerable changes had been manifest in the intervening grids (18 grids were administered over a period of nine months). The patient's clinical condition fluctuated markedly during treatment, but it eventually settled at a level of severe agoraphobia, identical with that which had caused her admission.

A MEANING OF SEX

At the beginning of psychotherapy, a frigid woman's ideas about sex were examined by grid technique. "Sex" was embodied in constructs such as *keen on sex, sexually attractive*, and so forth. The elements were personal acquaintances, and constructs such as *powerful personality, good, make you feel uncomfortable* (often thought to be a "threat" construct), were supplied. The initial grids were analyzed by the method which anchors the factors into specific constructs; most of the variance could be accounted for by two orthogonal dimensions, *good-bad* and *powerful personality-weak personality*. On graphical representation, sex-linked constructs initially appeared in the *bad-powerful* quadrant. As psychotherapy proceeded, sex-linked constructs moved steadily in a diagonal direction into the *good-weak* quadrant (see Fig. 10).

FIG. 10

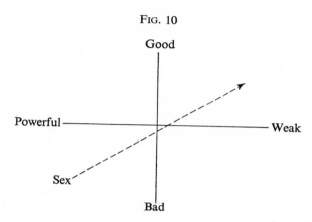

These grid changes were seen as relating to the psychotherapeutic process in two ways. In terms of outcome, the patient moved from a situation in which she was entirely unable to tolerate sexual intercourse, and expressed her disgust strongly enough to threaten her marriage, to a situation in which she regarded intercourse as an acceptable but unexciting domestic chore. The form of psychotherapy used had concentrated heavily on neutralizing the idea of sex by exhaustive discussions of sexual matters, and by repeated hypnotic sessions, during which the patient imagined sexual intercourse while in a completely relaxed and undisturbed state. It may well have been that the psychotherapy succeeded, in the sense that sex had ceased in any way to frighten the patient, but that, in making sex unfrightening, the psychotherapist had also made it uninteresting. More attention to the grid as a guide to psychotherapy, and less as a measure of outcome, might have forewarned the therapist of this possibility.

THE CONCEPT OF MALE–FEMALE

Salmon (1963) studied the case of a young woman who appealed to the psychiatrist for surgery to change her sex to male, on the grounds that she was "really a man." Rather than accept this request, the psychiatrist wanted to know if psychotherapy was likely to be effective in enabling her to adjust to a feminine role. Her occupation (mechanic), her dress and her manner were indeed "masculine," and the relevant question seemed to be how far she did in fact see herself in masculine terms. If the "masculine" construction was reasonably complete, then psychotherapy would probably not prove effective. Two grids were administered, in one of which the elements were photographs of women, and in the other, of men. Grid analysis of her construing of photographs of men showed that she had a highly organized way of construing them. Analysis of her female photograph sorting showed little structure. This suggested a dubious prognosis, since in order to view herself as a woman the patient would have needed to acquire an entirely new conceptual framework, in which women *in general* could be encompassed.

In this case, an answer was sought to the psychiatric question, in terms, not of the *content* of the patient's construing, but of the degree of *structure* in her construing of men and women. It seemed that to suggest to this woman that she became feminine would have been to present her with a meaningless idea.

VALIDATION AND SINGLE CASE STUDIES

The limited extent and nature of construct theory and grid work with single cases is highlighted by reviewing the studies cited in the light of Kelly's criteria for a useful clinical test.

Kelly stressed that a good clinical test should define the patient's problems in *usable* terms. This involves two acts of translation: translation of the patient's problem (or, more frequently, the psychiatrist's version of this problem) into grid terms, and translation of grid findings into terms which can be understood and used by the patient and those responsible for treatment. In the case of the agoraphobic woman, translation into grid terms involved embodying the phrase *"can go anywhere with confidence"* (in which she described her aspiration, as contrasted with her present state) as a construct in the grid, and examining its meaning in relation to other supplied and elicited constructs. The initial grid showed the construct to be orthogonal to the other constructs defining herself. This was translated into treatment terms, by arguing that therapy should focus on the agoraphobic problem (e.g. as in certain behaviour therapy techniques), since this was viewed by the patient as unrelated to other aspects of her personal life. In fact, a mixture of therapies was applied, which makes it impossible to say how useful the simple grid inference would have been.

Little is known about how to make predictions from psychiatric or life problems to the grid, or inferences from grid data, back to other situations. There is a temptation to be very simple-minded and assume, for example, that knowledge of whether a man is frightened by women can be gained by inserting the construct *frightening people*, and checking the relationship between this and the construct *male-female*. Such an assumption of one-to-one correspondence ignores questions such as; In what context is he frightened by females? What does he mean by frightened? Are there other aspects of females more important to him than their capacity to frighten?

The quoted agoraphobic case involved such a simple-minded translation. As a practical step towards avoiding the temptation to embody the question or categorization on the psychiatric referral sheet as a construct in the grid, grid construction should be preceded by extensive discussion with the patient. Such discussion should allow the patient to express his ideas of what his problems are, and how they affect his life situation. The hypotheses and content of the grid should derive as much from this discussion as from the official conceptualization of the problem.

Kelly next suggested that a good clinical test should reveal the pathways along which the patient is free to move and, by so doing, should reveal those of his resources and problems which may be overlooked by the therapist. In the case of the woman seeking surgery to change her sex, a negative point was established, indicating ways in which the patient probably could not modify her outlook. The study was incomplete, in that some of her limitations were noted, but her potential for elaborating her masculine role was unexplored.

One of Kelly's criteria for a good clinical test – that it should furnish hypotheses which may be subsequently tested out – does seem to be relatively well met in single case grid studies. Indeed, one of the problems of such studies seems to be the number of hypotheses which can be developed. Since tests of significance can be used on the data of single grids, there is some danger that hypotheses will too often be generated by one grid and tested in the next, rather than checked against the patient's ongoing behaviour outside the test situation.

In all the cases discussed, a divorce between investigation and treatment has made it impossible to assess the potential usefulness of grid method. For Kelly, the context of grid method was American clinical psychology, where investigation and psychotherapy are often integral procedures carried out by the same person – the clinical psychologist. Although for British clinical psychologists the situation is changing, they are still largely limited to assessment, as distinct from treatment. This makes it singularly difficult for them to assess the clinical usefulness of grid method. The grid's content is liable to be dictated by a psychiatric formulation of the problem; translation into and out of grid language must cope with psychiatric categories and, above all, the testing out of grid predictions is blurred by treatment regimes based on a variety of unrelated considerations. The whole business of admission testing, as opposed to longitudinal study and measurement, with only a third-party relationship to treatment, renders grid method difficult to develop or evaluate. Where so much is outside the control of the assessor, the disentangling of significant and meaningful grid changes from random score fluctuation is difficult.

Many favourable reactions to the grid may be forthcoming, because its users find neatly drawn maps of the subject's psychological space intriguing, in the sense that a toy is intriguing, or because *post hoc* they convince themselves that what they see in the grid is what they always suspected in the patient. Probably some will approve of it, not because it gives them information in any scientific sense, but because it inspires them to think imaginatively about the patient, and thereby produce ideas about assessment and treatment, rather in the way in which reading a good novel might refresh their thinking.

Probably the most useful, if not the most frequent, ventures will be those in which the grid is used with a single patient where the approach has formal coherence, so that predictions are made before test, the lines of treatment appropriate to negation or support of the hypothesis are specified before test, and the criteria of successful outcome of these predictions are defined in advance.

CONCLUSIONS

In psychology, the validation of measures commonly involves three practices: the possible behaviours of subjects are grossly limited; the experimenter's predictions are made to cover relatively short periods of time; subjects are not credited with the ability to create and construe situations, or to predict and evaluate outcomes *in their own terms*.

So far, the grid has been largely validated in studies which accept these restrictive conventions. Although the number of grid studies is small, the grid appears to have reasonable validity in these terms.

In terms of construct theory, these modes of validation seem incomplete. Construct theory envisages each individual as developing and operating an elaborate, even though sometimes poorly articulated, construct system, designed to deal with many situations. Measures of such a system can only be minimally validated in artificial and restricting contexts. Construct theory directs primary attention to superordinate and role-governing constructs, and measures of these can only be adequately validated in process and longitudinal studies. In construct theory, validation and invalidation are active procedures of the individual, and not merely ends to be achieved, or the exclusive prerogative of scientists. In addition to measuring and monitoring the changing organization of a person's constructs, attention must be paid to the way he establishes and evaluates his own efforts towards personal validation.

From this point of view, the validating of grid method has not yet begun.

CHAPTER 9

Practical and Theoretical Problems in Grid Method

THERE IS some danger that grid method may suffer the fate of the Rorschach. It may surround itself with a mass of loose folk-lore and semi-norms which enable the psychologist to practise casual speculation disguised as systematic instrumental investigation. Grid techniques may often appear more acceptable and promising to the empiricist than they do to the personal construct theorist. The latter is necessarily aware of the complexity of personal construct systems, and thereby sensitive to the over-simplified pictures of fragments of personal construct systems which grids inevitably produce. What follows is an attempt to specify some of the more obvious problems in grid usage. An attempt will be made to show how the practical aspects of each problem relate to the theoretical assumptions of grid method.

ELICITING AND SUPPLYING CONSTRUCTS

Most grids deal in readily verbalized constructs, although construct theory argues for the importance of non-verbalized constructs, which are operating discriminations not conceptualized by the person. Grid procedure for eliciting constructs does not necessarily demand that verbal labels be produced (Scott, 1962 and 1963). Subjects can be encouraged to make sorts on the grounds that the elements "go together"; and verbal labelling can be omitted entirely, or attempted by the subject or the experimenter *after* sorting has been completed – this kind of procedure might be particularly suitable for children.

Kelly's argument for representative sorts in eliciting constructs has already been given; but the problem of defining "representative" in particular contexts still remains. In clinical work, "representative" may often be usefully interpreted to mean those figures or events which directly relate to the patient's problems; perhaps pressing for a series of relevant constructions by repeatedly juxtaposing key elements. Triads for elicitation need not be pre-determined. It may be useful suddenly to group figures which have been repeatedly construed in an extreme way during the grid procedure, in the hope that more superordinate constructions may emerge.

Laddering, as a way of eliciting superordinates, presents the problem that "Why?" is not a guaranteed eliciter of superordinates; nor do "How do you know that?," or "What evidence is there for?" guarantee subordinates. If the issue is vital, implication counts or resistance to change checks may be necessary.

The problems which arise when constructs are supplied by the experimenter, rather than elicited from the subject, are obvious – any assurance that the constructs are a meaningful part of the subject's repertoire is forfeited, and some of the grid matrix variance will inevitably reflect a degree of failure by the subject to translate them into his own terms (see Isaacson and Landfield, 1965, and Cromwell and Caldwell, 1962). Yet in experiments with specific hypotheses and in those involving group comparisons, construct supplying seems useful. Tactics which reduce, though they do not eliminate, distortion effects in supplied construct grids, are suggested.

In any grid or grid series involving supplied constructs, additional elicited constructs from the subject can be used. The presence of such individually varying elicited constructs does not affect the calculation of relationships between the standard constructs; but it does provide a means of checking something of the meaningfulness of the supplied constructs. A markedly lower level of intercorrelation between supplied than between elicited constructs could indicate that the supplied constructs were largely verbiage for the subject. An individual examination of supplied/elicited construct relationships in the grid matrix might yield information as to any unusual meanings which had been attached to the supplied labels.

Pre-test interviewing of single subjects or groups on the topics covered in the grid might yield information as to the common vocabulary available, and increase the experimenter's chances of couching supplied constructs in terms meaningful to his subject.

To repeat a previous argument – the experimenter must consciously guard against the temptation to supply constructs which are a naïve equivalent of the psychological dimensions in terms of which he is framing the experiment. There is danger that the experimenter who regards, say, *dominant-passive* as a major psychological differentiation, and who wishes to explore this by grid method, will simply insert *dominant-passive*, or a verbal equivalent, as a construct in the grid. He might then include *like I am*, and assume that observed grid relationships between the two will index the subject's "dominance-passivity" level. What would be required here would be a very elaborate series of hypotheses as to the kind of construct systems (in both structural and content terms) which would underly "dominant" or "passive" behaviour. The psychologist's theoretical constructs cannot necessarily be used as grid material.

ELEMENT SAMPLES

In grid studies the problem under investigation determines the "relevant" sample of elements. Mitsos (1958) provided some experimental support for Kelly's contention that a wide range of role titles (as opposed to a random selection of acquaintances) would elicit elements of general significance in the subject's life. There has been an increasing tendency to use an undifferentiated list of elements provided by the subject; this achieves neither specific relevance to problem areas nor general representativeness.

Another technique which evades the issue of representativeness of elements is the increasing use of photographs of unknown people, which converts the task to one of "judgment of character from faces". This practice was originally developed for a particular purpose in grid investigations of thought disorder.

Bannister (1962) argued that thought-disordered schizophrenics might be giving *remembered* judgments of people which might intercorrelate to a greater degree than new judgments forced on them by novel (photograph) material. However, the practice of using photographs has become more general; this raises the problem of the equivalence or non-equivalence of using photographs and people as elements – a problem which continuing use of both seems to have been ignored.

ELEMENT ALLOTMENT

Grid studies seem to involve, interchangeably and presumably for reasons of convenience, the four major methods of element allotment so far developed – free dichotomizing, split-half, rank order and rating. *A priori* arguments have been put forward for advantages and disadvantages in relation to each method, but little is known about their degree of equivalence. Mair and Boyd (1967) compared a rank order and a split-half technique, and found considerable disparity between the patterns of construct interrelationship. Simple comparison studies of different element allotment methods may be less useful than studies in which the results of different methods are compared in terms of their predictive usefulness.

RANGE OF CONVENIENCE

Probably the most clear-cut rule in grid construction is that which states that all the elements used for sorting in a grid must be within the range of convenience of the constructs involved. Yet despite its apparent simplicity, this rule can be a snare and a delusion. Ranges of convenience for constructs, like other aspects of personal construct systems, are idiosyncratic to the subject. If he is a "good" subject, i.e. one who thoroughly carries out the instructions given to him, he may quietly produce what, in terms of his personal system, is non-sense. Even direct enquiry does not solve the problem entirely. Kelly has stressed that every construct has a focus of convenience and a range of convenience. A subject may be working with elements which are entirely within the focus of convenience of some constructs and which are only just within the range of convenience of others. The results might then show a greater degree of tightness and articulation for the former constructs, relative to the latter.

Yet a further source of confusion may arise from the different contexts in which an individual may use any single construct. For a given subject, the construct *mature-immature* may have one set of implications when it is applied to members of his own family, a rather different set of implications when it is applied to people in general, implications which are different again when it is applied to nations, and yet a further set of implications when it is used to subsume works of art. The picture of relations between constructs derived may depend a great deal on the context in which the subject was asked to use them. He may well have shifted from one context to another as he handled different constructs, and thus produced a confused and mixed reflection of the relationships between them. This may be a greater danger in the relatively context-free Implication Grid method. Understanding in what way, and to what extent, grids can reflect the construct systems of individuals or the modal systems of groups, must involve examining, in great detail, the account given by subjects of what they think they are doing in a grid situation, and finding ways of comparing this with the test outcome.

CONSTRUCT BIPOLARITY

One of the original features of grid form which has been ignored in more recent studies is the insistence that the subject specify both poles of each construct. This problem particularly arises when constructs are supplied. While the supplied emergent pole of a construct may be translated by the subject into his own terms, the supplying of a contrast pole may saddle the subject with what, for him, are poles of two different constructs, causing him to work his way round a psychological corner when ranking or allotting his elements. It would seem advisable to check on the subject's view of the contrast when constructs are being supplied.

This advice does not seem completely to solve the problem, as shown by Mair (1967). Here, the emergent poles of five constructs were supplied, and each individual's contrast poles elicited. Grid sorts using each pole of each construct independently were completed by the subjects. It was found that many elements placed under one pole of a construct were later placed under its contrast (e.g. elements categorized as *energetic* were later categorized as *lethargic*). The practical effects of this overlap for both content and structural measures were illustrated and discussed.

WHOLE-FIGURE CONSTRUCTS

In an attempt to gain some global picture of how the subject construes himself or some key figures such as his father or his mother, the practice has developed (Bannister 1965) of presenting the subject with a construct such as *like me in character*, or *like my father*, and hopefully assuming that the relationships between this construct and others within the grid, will index the subject's self-perception or, in some manner, his total perception of significant others in his life. This assumption is debatable, since the subject can hardly handle such whole-figure constructs in any total sense, but must break them down to the idea of *like my father in respect of dimension X* or *like I am in character as far as dimension Y is concerned*. Mair (1967a) studied sorts based independently on *most like I am* and *least like I am*, and afterwards asked his subjects to explain the basis for every choice they had made. No subject consistently used only one dimension as a basis for sorting people as like or unlike himself. When the various dimensions underlying *like me* and *unlike me* were used as constructs for further grid sorts by each individual, expected intercorrelations failed to appear. Any relationship scores between this type of whole-figure construct and other constructs may be difficult to interpret. There is some indirect evidence in the same study that "ideal" figure constructs (e.g. *like I'd like to be*) may prove more manageable for subjects, and more useful to experimenters.

TYPES OF CONSTRUCT RELATIONSHIP

Different types of construct relationship have been described (parallel, orthogonal, reciprocal, ambiguous) but, at present, grids, other than the Implication Grid, compound these various relationships into a single index of association – an index which is representative in the case of reciprocal construct relationships, but clearly distorting in the case of other types of relationship.

As an example of the kind of information which is thus lost, consider the question of contradiction within the network of constructs operated by an individual. Traditional logic is a product of man, but does not in itself necessarily describe man. Construct systems may sometimes be "short-circuited." A system may exist, in which $A+$ implies $B+$, $B+$ implies $C+$, $C+$ implies $X+$ and $X+$ implies $A-$. Thus, in situations where the A,B,C constructs are in operation, the individual is able to see his environmental alternatives clearly; but if a situation arises in which he tries to use both

A,B,C and X,Y, and Z constructs, then he will be faced with signposts which point in opposite directions, indicating a point of logical intransitivity in the system. This might be no great problem if one group of constructs is clearly superordinate to the other. If superordinancy is not well articulated, he may become hostile in Kelly's sense of the word. Possibly, one reason why conflict is so often thought of as "unconscious" is that many may have a clear picture of the first, second and third order implications of their constructions in any given situation, but are vague as to the 20th, 21st and 22nd order implications which follow from the elaborated network of their construct relationships.

In terms of grids as currently used, it is difficult to locate or assess contradiction, since they impose a kind of pseudologic on the system. If, for example, a rank order grid is used, then the network of construct relationships is expressed as a matrix of correlations. The mathematical rules for computing this matrix preclude the possibility of contradiction. No correctly calculated matrix can give correlations of the kind: A correlates $0 \cdot 9$ with B, B correlates $0 \cdot 9$ with C and C correlates $-0 \cdot 9$ with A. But the fact that the construing subsystem "mathematics" cannot carry such contradictory implications should not imply that no contradictory implications exist within construct systems.

MEASURING THEORETICAL CONSTRUCTS

A number of important theoretical constructs have proved difficult to translate into agreed and intercorrelating grid measures. Different measures have been suggested for the dimensions of core-peripheral, tight-loose, permeable-impermeable and superordinate-subordinate. For example, superordinate constructs have been defined as those constructs loading heavily on the first factor in a cluster-analyzed grid, or as the hypothetical construct explaining the first factor, or as the construct first extracted by the Anchor method, or as the constructs which have most resistance to change, have most implications and occur late in laddering. Bannister and Salmon (1967) intercorrelated a number of hypothesized measures of superordinancy, involving factor analysis, range of convenience, laddering and the subject's own rating of constructs as "important". Although factor analytic measures predictably intercorrelated, the measures, in general, showed insignificant relationships. Until the various operational definitions of major constructs of the theory are more carefully derived from an examination of the logic of the theory, confusion is likely to increase.

One of the most notable features of the development of repertory grid techniques to date has been the proliferation of forms of cluster analysis, Following Kelly's original non-parametric factor analysis (Kelly 1955), work has been done using further factor analytic techniques by Fager (1962) and

J. Kelly (1963), a form of Principal Component analysis (Slater, 1965) and cluster analysis techniques applicable to grids, such as those of Bromley (1966), Bannister (1965a), Constantinescu (1967) and Stringer (1967), to say nothing of the occasional use of general clustering techniques such as Thurstone's Centroid method.

At first glance, this might seem a very promising development in grid methodology. Many of the techniques possess the kind of mathematical sophistication which is much admired in psychological circles. Since construct theory repeatedly stresses that construct systems are hierarchical, and since it is easy to equate the notion of key and central ideas in a person's thinking with the mathematically central constructs emerging from a cluster analysis, the trend seems full of promise. Yet, there is clearly a danger, in any quantification system in psychology, of calculating particular quantities *because they can be calculated*. Until much more is understood of the psychological processes of subjects using their constructs in completing grids, it would seem unwise to blur the primary data by complex and extensive mathematical analyses.

CONCLUSIONS

It seems clear that the grid will never be a very handy or easy tool of psychological investigation. Yet the problems it presents can initially be investigated by the relatively simple technique of listening to the subject. Given a situation in which the subject is allowed to make a running commentary on the nature of the grid operations he is carrying out, and to deliver a further commentary on the conclusions the psychologist has reached, a better understanding of the relationship between grid results and construing might be achieved. In particular cases or investigations, further conventional ground might usefully be yielded by bringing in the subject as a partner in the design of the grid. This might ensure that the grid met the requirements of both experimenter and subject; and it would acknowledge the special relationship which should exist between the psychologist and those he studies.

CHAPTER 10

Retrospect and Prospect

THE USES of construct theory ideas and grid methods have inevitably been modified by traditional psychological assumptions and research methods. Some will approve of this process, regarding it as a necessary integration, while others may fear that the distinctive features of the new approach may become blurred and only a lowest common denominator retained. Bieri seems to hold the first view and his studies provide an interesting illustration of the amalgamation of old and new in his use of the concept of cognitive complexity-simplicity (Bieri, 1955 and 1961, *et seq.* reviewed Bonarius, 1965; Crockett, 1965 and Jaspars, 1966).

A marked characteristic of this work is the increasing tendency, as the studies proceed, to view cognitive complexity-simplicity as a *trait*. In Bieri and Blacker (1956) an attempt is made to establish the generality of the dimension by showing a correlation between cognitive complexity in the perception of people and Rorschach ink blots. In Bieri and Messerley (1957) the dimension of cognitive complexity-simplicity is related to the more traditional trait concept of introversion-extraversion. The habits of trait psychology seem to have led the experimenters from an initial observation about the mathematical characteristics of a single grid to a position where they speak of individual persons as being, in a generalizable and long term sense, either cognitively simple or cognitively complex and as occupying a relatively fixed position on the dimension. In contrast, construct theory stresses that the structural qualities of a construct system change continuously over time with the varying validational fortunes of expectations derived from the constructions. Additionally, in presenting his idea of range of convenience, Kelly argues that a single construct system may be viewed as consisting of a number of subsystems. A subsystem can be operationally defined as a group of constructs whose internal relationships and implications are stronger than the relationships between the group and a further group of constructs with similarly high internal relationships. In such terms, it is not difficult to envisage a single individual as being either cognitively complex or cognitively simple, depending on which of his subsystems is under consideration. Many psychological approaches contain concepts such as "areas of interests," "aptitude" or "stronger or weaker motives," all of which acknowledge varying structural qualities within individual systems.

The cognitive complexity studies can be compared with two other studies which stand in contrast to the *trait* approach.

Runkel and Damrin (1961) studied trainee teachers at three stages during their training, on entering, about half-way through and on emerging. They asked the students to rank order items of information about pupils which teachers might require, from those they would consider it most important to know, down to those they would consider more or less irrelevant to problems of teaching. Subjects carried out this task at the three points in their training programme and each subject's ranking was analyzed by an unfolding technique which disclosed how many discernible dimensions underlay the test decisions. The elements for sorting in this form of grid were types of information relevant to the chosen career of the subjects, and the form of analysis allowed for a simple-complex scoring to be made for each subject. The results showed that, in general, there was a curvilinear (U-shaped) relationship between time in training and the cognitive complexity scores. Initially the student teacher arrived on the course with a fairly large number of constructs which he tried to apply to the elements under view; in the middle of his training period these seemed to have shrunk to a relatively small number of dimensions. On emerging from training these had again been elaborated. This suggests that the aim of training might have been first to beat all the nonsense out of the trainee and get him to concentrate on one or two "important" things. When the subject had recovered from the impact of this focusing, he could again individually elaborate his construction of the teaching situation.

It is difficult to see how a notion of people as *typologically* complex or simple could subsume the kind of observations made in this study or the findings of similar process studies (Bannister, 1963 and 1965).

Hall (1966) administered grids to 110 subjects, each grid embodying ten elements and twenty elicited constructs. Each subject completed five grids on five sets of elements:

(i) Ten significant people in the subject's life, (ii) ten commonly known animals selected by the subject from a list provided, (iii) ten swatches of fabric, (iv) ten small coloured plastic chips and (v) ten art prints. For each grid a measure of cognitive complexity-simplicity was derived in terms of the amount of variance accounted for by the first factor, using Cromwell's (1960) factoring method.

For each subject, complexity scores derived from each type of grid were intercorrelated. In males, correlations ranged from 0·12 (between people and art prints), to 0·54 (people and colours). Eight out of the ten correlations were significant for men at or beyond the 5% level of confidence. There were no significant correlations for women.

Both men and women were most complex on art prints. Women were significantly ($p < 0.01$) more complex on each of the other four realms than on people. The mean complexity scores of men and women differed significantly only for people sorting ($p < 0.05$). The difference in the total cognitive complexity-simplicity between men and women was significant ($p < 0.01$) with men being the more complex.

The most significant aspect of the research is its contradiction of the *generalized* notion of cognitive complexity-simplicity. Correlations between subsystems did not exist for women at all, and were low for men. Here a static test situation was used with no attempt being made to vary validational fortunes, a process which might well have reduced even the low correlations which did appear.

Each of the major constructs described in construct theory (permeability, dilation, etc.) could be treated in a trait fashion similar to that favoured by Bieri. Such a trend would be a negation of Kelly's view of these constructs as dimensions in terms of which people change. He did not regard them as categories for pinpointing static "types."

Grid methods have been used too often to measure "attitude" or "meaning" in familiar research designs, and little attention has been given to the new areas which the method and its parent theory open up. Kelly envisaged the grid as a means whereby patients in psychotherapy could themselves explore aspects of their own construing which were poorly articulated. Little has been done in these terms in psychotherapy, and no studies use the grid in this way to examine and make more explicit the processes of normal construing. Such studies would also change the role relationship between experimenter and subject so that the experimenter would gain information to the extent that his subject was enabled to gain a greater understanding of his own system. Too much attention has been paid to the grid as a cross-sectioning and static mapping device, and too little attention has been given to the *use* made by people of constructs elicited by the grid or to the *changes* in construing following the new validational experiences which use provides.

In Britain, at least, one of the most marked effects that traditional psychological frameworks have had on investigations of personal constructs has been to focus attention on grid method and away from the underlying point of view. The important thing is to explore construct systems in action and grid method, *along with many others*, may be called into service where appropriate.

Since construct theory is not committed to a specific area of study in psychology, it can offer explanations in a variety of fields and its methods are potentially applicable to diverse problems. What follows is a speculative commentary on some of the traditionally formulated areas in psychology where the use of construct theory ideas and methods may prove useful and may change points of emphasis.

CHILD DEVELOPMENT

A great deal of attention has been given to the problem of how the child progressively orders his universe, attaches significance to himself and others and conceptualizes the multiple moral, mathematical and personal relationships projected by his society.

A child's construct system might be serially examined as it undergoes varying validational experience in order to examine the development of construct systems. In terms of construct theory an initial argument might be that the development of the child would be characterized by a progressive vertical growth of the construct hierarchy. Repeated measurement (e.g. by "laddering") might show an increase in the number of links between concretistic constructions of events and the superordinate abstractions used to weld these events together and give them overall significance. Some aspects of construing in children have already been explored with grid methods by Ravenette (1964) and Salmon (1967).

INTERPERSONAL RELATIONS

One interesting characteristic of grids where groups are concerned, is their capacity to serve simultaneously as rating scales of elements and as measures of construct relationships, where members of a group use each other as the elements for the grid. Within family groups, for example, it would be possible to administer grids in which the elements were members of the family and the constructs were common for the group. A picture (which could be reviewed over time) of the position which each member of the family occupied within the construct space of other members, and the structural and content similarities and dissimilarities of the goggles through which each family member was viewing the others, could be derived. The effect of similarities and differences on communication and upon what each could hope for in the way of meaningful validation or invalidation from his family, or fear in the way of unconstruable behaviour, might be indexed and examined. Some possible long term effects of family experience on modes of construing is explored by Morse (1966).

The *process* view of person perception which construct theory encourages, directs attention not simply to the way other people are perceived but to the way in which difficulties in the perception of others leads to further *evolution* in the "person perception system" as a whole. Adams-Webber (1967) implies that particular elements in any individual's grid (where the elements are people known personally to the subject) can be seen as centres of actual chaos and simultaneously foci of potential structure. This was first noted as an "artefact" of computer programmes for the cluster analysis of grids. In studying principal component analysis data on individual subjects, it was noticed that for some subjects a particular element (person) tended to defy the pattern of qualities defined by the first component (the component accounting for the most variance) in the grid matrix. The first component, in terms of the constructs defining it, would prescribe a particular combination of qualities, and there would be some figure with a profile of qualities at variance with this prescription. Such an unpredictable figure might be seen as *kind* and *hypocritical* and *stupid* and *successful* by a subject who lived in a world where he expected kind people to be sincere and stupid people to fail. This figure was usually the element most loaded on the second component, which appeared to be designed specifically to account for this unpredictable and troublesome figure. In one sense this is an artefact – programmes for cluster analysis, having extracted a first component, tend to take as their starting point for extracting a second component, those elements least accounted for by the first. It can be argued that the principal component analysis programme (being produced by a person) reflects the construing processes of people. It may well be that the attempt to understand people who puzzle, confuse and threaten, initiates the elaboration of new constructs and construct relationships. Intransitivity or contradiction, as defined in Implication and Resistance to Change grids and discussed in the fragmentation corollary, may well prove a starting point for many fruitful psychological studies.

CLINICAL PROBLEMS

A psychiatric patient's conception of himself, his view of his total situation as a psychiatric patient, and his conception of "treatment" affects his responses to the hospital regime and the outcome of therapy. That this problem is generally neglected may be due to the persistent attempt by orthodox psychiatry to work within the intellectual framework originally developed for general medicine. This is an outstanding characteristic of psychiatry and manifests itself in constructs directly carried over from general medicine, e.g. *patient, illness, hospital, doctor, treatment, diagnosis, prognosis, nurse.* In general medicine the "illness" is, strictly speaking, no concern of the patient; it is the business of the doctor and the patient is involved only insofar as he wishes to be rid of his "illness," and is willing to submit himself to the doctor's expertize. When this posture is carried over by both patients and psychiatrists into the field of "mental illness" it runs counter to Kelly's dictum that a man is strictly speaking, the only informed expert on himself.

Apart from adverse critical analyses of the orthodox psychiatric stance (e.g. Szasz, 1960; Laing and Esterson, 1964; Siegler and Osmond, 1966) many of the tactics and strategies of psychiatry covertly admit the limitations of the general medical framework. The development of group psychotherapy procedures, in which patients are specifically encouraged to review their own ideas of their condition in terms of the views of other patients, is a direct recognition of the patient's interpretative involvement in his own "illness." A number of techniques of individual psychotherapy (e.g. rational psycho-therapy, Ellis, 1957) and counselling practices generally, focus on the articula-tion of the patient's outlook as both a definition of, and remedy for, the "illness." The justification of industrial rehabilitation units in terms of their "ability to restore work habits," and of community therapy projects in terms of their contribution towards the development of "social skills and attitudes," inevitably dilute the illness concept by reference to social processes as of primary relevance. Placebo research (while often limited to efforts to partial out placebo response so that the value of "true" treatment can be assessed, and while carrying with it overtones of the curious notion that when men are being "psychological" they are being fooled) recognizes the patient's view of his treatment as a significant factor. Perhaps the whole movement towards making life liveable for patients in psychiatric hospitals is born of an aware-ness that even more than time spent in a general hospital, time spent in a psychiatric hospital cannot be regarded as time sliced out of living in order to have "treatment." It is time entirely filled by events relevant to the person's life.

In this context, grid method offers lines of attack. If psychiatrists construe their treatments as "physical" and "psychological," then outcome could be examined in relation to the patient's view of his condition along these dimensions. If the patient regards his condition as an "illness" of mysterious origin, unrelated to his present outlook or past way of life, or if he has been persuaded by the hospital to accept such a view, then he may well respond to equally mysterious electricity or equally mysterious chemicals as the appro-priate agents of recovery. Conversely, if in grids whose constructs embody his *complaints* and his *philosophy*, close relationships between the two are found, then physical treatment might be outside the range of convenience of the constructs he is using to subsume his "illness", and possibly lack efficacy. Alternatively, since clinicians are publicly committed to the idea of *changing* their patient's in some respect or other, it might be relevant in terms of constructs which the patient uses along a time line (like I used to be, like I am, like I would like to be) to examine whether change, as such, is any part of the patient's expectations. Grids can accept treatments, hospital personnel, lists of self reported complaints and symptoms, other patients and so forth as elements, and matrices of relationships between constructs subsuming such elements might depict the patient as a man in a human situation rather than a patient suffering from an illness.

Any area of psychological investigation which is thought to hinge on a single major superordinate construct (such as *male-female, child-adult, rich-*

poor) is clearly open to study in grid terms by using elements selected in terms of this dimension, and constructs whose capacity to imply, or failure to imply this superordinate, will have far reaching consequences for the construct system as a whole.

Bannister and Salmon (1963) asked a group of homosexual men and a group of heterosexual men to construe photographs of women in terms of supplied sex relevant constructs (e.g. *attractive, pretty*) and generally evaluative constructs (e.g. *kind, good*), and the relationships between these constructs for both groups were examined. There was an initial indication that the difference between the two groups did not lie in the links *within* either the sex relevant constructs or within the evaluative constructs, but in the cross linkages between both. Homosexual men appeared to use these sexual constructs in a more "technical" way so that they were not cross related to the evaluative constructs. The study illustrates grid possibilities in the investigation of sexual construing. Grids using the two sexes as elements and constructs with and without sexual implications, can yield comparable pictures of the way in which *male-female* as a major superordinate construct is located within the person's overall construct system. They may indicate the kind of expectations which a given individual is likely to have where sexual roles are concerned, and the kinds of sexual undertaking which for him may be inevitable, unacceptable or literally unthinkable.

Problems need not only be viewed descriptively but can be looked at in process and development terms. Age group examination in order to assess at what stage and in what form the superordinate construct is developed, and by contrast at what age and in what way "deviant" constructions evolve, could be undertaken.

MEMORY

Psychologists have often stressed that remembered accounts of past events change over time. It has frequently been noted that the changed accounts are themselves coherent (rather in the manner that group transmitted messages in rumour experiments come out at the far end as internally coherent but different from the original input). This kind of change is regarded as showing both loss and distortion. This view seems founded on the idea that the original events were "real" in the sense that there was one absolutely accurate and truthful account which could have been "recorded," compared with which all others are "distortions." In experimental work this "true account" is the experimenter's prescription of the task.

A construct theory approach might make sense of the process of changing accounts without recourse to the notion of a "true account." If a man of twenty is asked to describe what his life was like when he was eight years old and is asked the same question at the age of fifty, the two accounts may not tally. The discrepancy does not have to be explained in terms of "loss" and "distortion." It can be argued that in the intervening years his personal construct system has altered and his view of what is important and unimportant, and what is signified by events, and what events are causally related, may all have changed. Thus, when he gives his new account, certain events will have dropped out of the picture because they are now too trivial in terms of his new construing to be "remembered," other events previously not part of the account may now be presented as of great significance. From a construct theory point of view, *remembering* and *understanding* are inextricably related. From this point of view there is little point in studying how much of some material is retained by a subject unless a parallel investigation has been made of the way in which the person *construed* the material.

LEARNING

Simple and allegedly basic conditioning experiments tend to assume agreement between experimenter and subject as to what constitutes the stimulus. If an attempt were made to condition a subject to blink at the presentation of prime numbers by presenting number series, and relating the puff of air to the occurrence of a prime number, the acquisition of a conditioned response would depend on whether the subject initially had or had not constructions which enabled him to identify prime numbers. If he had no such construction, then he might well condition to particular prime numbers (but he would not generalize to new prime numbers when they occurred), or he might condition to odd numbers. Learning experiments often avoid the problem by using as the experimental stimuli elements about which there is such high consensual agreement that subject-experimenter differences in construing are unlikely to occur, e.g. electric shock, coloured lights. The introduction of grid method might enable the experimenter to widen his repertoire of stimuli while providing him with information about the subject's construing system which might enable him to keep them within the range of convenience of the subject's construing. "Units" might then be "units" for both experimenter and subject.

It might enable him to avoid tautology where concepts such as "punishment" and "reward" are concerned. The tautology being that punishment is what the subject avoids and reward is what the subject seeks, and of course what the subject avoids is punishment and what the subject seeks is reward, and concensus of opinion is used to escape the logical difficulty. Borger and Seaborne (1966) admitted this problem when they pointed out that "when we couple a sexually exciting stimulus with shock, (learning) theory does not explain precisely why this should make the stimulus aversive rather that provide the shock with erotic significance."

Grid methods might allow an identification of punishment and reward in terms of each individual's construct system, and again widen the repertoire of stimuli so that learning experiments were not chained to the socially agreed minutiae of life. Given such additions to the methodology of learning experiments, it would then be of more than passing interest to see how long the grid and its construct theory implications continued to be subsumed by super-ordinate constructs such as "punishment" and "reward." Eventually the notion that what the subject (like the experimenter) is seeking, is a meaningful view of his situation, and what he is avoiding is loss of significance, might replace the current view.

Mair (1964) began with a traditional paired-associate learning study, but found that the inclusion of grid measures and personal construct theory ideas highlighted the inadequacy of his conventional research design. The design accepted that subjects approach an experimental situation by trying to make sense of it, but it did not allow for change in their view of themselves and the experiment while they were completing the experimental tasks. This continuous reconstruction is to be expected from a construct theory viewpoint, but was not allowed for in this experimental design, nor is it usually envisaged in experiments on learning. Attention to the kind of research strategy described in some detail by Kelly (1965) could obviate this type of shortcoming.

CONCLUSIONS

Personality theorists seem divided on the question of whether personality changes. However, personality tests tend not to explore change but to write it off as error variance. Change seems only to be envisaged when some unusual intervention in the person's life has been made. English and English (1958) pointed out that the meaning of personality is influenced by the way it is studied. Perhaps, more emphatically, the meaning of personality is *decided* by the way it is studied, and already a position has been reached in which the assumptions underlying personality test construction often demand that personality be viewed as static. Thus the history of personality tests may follow that of intelligence tests. Early on, intelligence in adults was regarded as a stable and unchanging characteristic. In line with this assumption came the practice of altering the item content and format of intelligence tests until relative stability, given age weighting of test scores, was achieved. Then anyone who was prone to promote a particular construction to a law of nature, felt entitled to claim that intelligence did not change. The following through of an assumption in this way is reasonable provided that it is recognised that alternative assumptions could have been made and, as a result, different outcomes achieved.

Construct theory implies that a man's personality is the way in which he views, experiences and experiments with the world, and it differs from other theories in explicitly specifying different kinds and degrees of change. It can deal with the question of change and stability in personality by arguing that a man's subordinate constructions change relatively rapidly while his super-ordinate constructions change relatively slowly. As between one man and another, the man with a permeable construct system may change rapidly relative to the man with an impermeable construct system. Change within aspects of a personality and between personalities is theoretically definable in construct theory terms and potentially assessable in grid terms. People interpret and change their interpretations. A psychology of personal constructs is concerned with understanding the why and the how of change, rather than with describing states.

Kelly (1961) commented on the relationship between tests and theories.

"First of all, theoretical inventions are used to make predictions. Then, still using inventions – but of a more instrumental type, we examine the outcomes to see if there is any correspondence between what we have predicted and what our instrumentalized perceptions tell us has occurred. If we find such a correspondence we call it a discovery. We do not discover our theory; we do not discover our prediction; we do not even discover the ensuing event. What is discovered is a correspondence – a practical correspondence – between what our theoretical invention leads us to anticipate and what subsequently our *instrumental invention* leads us to observe."

Grids are instrumental inventions appropriate to the theoretical invention of personal construct theory. Psychologists who use them may initially value the direct information they provide, but may eventually see as more significant the changes in approach to people which their use involves. It is not grid method as such, which is important, it is the exploration of personal constructs.

APPENDIX

Formal Content of Personal Construct Theory

Fundamental Postulate. A person's processes are psychologically channelized by the ways in which he anticipates events.

Construction Corollary. A person anticipates events by construing their replications.

Individuality Corollary. Persons differ from each other in their constructions of events.

Organization Corollary. Each person characteristically evolves for his convenience in anticipating events, a construction system embracing ordinal relationships between constructs.

Dichotomy Corollary. A person's construction system is composed of a finite number of dichotomous constructs.

Choice Corollary. A person chooses for himself that alternative in a dichotomized construct through which he anticipates the greater possibility for the elaboration of his system.

Range Corollary. A construct is convenient for the anticipation of a finite range of events only.

Experience Corollary. A person's construction system varies as he successively construes the replications of events.

Modulation Corollary. The variation in a person's construction system is limited by the permeability of the constructs within whose ranges of convenience the variants lie.

Fragmentation Corollary. A person may successively employ a variety of construction subsystems which are inferentially incompatible with each other.

Commonality Corollary. To the extent that one person employs a construction of experience which is similar to that employed by another, his processes are psychologically similar to those of the other person.

Sociality Corollary. To the extent that one person construes the construction processes of another he may play a role in a social process involving the other person.

Formal Aspects of Constructs

Range of Convenience. A construct's range of convenience comprises all those things to which the user would find its application useful.

Focus of Convenience. A construct's focus of convenience comprises those particular things to which the user would find its application maximally useful. These are the elements upon which the construct is likely to have been formed originally.

Elements. The things or events which are abstracted by a person's use of a construct are called elements. In some systems these are called objects.

Context. The context of a construct comprises those elements among which the user ordinarily discriminates by means of the construct. It is somewhat more restricted than the range of convenience, since it refers to the circumstances in which the construct emerges for practical use, and not necessarily to all the circumstances in which a person might eventually use the construct. It is somewhat more extensive than the focus of convenience, since the construct may often appear in circumstances where its application is not optimal.

Pole. Each construct discriminates between two poles, one at each end of its dichotomy. The elements abstracted are like each other at each pole with respect to the construct and are unlike the elements at the other pole.

Contrast. The relationship between the two poles of a construct is one of contrast.

Likeness End. When referring specifically to elements at one pole of a construct, one may use the term "likeness end" to designate that pole.

Contrast End. When referring specifically to elements at one pole of a construct, one may use the term "contrast end" to designate the opposite pole.

Emergence. The emergent pole of a construct is that one which embraces most of the immediately perceived context.

Implicitness. The implicit pole of a construct is that one which embraces contrasting context. It contrasts with the emergent pole. Frequently the person has no available symbol or name for it; it is symbolized only implicitly by the emergent term.

Symbol. An element in the context of a construct which represents not only itself but also the construct by which it is abstracted by the user is called the construct's symbol.

Permeability. A construct is permeable if it admits newly perceived elements to its context. It is impermeable if it rejects elements on the basis of their newness.

Constructs classified according to the Nature of their Control over their Elements

Preemptive Construct. A construct which preempts its elements for membership in its own realm exclusively is called a preemptive construct. This is the "nothing but" type of construction—"If this is a ball it is nothing but a ball."

Constellatory Construct. A construct which fixes the other realm membership of its elements is called a constellatory construct. This is stereotyped or typological thinking.

Propositional Construct. A construct which carries no implications regarding the other realm membership of its elements is a propositional construct. This is uncontaminated construction.

General diagnostic Constructs

Preverbal Constructs. A preverbal construct is one which continues to be used, even though it has no consistent word symbol. It may or may not have been devised before the client had command of speech symbolism.

Submergence. The submerged pole of a construct is the one which is less available for application to events.

Suspension. A suspended element is one which is omitted from the context of a construct as a result of revision of the client's construct system.

Level of cognitive Awareness. The level of cognitive awareness ranges from high to low. A high-level construct is one which is readily expressed in socially effective symbols; whose alternatives are both readily accessible; which falls well within the range of convenience of the client's major constructions; and which is not suspended by its superordinating constructs.

Dilation. Dilation occurs when a person broadens his perceptual field in order to reorganize it on a more comprehensive level. It does not, in itself, include the comprehensive reconstruction of those elements.

Constriction. Constriction occurs when a person narrows his perceptual field in order to minimize apparent incompatibilities.

Comprehensive Constructs. A comprehensive construct is one which subsumes a wide variety of events.

Incidental Constructs. An incidental construct is one which subsumes a narrow variety of events.

Superordinate Constructs. A superordinate construct is one which includes another as one of the elements in its context.

Subordinate Constructs. A subordinate construct is one which is included as an element in the context of another.

Regnant Constructs. A regnant construct is a kind of superordinate construct which assigns each of its elements to a category on an all-or-none basis, as in classical logic. It tends to be non-abstractive.

Core Constructs. A core construct is one which governs the client's maintenance processes.

Peripheral Constructs. A peripheral construct is one which can be altered without serious modification of the core structure.

Tight Constructs. A tight construct is one which leads to unvarying predictions.

Loose Constructs. A loose construct is one leading to varying predictions, but which retains its identity.

Constructs relating to Transition

Threat. Threat is the awareness of an imminent comprehensive change in one's core structures.

Fear. Fear is the awareness of an imminent incidental change in one's core structures.

Anxiety. Anxiety is the awareness that the events with which one is confronted lie mostly outside the range of convenience of his construct system.

Guilt. Guilt is the awareness of dislodgment of the self from one's core role structure.

Aggressiveness. Aggressiveness is the active elaboration of one's perceptual field.

Hostility. Hostility is the continued effort to extort validational evidence in favor of a type of social prediction which has already been recognized as a failure.

C-P-C Cycle. The C-P-C Cycle is a sequence of construction involving, in succession, circumspection, preemption, and control, and leading to a choice precipitating the person into a particular situation.

Creativity Cycle. The Creativity Cycle is one which starts with loosened construction and terminates with tightened and validated construction.

REFERENCES

Adams-Webber, J. (1967). Construct and Figure Interactions within a Personal Construct System: An extension of repertory grid technique. Unpublished Ph.D. Thesis. Brandeis University, Mass.

Al-Issa, I. and Robertson, J. P. S. (1964). Divergent thinking abilities in chronic schizophrenics. *J. clin. Psychol.* **20**, 4, 433.

Anastasi, A. (1961). *Psychological Testing.* Macmillan, New York and London.

Arthur, A. Z. (1963). Delusions: a theoretical, methodological and experimental study. Unpublished Ph.D. Thesis. University of London.

Asch, S. E. (1946). Forming impressions of personality. *J. abnorm. soc. Psychol.* **41**, 258.

Ashcroft, C. W. (1963). The relationship between conceptions of human nature and judgments of specific persons. Unpublished Ph.D. Thesis. George Peabody College for Teachers, Nashville.

Atkinson, J. W. (1958). *Motives in Fantasy, Action and Society.* (J. W. Atkinson, ed.) Van Nostrand, Princeton.

Bannister, D. (1959). An application of personal construct theory (Kelly) to schizoid thinking. Unpublished Ph.D. Thesis. University of London.

Bannister, D. (1960). Conceptual structure in thought disordered schizophrenics. *J. ment. Sci.* **106**, 1230.

Bannister, D. (1962). The nature and measurement of schizophrenic thought disorder. *J. ment. Sci.* **108**, 825.

Bannister, D. (1962a). Personal construct theory: a summary and experimental paradigm. *Acta Psychol.* **20**, 2, 104.

Bannister, D. (1963). The genesis of schizophrenic thought disorder: a serial invalidation hypothesis. *Brit. J. Psychiat.* **109**, 680.

Bannister, D. (1965). The genesis of schizophrenic thought disorder: re-test of the serial invalidation hypothesis. *Brit. J. Psychiat.* **111**, 377.

Bannister, D. (1965a). The rationale and clinical relevance of repertory grid technique. *Brit. J. Psychiat.* **111**, 977.

Bannister, D. (1966). Psychology as an exercise in paradox. *B.P.S. Bull.* **19**, 63, 21.

Bannister, D. (1966a). A New Theory of Personality. In *New Horizons in Psychology.* (B. M. Foss, ed.) Penguin Books, Middlesex.

Bannister, D. and Fransella, Fay (1966). A grid test of schizophrenic thought disorder. *Brit. J. soc. clin. Psychol.* **5**, 95.

Bannister, D. and Fransella, Fay (1967). *A grid test of schizophrenic thought disorder: a standard clinical test.* Psychological Test Publications: Barnstaple.

Bannister, D. and Salmon, P. (1963). Homosexual construing in grid terms. Unpublished study.

Bannister, D. and Salmon, P. (1966). Schizophrenic thought disorder: specific or diffuse? *Brit. J. med. Psychol.* **39**, 215.

Bannister, D. and Salmon, P. (1967). Measures of superordinacy. Unpublished study.

Bartlett, F. C. (1932). *Remembering: An Experimental and Social Study.* Cambridge University Press, London

Bateson, G., Jackson, D., Haley, J. and Weakland, J. (1956). Towards a theory of schizophrenia. *Behav. Sci.* **4**, 251.

Bender, M. P. (1968). Friendship formation, stability and communication amongst students. Unpublished M.A. Thesis. University of Edinburgh.

Bennion, R. C. (1959). A study of relative readiness for changing anticipations following discredit to situational behaviors: hostility and the constellatoriness of personal constructs. Unpublished M.A. Thesis. Ohio State University.

Bieri, J. (1955). Cognitive complexity-simplicity and predictive behavior. *J. abnorm. soc. Psychol.* **51**, 263.

Bieri, J. (1961). Complexity-simplicity as a personality variable in cognitive and preferential behavior. In *Functions of Varied Experience.* (D. W. Fiske and S. Maddi, eds.) Dorsey.

Bieri, J. and Blacker, E. (1956). The generality of cognitive complexity in the perception of people and inkblots. *J. abnorm. soc. Psychol.* **53**, 112.

Bieri, J. and Messerley, S. (1957). Differences in perceptual and cognitive behavior as a function of experience type. *J. consult. Psychol.* **21**, 217.

Binner, P. R. (1958). Permeability and complexity: two dimensions of cognitive structure and their relationship to behavior. Unpublished Ph.D. Thesis. University of Colorado.

Block, J. (1955). The difference between Q and R. *Psych. Rev.* **62**, 5, 356.

Bonarius, J. C. J. (1965). Research in the personal construct theory of George A. Kelly. In *Progress in Experimental Personality Research.* Vol. 2. (B. A. Maher, ed.) Academic Press, New York and London.

Borger, R. and Seaborne, A. E. M. (1966). *The psychology of learning.* Penguin Books, Middlesex.

Bousfield, W. A. (1961). The problem of meaning in verbal learning. In *Verbal learning and verbal behaviour.* (C. N. Cofer, ed.) McGraw-Hill, New York.

Bridges, D. V. (1965). An application of repertory grid technique to schizophrenic thought disorder.Unpublished B.A. dissertation. University of Reading.

Bromley, D. B. (1966). Rank order cluster analysis. *Brit. J. math. stat. Psychol.* **19**, 1, 105.

Brown, R. W. (1958). Is a boulder sweet or sour? *Contemp. Psychol.* **3**, 5, 113.

Bruner, J. S. (1957). On perceptual readiness. *Psychol. Rev.* **64**, 123.

Bruner, J. S., Shapiro, D. and Tagiuri, R. (1958). The meaning of traits in isolation and in combination. In *Person perception and Interpersonal behavior.* (R. Tagiuri and L. Petrullo, eds.) Stanford University Press.

Bruner, J. S. and Tagiuri, R. (1954). The perception of people. In *Handbook of Social Psychology.* (G. Lindzey, ed.) Addison-Wesley, Cambridge, Mass.

Brunswick, E. (1956). *Perception and the representative design of psychological experiments.* Berkeley and Los Angeles, University of California.

Caine, T. M. and Smail, D. J. (1967). Personal relevance and the choice of constructs for the repertory grid technique. *Brit. J. Psychiat.* **113**, 517.

Carroll, J. B. (1959). The measurement of meaning, a review. *Language* **35**, 1, 58.

Carver, M. V. (1967). The critical evaluation of films by repertory grid. Unpublished Ph.D. Thesis. University of London.

Constantinescu, P. (1967). A method of cluster analysis. *Brit. J. math. stat. Psychol.* **20**, 93.

Cook, J. M., Heim, A. W. and Watts, K. P. (1963). The Word-in-Context: a new type of verbal reasoning test. *Brit. J. Psychol.* **54**, 3, 227.

Coombs, C. H. (1964). *A Theory of Data.* Wiley, New York.

Costello, C. G. (1966). *Psychology for Psychiatrists*. Pergamon Press.

Crisp, A. H. (1964). An attempt to measure an aspect of "transference". *Brit. J. med. Psychol.* **37**, 17.

Crockett, W. H. (1965). Cognitive complexity and impression formation. In *Progress in Experimental Personality Research*. Vol. 2. (B. A. Maher, ed.) Academic Press, New York and London.

Cromwell, R. L. (1960). Factoring the Rep. Test. Unpublished manuscript, George Peabody College for Teachers, Nashville.

Cromwell, R. L. and Caldwell, D. F. (1962). A comparison of ratings based on personal constructs of self and others. *J. clin. Psychol.* **18**, 43.

Cronbach, L. J. (1955). Processes affecting scores on "understanding of others" and "assumed similarity". *Psychol. Bull.* **52**, 177.

Cronbach, L. J. (1961). *Essentials of Psychological Testing*. Harper and Row, New York and London.

Cronbach, L. J. and Meehl, P. E. (1955). Construct validity in psychological tests. *Psychol. Bull.* **52**, 281.

Dalziel, F. R. (1960). An experimental study of the concept of meaning. Unpublished Ph.D Thesis. University of Aberdeen.

Deese, J. (1965). *The structure of associations in language and thought*. Johns Hopkins Press, Baltimore.

Drewery, J. and Rae, J. B. (1968). A group comparison of psychiatric and non-psychiatric marriages using the interpersonal perception technique. *Brit. J. Psychiat.* (In Press).

du Mas, F. (1955). Science and the single case. *Psych. Rep.* **1**, 65.

Ellis, A. (1957). Rational psychotherapy and individual psychology. *J. Indiv. Psychol.* **13**, 38.

English, H. B. and English, A. C. (1958). *A comprehensive dictionary of psychological and psychoanalytic terms*. Longmans.

Epstein, S. (1953). Over-inclusive thinking in a schizophrenic and a control group. *J. consult. Psychol.* **17**, 384.

Fager, R. E. (1962). Program for the analysis of repertory grids on the 1620 IBM computer. Unpublished manuscript. Syracuse University.

Fjeld, S. P. and Landfield, A. W. (1961). Personal construct consistency. *Psych. Rep.* **8**, 127.

Foulds, G. A. and McPherson, F. M. (1966). Thought process disorder among schizophrenics. *B.P.S. Bull.* **19**, 63, A18.

Fransella, Fay (1965). The effects of imposed rhythm and certain aspects of personality on the speech of stutterers. Unpublished Ph.D. Thesis. University of London.

Fransella, Fay (1966). The stutterer as subject or object. Proc. Internat. Seminar on Stuttering and Behaviour Therapy. Carmel, California.

Fransella, Fay and Adams, B. (1965). An illustration of the use of repertory grid technique in a clinical setting. *Brit. J. soc. clin. Psychol.* **5**, 51.

Fransella, Fay and Bannister D. (1967). A validation of repertory grid technique as a measure of political construing. *Acta. Psychol.* **26**, 97.

Garskof, B. E. and Houston, J. P. (1963). Measurement of verbal relatedness: an idiographic approach. *Psych. Rev.* **70**, 277.

Giles, P. G. (1961). The validity of the role construct repertory test as a measure of sexual identification. Unpublished M.A. Thesis. Washington State University.

Gottesman, L. E. (1962). The relationship of cognitive variables to therapeutic ability and training of client centred therapists. *J. consult. Psychol.* **26**, 119.

Gulliksen, H. (1958). How to make meaning more meaningful. *Contemp. Psychol.* **3**, 5, 115.

Haire, M. and Grunes, W. F. (1950). Perceptual defences: processes protecting an organized perception of another personality. *Hum. Relat.* **3**, 403.

Hall, M. F. (1966). The generality of cognitive complexity-simplicity. Unpublished Ph.D. Thesis. Vanderbilt University.

Hays, W. L. (1958). An approach to the study of trait implication and trait similarity. In *Person Perception and Interpersonal Behavior*. (R. Tagiuri and L. Petrullo, eds.) Stanford University Press.

Hess, H. F. (1959). Level of cognitive awareness: its measurement and relation to behavior. Unpublished Ph.D. Thesis. University of Colorado.

Hinkle, D. N. (1965). The change of personal constructs from the viewpoint of a theory of implications. Unpublished Ph.D. Thesis. Ohio State University.

Hunt, D. E. (1951). Studies in role concept repertory: conceptual consistency. Unpublished M.A. Thesis. Ohio State University.

Isaacson, G. S. and Landfield, A. W. (1965). Meaningfulness of personal *versus* common constructs. *J. Indiv. Psychol.* **21**, 160.

Jaspars, J. M. F. (1963). Individual cognitive structures. Proc. 17th Internat. Cong. Psychol. Washington.

Jaspars, J. M. F. (1966). *On Social Perception*. University of Leiden: Holland.

Jessor, R. (1958). The problem of reductionism in psychology. *Psych. Rev.* **65**, 3, 170.

Jessor, R. and Hammond, K. R. (1957). Construct validity and the Taylor Anxiety Scale. *Psych. Bull.* **54**, 161.

Jones, H. G. (1963). Conceptual analysis in the assessment of personality. Proc. B.P.S. Conf. Psychological assessment of personality: Swansea.

Jones, R. E. (1954). Identification in terms of personal constructs. Unpublished Ph.D. Thesis. Ohio State University.

Jones, R. E. (1961). Identification in terms of personal constructs. *J. consult. Psychol.* **25**, 276.

Kelly, G. A. (1955). *The Psychology of Personal Constructs*. Vols. I and II. Norton, New York.

Kelly, G. A. (1958). Man's construction of his alternatives. In *The Assessment of Human Motives*. (G. Lindzey, ed.) Rinehart, New York.

Kelly, G. A. (1961). The Abstraction of Human Processes. Proc. XIVth Internat. Cong. Applied Psychol. Copenhagen.

Kelly, G. A. (1961a). Theory and therapy in suicide: the personal construct point of view. In *The Cry for Help*. (N. Farberow and E. Shneidman, eds.) McGraw-Hill, New York.

Kelly, G. A. (1962). Europe's matrix of decision. In *Nebraska Symposium on Motivation*. (M. R. Jones, ed.) University of Nebraska Press, Lincoln.

Kelly, G. A. (1963). *A theory of personality*. Norton, New York.

Kelly, G. A. (1963a). Comments on Aldous, the personable computer. In *Computer Simulation of Personality*. (S. S. Tomkins and S. I. Messick, eds.) Wiley and Sons, Ltd.

Kelly, G. A. (1963b). Non-parametric factor analysis of personality theories. *J. indiv. Psychol.* **19**, 115.

Kelly, G. A. (1963c). The Autobiography of a Theory. Unpublished manuscript. Ohio State University.

Kelly, G. A. (1964). The language of hypothesis. *J. indiv. Psychol.* **20**, 137.

Kelly, G. A. (1965). The strategy of psychological research. *B.P.S. Bull.* **18**, 1.

Kelly, G. A. (1966). A brief introduction to personal construct theory. Unpublished manuscript. Brandeis University.

Kelly, J. V. (1963). A programme for processing George Kelly's Rep Grids on the IBM 1620 computer. Unpublished manuscript. Ohio State University.

Knowles, J. B. and Purves, C. (1965). The use of repertory grid technique to assess the influence of the experimenter-subject relationship in verbal conditioning. *B.P.S. Bull.* **18**, 59, 23A.

Laing, R. D. and Esterson, A. (1964). *Sanity, Madness and the Family*. Tavistock Publications, London.

Laing, R. D., Phillipson, H. and Lee, A. R. (1966). *Interpersonal Perception*. Tavistock Publications, London.

Landfield, A. W. (1954). A movement interpretation of threat. *J. abnorm. soc. Psychol.* **49**, 529.

Landfield, A. W. (1955). Self-predictive orientation and the movement interpretation of threat. *J. abnorm. soc. Psychol.* **51**, 434.

Landfield, A. W. (1961). The science of psychology and the psychology of science. *Percep. Mot. Skills* **13**, 319.

Landfield, A. W. (1967). Grid relationship scoring used with a Rep test modification. *Psychol. Rep.* 21, 19.

Landfield, A. W. and Fjeld, S. P. (1960). Threat and self-predictability with predictability of others controlled. *Psych. Rep.* **6**, 333.

Landfield, A. W. and Nawas, M. M. (1964). Psychotherapeutic improvement as a function of communication and adoption of therapist's values. *J. counsel. Psychol.* **11**, 336.

Lederman, D. G. (1957). Sexual identification on the role construct repertory test. Unpublished M.A. Thesis. Ohio State University.

Levy, L. H. (1954). A study of the relative information value of constructs in personal construct theory. Unpublished Ph.D. Thesis. Ohio State University.

Levy, L. H. (1956). Personal constructs and predictive behaviour. *J. abnorm. soc. Psychol.* **53**, 54.

Levy, L. H. and Dugan, R. D. (1956). A factorial study of personal constructs. *J. consult. Psychol.* **20**, 53.

Lidz, T. (1964). *The family and human adaptation*. Hogarth, London.

Lynn, D. B. (1957). The organism as a manufacturer of theories. *Psych. Rep.* **3**, 353.

Mair, J. M. M. (1964). Paired-associate learning in neurotics: an investigation of individual differences and the effects of repeated failure. Unpublished Ph.D. Thesis. University of London.

Mair, J. M. M. (1964a). The derivation, reliability and validity of grid measures: some problems and suggestions. *B.P.S. Bull.* **17**, 55, 7A.

Mair, J. M. M. (1964b). The concepts of reliability and validity in relation to construct theory and repertory grid technique. In *Brunel Construct Theory Seminar Report*. (N. Warren, ed.) Brunel University.

Mair, J. M. M. (1966). Prediction of choice behaviour. Unpublished study.

Mair, J. M. M. (1966a). Prediction of grid scores. *Brit. J. Psychol.* **57**, 1 and 2, 187.

Mair, J. M. M. (1967). Some problems in repertory grid measurement. I. The use of bipolar constructs. *Brit. J. Psychol.* **58**, Nos. 3 and 4.

Mair, J. M. M. (1967a). Some problems in repertory grid measurement. II. The use of whole-figure constructs. *Brit. J. Psychol.* **58**, Nos. 3 and 4.

Mair. J. M. M. and Boyd, P. R. (1967). A comparison of two grid forms. *Brit. J. soc. clin. Psychol.* **6**, 220.

Mair, J. M. M. and Crisp, A. H. (1968). Estimating psychological organization, meaning and change in relation to clinical practice. *Brit. J. med. Psychol.* (In Press).

Marshall, G. R. and Cofer, C. N. (1963). Associative indices as measures of word relatedness: a summary and comparison of ten methods. *J. verb. Learn. verb. Behav.* **1**, 408.

Mayo, C. A. (1960). Cognitive complexity and conflict resolution in impression formation. Unpublished Ph.D. Thesis. Clark University.

Mischel, T. (1964). Personal constructs, rules and the logic of clinical activity. *Psych. Rev.* **71**, 3, 180.

Mitsos, S. B. (1958). Representative elements in role construct technique. *J. consult. Psychol.* **22**, 311.

Morse, E. L. (1966). An exploratory study of personal identity based on the psychology of personal constructs. Unpublished Ph.D. Thesis. Ohio State University.

McClelland, D. C., Atkinson, J. W. Clark, R. A. and Lowell, E. L. (1953). *The Achievement Motive.* Appleton-Century-Crofts: New York.

McFall, R. M. (1965). Unintentional communication, the effect of similarity and dissimilarity in subjects' and experimenters' construing. Unpublished Ph.D. Thesis, Ohio State University.

McQuitty, L. L. (1957). Elementary linkage analysis for isolating orthogonal and oblique types and typal relevancies. *Educ. psychol. measur.* **17**, 207.

Newman, D. K. (1956). A study of factors leading to change within the personal construct system. Unpublished Ph.D. Thesis. Ohio State University.

Oliver, W. D. and Landfield, A. W. (1963). Reflexivity: an unfaced issue of psychology. *J. indiv. Psychol.* **20**, 187.

Oppenheim, A. N. (1966). *Questionnaire Design and Attitude Measurement.* Heinemann, London.

Osgood, C. E. (1962). Studies on the generality of affective meaning systems. *Am. Psychol.* **17**, 1, 10.

Osgood, C. E. and Luria, Z. (1954). A blind analysis of a case of multiple personality using the semantic differential. *J. abnorm. soc. Psychol.* **49**, 579.

Osgood, C. E., Suci, G. J. and Tannenbaum, P. H. (1957). *The Measurement of Meaning.* Urbana, University of Illnois.

Payne, D. E. (1956). Role constructs *versus* part constructs and interpersonal understanding. Unpublished Ph.D. Thesis. Ohio State University.

Pedersen, F. A. (1958). A consistency study of the R.C.R.T. Unpublished M.A. Thesis. Ohio State University.

Poch, S. M. (1952). A study of changes in personal constructs as related to interpersonal prediction and its outcome. Unpublished Ph.D. Thesis. Ohio State University.

Ravenette, T. (1964). Some attempts at developing the use of the repertory grid technique in a child guidance clinic. In *Brunel Construct Theory Seminar Report.* (N. Warren, ed.) Brunel University.

Runkel, P. J. and Damrin, D. E. (1961). Effects of training and anxiety upon teachers' preference for information about students. *J. educ. Psychol.* **52**, 254.

Russell, W. A. (1961). Assessment *versus* experimental acquisition of verbal habits. In *Verbal learning and verbal behaviour.* (C. N. Cofer, ed.) McGraw-Hill, New York and London.

Ryle, A. (1967). A Repertory Grid Study of the Meaning and Consequences of a Suicidal Act. *Brit. J. Psychiat.* **113**, 1393.

Salmon, Phillida. (1963). A clinical investigation of sexual identity. Unpublished case study.

Salmon, Phillida. (1967). A study of the social values and differential conformity or primary schoolboys, as a function of maternal attitude. Unpublished Ph.D. Thesis. University of London.

Salmon, Phillida., Bramley, J. and Presly, A. S. (1967a). The Word-in-Context Test as a measure of conceptualisation in schizophrenics with and without thought disorder. *Brit. J. med. Psychol.* 40, 253.

Scott, W. A. (1962). Cognitive complexity and cognitive flexibility. *Sociometry*, **25**, 405.

Scott, W. A. (1963). Cognitive complexity and cognitive balance. *Sociometry* **26**, 66.

Sechrest, L. B. (1962). Stimulus equivalents of the psychotherapist. *J. indiv. Psychol.* **18**, 172.

Sechrest, L. B. (1963). The psychology of personal constructs: George Kelly. In *Concepts of Personality* (J. M. Wepman and R. W. Heine, eds.) Aldine, Chicago.

Semeonoff, B. (ed.) (1966). *Personality Assessment.* Penguin Books, Middlesex.

Shapiro, M. B. (1961). A method of measuring psychological changes specific to the individual psychiatric patient. *Brit. J. med. Psychol.* **34**, 151.

Siegler, M. and Osmond, H. (1966). Models of Madness. *Brit. J. Psychiat.* **112**, 1193.

Slater, P. (1965). *The Principal Components of a Repertory Grid.* Vincent Andrews and Co. London.

Slater, P. (1967). *Notes on Ingrid 67.* Biometrics Unit, Maudsley Hospital, London

Smith, R. G. (1962). A semantic differential for speech correction concepts. *Speech Monogr.* **29**, 32.

Stephenson, W. (1953). *The study of behavior: Q-technique and its methodology.* University of Chicago Press.

Stringer, P. (1967). Cluster analysis of non-verbal judgements of facial expressions. *Brit. J. math. stat. Psychol.* 20, 71.

Strodtbeck, F. (1951). Husband-wife interaction over revealed differences. *Am. soc. Rev.* **16**, 468.

Szasz, T. S. (1960). *The Myth of Mental Illness.* Secker and Warburg, London.

Tannenbaum, P. H. (1956). Music background in the judgement of stage and television drama. *Audio-vis. Commun. Rev.* **4**, 2, 92.

Thouless, R. H. (1951). Methodology and research in psycho-pathology. *Brit. J. med. Psychol.* **24**, 1, 8.

Todd, F. J. and Rappoport, L. A. (1964). A cognitive structure approach to person perception: a comparison of two models. *J. abnorm. soc. Psychol.* **68**, 469.

Vernon, P. E. (1964). *Personality Assessment.* Methuen, London.

Warren, N. (1964). Constructs, Rules and the Explanation of Behaviour. In *Brunel Construct Theory Seminar Report.* (N. Warren, ed.) Brunel University.

Warren, N. (1966). Social class and construct systems: an examination of the cognitive structure of two social class groups. *Brit. J. soc. clin. Psychol.* **5**, 254.

Wishner, J. (1960). Re-analysis of "Impressions of Personality". *Psych. Rev.* **67**, 96.

Zajonc, R. B. (1960). The process of cognitive tuning in communication. *J. abnorm. soc. Psychol.* **61**, 159.

AUTHOR INDEX

Numbers in italics indicate the page numbers in the References

SUBJECT INDEX